American Society Since 1945

American Society Since 1945

Edited with an Introduction by
William L. O'Neill

❧ a New York Times Book

Quadrangle Books
CHICAGO

Contents

3. Right and Left

4. From Civil Rights to Black Power

5. Where Are We Now?
from The Theater for Ideas

American Society Since 1945

Introduction

Origins of the Postwar Era

WHEN WORLD WAR II ended everyone thought the postwar era would now begin. They were wrong. The war had brought prosperity and excitement to many Americans, tragedy to a few, but a sense of the future's possibilities to almost no one. Psychologically, most people were still living in the 1930's. Repeated assurances by important men that a bright new world was emerging from the ruins of war promoted spurts of optimism without erasing the emotional scars left by the Depression. The period immediately after the war was marked, therefore, by a wildly fluctuating public temper. On the one hand, it was believed, the technological and productive triumphs of the war economy guaranteed a richly improved way of life for all Americans. On the other hand, the end of war contracts and the demobilization of twelve million servicemen and -women was certain to touch off a recession, if not a depression, and some unemployment could hardly be avoided. Under these circumstances a measure of folk cynicism was clearly in order. Indeed, it was not only understandable but wholesome as well. Fearing the worst, Americans were able to accept the shortages, dislocations, and uncertainties that followed the war with remarkable composure.

A variety of anticipated problems—the veteran question, for example—never materialized. People hoped that ex-warriors, ennobled by their services to the cause of peace and freedom, would dig in and help reconstruct the nation. Perhaps, however, their foreign adventures had brutalized and traumatized them in a variety of unpleasant ways making them unfit to participate in American society. At the very least, a long period of adjustment was expected. Here, again, everyone guessed wrong. The veteran problem turned out to be no problem at all. Except for a troubled handful, most veterans wanted nothing more than to pick up where they had left off before induction, or to make up for civilian joys lost while in uniform. There were a few manifestoes along the lines of "What G.I. Joe Expects from America," a few attempts to organize veterans for social action, but for the most part they seemed happy to settle down to work or study. Congress wisely passed legislation (known as the G.I. Bill of Rights) that modestly assisted these ambitions. Of all the surprising developments in the postwar years, the easy accommodation of this mass of men was perhaps the most astonishing. A country worried about unemployment, plagued by a shortage of housing, with woefully inadequate college facilities, was able to find enough homes, jobs, and desks to meet the veterans' most urgent needs. Housing was inadequate for years after the war, but the economic boom provided jobs for nearly everyone, and the colleges rose to the occasion in splendid fashion. With little help from the federal government they nonetheless made do by doubling up faculties, constructing temporary buildings, and showing an entirely unexpected inventiveness and flexibility. Within a few years the entire crop of veterans had been processed in what was surely American higher education's finest hour.

Unfortunately, not all the gloomy prophecies of 1945 and 1946 were ill-founded. The early decisions to eliminate rationing and end price and wage controls were opposed by critics who believed that planning for peace was as important as planning for war. But pressure from consumers hungry for goods, producers eager to profit from their wants, and workers restive under wage restraints prevailed. The consequences were not only predictable but predicted. Prices rose, profiteers multiplied, inflation mounted, and in 1946 a wave of strikes angered consumers who resented the interrupted flow of still scarce goods. Congress retaliated with the Taft-Hartley law. While the act (which permitted individual states to legislate anti-union open-shop laws and authorized the President to suspend national strikes for a limited period of time) was not, as some charged, a "slave labor bill," it did weaken the unions to a degree. Even more, it demonstrated the essentially negative role played by government in these years. Apart from a few useful measures like the

G.I. Bill, and some purely ceremonial deeds like the Employment Act of 1946, government contented itself with repealing controls, sniping at organized labor, and protecting itself against the (largely imaginary) threat of subversion. All the same, shortages and temporary dislocations notwithstanding, reconversion proceeded apace. By about 1948 the essential job of adjusting to a peacetime economy had been accomplished. Unemployment remained low while production and income rose. People were slow to understand that the Depression would not return, but in time it became clear that the problems of the forties and fifties would be quite different from those of the past. At this point, the postwar years really began.

Before discussing the new era, let us consider for a moment the general failure to anticipate it. The prophecy business is, of course, always a chancy one, but there were special reasons why Americans in 1945 had trouble understanding what was going on. The first problem involved the choice of a suitable model. Some people thought the 1940's were going to resemble the 1930's. For them unemployment, trade unions, and the whole complex of work and welfare matters seemed crucial. Knowing that not all questions had been answered by the New Deal, it was natural for them to feel that priority should be given to those structural weaknesses revealed by the Depression. They believed, in short, that the thirties had been a normal period in American history. Others believed that the postwar era was more likely to resemble the years after World War I: that the 1920's offered the best model for postwar planning. This was an ominous thought in several respects. Broadly speaking, there were two interpretations of the twenties. One view was articulated in an April 1946 issue of the *New York Times Magazine* by Charles Poore, who guessed that the flamboyant aspects of the "Roaring Twenties" were likely to be recapitulated. Dance crazes, fads, a stock market boom, and similar features of the affluent, hedonistic society were now in order. Another view was expressed in the same magazine six weeks later by a veteran who declared "Youth Will Not Permit Another 1920." He saw the twenties as a time of corruption and repression, of red scares and union busting. Neither view, of course, offered liberals much comfort. If these predictions were correct, the postwar era was going to be either trivial or reactionary, or both. Understandably, the inclination of serious people was to reject the twenties as a model for the postwar period.

In the event, they were mistaken. For several reasons the twenties were suggestive of America's postwar concerns. Prosperity became widespread, if not universal. Politics declined in interest and importance. Radicals and reformers were submerged in a sea of red-baiting and witch-hunting. General Eisenhower's administration fitted nicely into the Harding-Coolidge tradition. The American people turned their backs on most social issues and became absorbed in private pursuits—mainly the twin quests for security and pleasure. Popular culture, nurtured in the mass media's rich soil, mushroomed. In these and other ways the two postwar eras closely resembled one another. There were, however, important differences which most observers, whatever their feelings, missed. The prosperity of the 1920's, while very real, had been thinly rooted. It was the decade when America came of age and assumed its modern form—and in this sense it was a normal epoch while the Great Depression was abnormal—but modernity was unevenly expressed. Unemployment was high throughout the twenties, reaching 10 per cent at the end, income remained roughly constant, and population growth was slight. The stock market was uncontrolled to the point where paper values often had only a slight relationship to real assets. These and other weaknesses finally asserted themselves after 1929. Reasoning from this experience, Americans who grasped the parallel between 1920 and 1945 or 1950 expected a severe recession sooner or later.

A number of things had happened in the thirties and early forties, however, which few allowed for. The sector of the work force that was unionized had greatly increased. Although only a minority of working men belonged to unions, enough were organized to exert a stabilizing effect on the economy. Their wages and jobs were protected by union contracts. When they were laid off or on strike, unemployment compensation and strike funds provided them with incomes. Thus, fluctuations in the economy were cushioned as they had not been earlier. Social security payments, which continued regardless of business downturns, further stabilized the economy. The stock market was regulated so that paper values and actual worth bore some relationship to each other, making a repetition of the 1929 crash unlikely. The minimum wage, while restricted, established income floors in many occupations and increased the work force's buying power. Federal spending for armaments continued at a high level. Finally, an enormous and wholly unexpected population explosion stimulated the demand for a great range of goods and services while forcing cities and states to greatly increase their expenditures over a long period. Thus, even though government's response to social and economic problems in the forties and fifties was sluggish and ineffective, much had already been done (mainly by the New Deal) to protect the country against its own successes.

This was the atmosphere in which the postwar era began. Having braced themselves for depression, the American people were startled by prosperity. Poverty was not, of course, abolished, but the postwar poor, as Michael Harrington and others pointed out later, were invisible. Unlike the unemployed and the underemployed of the 1930's, the poor were now confined mainly to segregated minority groups —Negroes, Mexican Americans, Indians, Puerto Ricans—shut away in urban and rural ghettos. In the forties and fifties they lacked the organization and drive which in the 1960's enabled them to break out of obscurity. In the postwar era, therefore, it was the new affluence, not the old poverty, that captured the public's imagination.

The Nineteen Fifties

Even for those who lived through it, the decade of the 1950's (that is, the period that began around 1948 and ended in 1960 or 1961) has an aura of unreality. Could we really have believed that J. D. Salinger was a writer of great moral power and acumen? Did we honestly think America ripe for subversion? Was Elvis Presley actually considered a threat to established morals? Alas, these and other views, which now seem ludicrous at best, were held not only by the uninformed and unenlightened but by people of taste and intelligence as well. How is such a peculiar state of affairs to be explained?

To begin with, the Cold War had a depressing effect on American morale. World War II had been a great and terrible event, yet it had also been a reassuring one. The struggle was plainly and unambiguously fought between the forces of good and evil. Truth crushed to earth rose again and overcame error with fire and the sword. Both the physical power and the ideology of fascism were destroyed. Even more, all this was accomplished with little sacrifice, while the high level of American prosperity during the war was further evidence of divine favor. The Cold War changed all this. Russia's emergence as the chief threat to world peace and freedom, or so it was thought, retrospectively discredited the wartime coalition and, to a degree, the war effort itself. Unlike Nazism, communism seemed to have a broad and persistent popular appeal. The accomplishments of Soviet Russia, the rise of large Communist parties in Europe and elsewhere, and, most of all, the revolution in China undermined American self-confidence. While abroad the nation increasingly reacted to communism as if the challenge it posed was chiefly military, at home the threat was perceived differently. An excessively concrete foreign policy based on guns and money was matched by an excessively abstract domestic response concerned mainly with ideas. This reaction was based on the premise that communism had to be defeated ideologically as well as militarily. America needed to win what was commonly described as "the war of ideas." But in the nature of things, ideological warfare had to be waged mainly at home. It was easy to send troops to Europe and guns to Formosa; it was very difficult to get foreigners to read *Time* magazine, the *Saturday Evening Post,* and other vehicles of American popular thought. Thus, except for certain feeble propaganda efforts, the war of ideas was confined pretty much to our own mass media.

Considering how practical Americans are supposed to be, the great polemics of the 1950's were extraordinarily abstract. They generally revolved around two concepts, "totalitarianism" and "democracy," which everyone agreed were what the Cold War was all about. Democracy got rather short shrift. It had something to do with Abraham Lincoln, telephones, and air-conditioning, but its virtues were more taken for granted than analyzed. Totalitarianism, on the other hand, was exhaustively discussed. What made people want to "escape from freedom"? Was there such a thing as an "authoritarian personality"? (Indeed, there probably was, at least in America, judging by the classic study on this subject by T. W. Adorno and others, *The Authoritarian Personality*.) A vintage example of this genre was Eric Hoffer's *The True Believer,* which purported to demonstrate by the use of maxims, aphorisms, and the author's numerous and interesting personal prejudices how the weak-willed were seduced into worshiping false political gods. Although the book was in no way marred by factual evidence, and assumed everything that normally demands proof, it was vastly popular.

The effects of this mighty stream of literature condemning wrong thoughts and those who held them were profound. Most dramatic were the trials and investigations of the late forties and early fifties—the great witch-hunts. Nominally these efforts were directed against disloyal acts. In reality they were attempts, often successful, to proscribe false opinions. The best evidence for this is the absurd grounds on which so many prosecutions were based. Apart from a handful of legitimate espionage cases, none of which seriously compromised national security, most victims of the anti-red hysteria were guilty of little more than poor judgment. In the celebrated Hiss case, for example, the point at issue was whether or not Alger Hiss, while an officer of the Department of State in the 1930's, had passed some classified documents to Soviet agents. Robert Oppenheimer, invariably described as "the father of the A-bomb," was denied a security clearance for opposing development of the hydrogen bomb. Most victims were chosen because they had once belonged to the Communist party or its front groups in, usually, an open and legal fashion. Sometimes they were attacked through their associations with suspected communists or, as the phrase went, "fellow travelers." As their behavior was neither treasonous nor criminal, few were convicted on account of it. What could be done, however, was to publicize their opinions and associations in ways that subjected them to public humiliation and made them, as teachers, government workers, and especially entertainers, virtually unemployable.

In principle, of course, the Bill of Rights protected Americans from prosecution for their opinions, but it offered no defense against this sort of persecution. Moreover, the courts tended to accept broad definitions of the national security and narrow definitions of individual rights. Thus, injured persons could not usually secure a redress of their grievances, no matter how false the charges raised against them. And congressional committees could "try" an individual without the usual legal safeguards. Many liberals acquiesced in the suppression of dissent. Some were scared of being caught up in the popular mania themselves and joined the mob lest it turn on them. Others were convinced that the handful of Soviet sympathizers in America were a great enough menace to warrant extreme action. This faith in the power of American communism continued even after the American Communist party was effectively destroyed, its leaders jailed, and its apparatus riddled by FBI informers in the early fifties.

In theory, liberals were governed by Sidney Hook's famous maxim, "Heresy yes, treason no." But in an atmosphere where the power of totalitarian ideas was taken for granted, the distinction broke down. Whatever sophistries were advanced to explain why a given person should be jailed or fired from his job, it was clear to the average American that ideas, not actions, were being penalized. Having been assured by liberal and conservative anti-communists alike of the awful potency of false opinions, thousands of communities felt justified, even obliged, to search out and destroy the sources of ideological contagion. Teachers were fired, textbooks scrutinized for un-American ideas, and libraries censored. Even mild criticisms of American society opened one to attack, so few were made. Those liberals who supported the anti-communist crusade, for whatever reason, were themselves weakened by it. At a time when Presidents and cabinet officers were accused of treason, no liberal could be above suspicion, however strident his denunciations of communists and fellow travelers. After Henry Wallace's futile presidential campaign of 1948, and after the empty rhetoric of Harry Truman's Fair Deal died away, this intimidating atmosphere brought the process of reform pretty much to a halt.

The Cold War had other consequences for American life and thought. The attack on false ideas spilled over into an attack on all ideas. Adlai Stevenson's chief handicap as a presidential candidate in the 1950's was his status as an intellectual, or an "egghead," to use the era's favorite term. Many critics and social scientists came to accept this distrust of ideas as, in some measure at least, desirable. It was compared favorably to the European infatuation with ideas which allegedly had produced fascism and communism. The true American philosophy, it could now be seen, was pragmatism—which somehow always seemed to mean either selling out one's highest principles or operating largely on the basis of snap judgments. Problem-solving, an attribute of pragmatic men, was highly admired, but few problems were solved. As it turned out, what Daniel Bell called "the end of ideology" was not necessarily the beginning of wisdom. The denigration of intellect encouraged schools to place socialization ahead of education. The repudiation of moral passion and utopian politics enfeebled public life and generated a peculiar body of social thought.

Criticism did not, however, entirely die. On the left, C. Wright Mills produced several brilliant and passionate books, notably *The Power Elite*. At the other extreme, Russell Kirk, a fugitive blossom in the rank garden of reactionary thought, produced his first-rate study *The Conservative Mind*. These men, who combined a straightforward partisanship with high standards of intellectual rigor, were not typical of the fifties, however. More representative was William

Whyte's *The Organization Man,* which argued that variety and originality were giving way in every sphere of American life to conformity. A common type was emerging in business, government, and education. Everywhere the bureaucrat was replacing the pioneer. Even domestic life reflected this, for the new suburbs were but extensions of the corporate structure. This theme, and variations of it, dominated intellectual discourse in the fifties. Perhaps the most searching example of the genre was David Riesman's *The Lonely Crowd.* This book was rooted in that obsessive concern, typical of the period, with what was usually called "the national character." Riesman suggested that the nineteenth-century Americans were indoctrinated with a fixed set of values which, once absorbed, enabled them to move through life with certainty and sureness. The image he used to describe this "inner-directedness" was the gyroscope. Victorian man kept an even keel, regardless of circumstances, because his moral guidance system was invariable. Modern man, on the other hand, was "other-directed," instructed in relative moral principles and dependent on his peer group for direction. Instead of a gyroscope, he was fitted with a radar set.

This vein of criticism had several interesting features. Because it was neither reactionary nor progressive it did not point to any particular course of action. Indeed, it was programmatically sterile to the point of absurdity. William Whyte concluded his forceful critique of the organizational (we would now say corporate) society by showing how to cheat on personality tests. Otherwise, he had no important suggestions to make. *The Lonely Crowd,* after exposing the other-directed man, ended with a pious hope that someday a better type, the "autonomous man," would emerge and the American character assume a more pleasing shape. These formal studies were reinforced by novels like Sloan Wilson's *The Man in the Gray Flannel Suit* (which was to the fifties what *Babbitt* had been to the twenties) and by journalistic exposés such as Vance Packard's *The Hidden Persuaders.* This last indicates another effect of the social criticism of the 1950's. In the absence of a program there developed in some quarters a kind of centrist scapegoating. If a plan for reforming American society could not be found, one could at least pinpoint the source of decay. Usually this turned out to be the advertising industry. Madison Avenue, home of many large advertising agencies, came to occupy the position once held by Wall Street in the mythology of popular social criticism. It stood for everything meretricious and corrupt in American life. Peopled entirely by men in three-button suits who carried attaché cases and drank martinis (or the even more sinister gibsons), it was the evil center of a giant, if amorphous, conspiracy which was converting a nation of eagles into a nation of hogs.

This is not to say that the advertising industry was in any respect admirable, but only to point out that the attack on it was characteristic of the fifties: the symptoms were mistaken for the disease. The real problems of the fifties were the same as those of the sixties, except almost no one could see them. The racial crisis, the urban crisis, even the war in Vietnam were building at the very time when Madison Avenue, automobiles with garish tail fins, and rigged television quiz shows occupied the critics' attention. The key issues were seen as essentially moral ones. Was the national moral fiber being undermined? (Strictly speaking, of course, fibers fray, but in the fifties moral fiber was always in danger either of being undermined or eroded.) Was abundance destroying those virtues that had made the country great? Did the youth of today lack the idealism of their predecessors (i.e., the middle-aged men asking this question)? Matters of this sort could neither be resolved nor made the basis of rational policies. The public discourse was thus mired in a welter of fuzzy generalizations. Once again, an era that proudly claimed to be pragmatic and unideological showed itself to be obsessed with abstract, not to say ethereal, propositions. When a handful of American prisoners of war defected to China, or when a member of a distinguished family of intellectuals was found to have conspired with the producers of a TV quiz show, these events were instantly recognized as signs of the general rot. To combat it people were urged to go to church more often, vote for General Eisenhower, and read books like Norman Vincent Peale's *The Power of Positive Thinking*.

In retrospect the era's problems were distressingly concrete. John Kenneth Galbraith made this clear in *The Affluent Society* which, while it appeared at the end of the fifties and used those protective mechanisms of wit and irony demanded by the times, anticipated the future's concerns. Galbraith argued that what ailed America was not private richness but public poverty. While private transportation (especially the auto industry) was given every sort of encouragement, public transit languished. While private housing was subsidized by government-guaranteed loans and burgeoned at a fantastic rate, public housing was neglected. During the Eisenhower years especially, a modified laissez faire (modified in the sense that government now underwrote a great variety of private enterprises) was pursued at the expense of all those social ills from which a profit could not be extracted. What C. Wright Mills called the "higher immorality" dominated life in the United States. Slums were ignored and caution urged upon civil rights workers lest "Southern moderates" become alienated. But most Americans had never had it so good, as politicians tirelessly reminded them.

In fact, domesticity was what the fifties were really all about. The decline of politics as a serious enterprise was accompanied by the privatization of everyday life. In a real sense the family became the chief unit of that private sector whose demands Galbraith spoke against. The neo-Victorian revival of family life in the fifties was, like the baby boom that accompanied it, unexpected and almost inexplicable. It was rooted in a demographic revolution of immense proportions. From the Civil War to World War I the trend had been toward smaller families. People married later and, partly because of this, had fewer children. At first, alarmists had raised the cry of "race suicide." The basic American stock, they warned, was on the verge of extinction through birth control, while the immigrant birthrate was rising. Simple arithmetic showed that if immigrants multiplied and Yankees subtracted, the former would soon overcome the latter. In the 1920's this particular anxiety faded (even though contraceptive devices were at last available) because immigration was restricted. Moreover, it was becoming evident that as immigrants improved their socio-economic status they tended to have fewer children. In the 1930's the marrying age rose sharply and the birthrate fell, as wedlock and paternity became luxuries that the economically depressed could ill afford. Even the divorce rate, which had been rising for almost a century, declined. World War II provoked a wave of sudden marriages followed in due course by a crop of babies. No one was surprised by this. In part it was thought to be a consequence of war-generated emotions, partly also a result of the new prosperity that allowed people who had deferred marriage in the thirties to consummate their relationships. Everyone was certain these changes were temporary, and that in the postwar era normal demographic patterns would be re-established. This was why the Census Bureau's director, in an article for the *New York Times Magazine,* estimated in 1946 that the population would not reach 163 million until 2000 A.D. No one was prepared, therefore, when the wartime pattern persisted into the 1950's. The marrying age for both men and women dropped, the birthrate soared. In the 1960's these trends finally began to reverse themselves, but by then almost an entire generation had passed.

What caused such an extraordinary phenomenon we do not really know. These great demographic movements remain as mysterious and little understood as the nature of life itself. Between the 1920's, a prosperous time when the population grew slowly, and the 1950's, when the population exploded, something of importance had happened at which we can only guess. One possibility is that the prosperity of the fifties was so much greater than that of the twenties that for the first time in perhaps a century large numbers of middle-class people felt able to indulge themselves in the luxury of large families. This does not, however, explain why they chose to spend their surplus on children as against other kinds of luxuries. A better guess concerns the changing roles and expectations of women in the past century. If we assume that women determine family size—a big assumption, for here also little is known—then a solution does offer itself. The middle-class family declined in size during the years— roughly from 1860 to 1920—when women were demanding, and to a degree getting, a larger measure of freedom. They entered the colleges and the professions, obtained jobs in large numbers, gained the vote, formed a great variety of volunteer associations, and in many other ways secured public rights that conflicted somewhat with their private obligations as mothers. Working women married later than those who did not work. College graduates married later still. We do not have to strain very hard, then, to argue that a cause-and-effect relationship existed between women's expanded public role and their diminished private role. In certain areas the connection was obvious. During the nineteenth century about half of all women college graduates never married. Later, as more women went to college, the ratio changed, but for years higher education correlated positively with spinsterhood.

In the 1920's, however, a counterreaction began. The percentage of women earning college degrees peaked. In 1920, 47 per cent of all students in institutions of higher learning were women; by 1950 they accounted for only 30 per cent of the student body. In 1930, 40 per cent of all bachelor's degrees were awarded to women, but in 1956 only a third of the recipients were female. In 1920 one out of every seven doctorates was given to women, but in 1956 women earned less than one out of ten. Similarly, the percentage of women professionals declined. While the female sector of the work force continued to grow, that growth was concentrated at the bottom of the occupational hierarchy. It had always been known that marriages and careers for women were not easily reconciled, but until the 1920's women increasingly chose the latter over the former. After 1920 the balance tilted, with marriages gaining the advantage over careers.

Almost certainly this reactionary development was stimulated by what Betty Friedan, in her admirable polemic, has called *The Feminine Mystique*. The feminist movement had defeated the nineteenth-century precept that "woman's place was in the home" by demonstrating that women could fill a great many other places just as well. Although the stream of propaganda directing women to marry early and raise numerous children never dried up entirely, and many women continued to observe its tenets, by 1920 feminism appeared to have won the war of ideas. But at the very moment of triumph, feminism was undone by a successful counterattack which used new ideas to advance the old principles. Emancipated individuals had demanded sexual freedom to liberate women from the tyranny of marriage. In the 1920's readers of Sigmund Freud argued that true sexual freedom took place within marriage, and, indeed, that motherhood was essential to real fulfillment. Feminists had sought to refute the old idea that child-rearing was woman's only duty by showing that women could enjoy the same accomplishments as men. Now they were overcome by the argument that women were completely unlike men and could achieve satisfaction only by living in harmony with their biological compulsions. Housekeeping became "domestic science," and businessmen eager to expand their markets advanced the notion that modern homemakers were actually managers of the family system, equal in skill and status with professional executives. With this positive effort came the charge that women who did not remain faithful to their feminine natures, who persisted in competing with men in the outside world, were victims of "penis envy," or its dread counterpart, "the castration complex."

Of course, women did not give up their public aspirations and return to domesticity because of the feminine mystique alone. Domestic life became more attractive, we can fairly assume, because by the 1920's women had accumulated enough practical experience to know that the joys of struggling in the marketplace were not so agreeable as feminists had led them to suppose. Many women found only routine jobs which were hardly worth the sacrifices they demanded. Others discovered that, even after they became fully qualified professionals, advancement was more difficult for them than for comparably equipped men. Also in the twenties the reform and service enterprises that had engaged masses of women in the Progressive era had grown stale and no longer commanded the enthusiasm of active young women. At this point, then, marriage and family life, cleansed, as it was thought, of their old imperfections by modern technology and more enlightened customs, took on a new lustre. This general response began in the twenties, was obscured by the thirties, but matured in the postwar era. Once middle-class women conceded that motherhood was their highest duty and most fulfilling role, the domestic explosion of the 1950's was inevitable.

The revival of domesticity affected many areas of the national life. After reaching an all-time high in 1946, the divorce rate fell sharply. The marriage rate and the birthrate shot up. The marrying age declined. "Going steady," as exclusive dating among adolescents was called, rose in popularity and became a kind of pseudo marriage that often led to the real thing. Families with large numbers of small children demanded separate houses with contiguous play areas. This promoted the development of great real estate subdivisions. The "tract," with its hundreds, even thousands, of similar dwellings, each with its own yard, became the standard form of middle-class and upper lower-class housing. Tracts were invariably located outside of cities, thus accelerating urban deterioration by taking the most important bloc of taxpayers out of the city while increasing the demand for urban transportation facilities. Tracts were usually closed to the flood of nonwhites pouring into the cities, thus the slums grew, imposing further strains on underfinanced city administrations and forcing increases in property taxes which accelerated the suburban movement. The federal government contributed its bit by subsidizing, especially through G.I. and FHA home loans, suburban construction, and later by subsidizing urban expressways which enabled larger numbers of people to live in tracts while working in the cities. More and more private automobiles washed into the city, poisoning the air and reducing the tax base further as expressways and parking lots displaced more productive facilities. An expanding population and a diminished living area put greater pressure on the slums. No private housing was built for low-income people, and public housing projects usually did not meet the needs even of those people who were displaced by their construction.

While this was going on the American people were preoccupied with what one popular women's magazine called "togetherness." "The family that prays together stays together," it was said, and families did, in truth, more praying than ever before. Or at least they went to church more often. The percentage of people who manifested a denominational affiliation increased. The burgeoning suburbs were festooned with new churches, which became as characteristic of life in the tract as the car pool, the shopping center, and the new elementary school. The automobile came fully into its own. Suburbs everywhere were poorly serviced by public transit authorities, so men commonly drove to work, singly or in combinations, and wives had to spend an important part of their time driving themselves and their children about. In fact, to live comfortably in the suburbs families really needed two cars, and, as more families bought them, the air became more poisonous and the traffic snarls more numerous and complex.

These developments did not escape notice. In two witty books, *The Crack in the Picture Window* and *The Insolent Chariots,* John Keats attacked the twin pillars of suburban life. Innumerable writers drew attention to the cloying domesticity, the smugness and self-satisfaction, the sterile homogeneity, and the aesthetic shortcomings of tract housing. None of the criticisms did the slightest good. For one thing, when the residential construction boom started in the late forties, it had to meet the needs of an entire generation. There had been no homebuilding since the twenties, and many Americans were frantic to escape their aging quarters. Whatever its flaws, tract housing was an improvement over what most new suburbanites were accustomed to. For another thing, they genuinely liked their new houses. This was a point that intellectuals and hardened city dwellers had difficulty in grasping. To their eyes the tracts were ugly and barren, the houses cheaply constructed, and the lots on which they stood offensively small. But the occupants loved them. Critics predicted that the tracts would degenerate into suburban slums. Some did, but more often the owners repaired their houses' defects, enlarged and improved them, and planted trees and shrubs, so that today the original subdivisions are more valuable, and much more attractive, than when they were first built.

Another feature of suburban life that escaped critics was the way in which the tracts satisfied their residents' needs for proprietorship and community. These are old wants in America. The pioneers pushed west in order to become freeholders, and the desire to own house and land, the visible symbol of independence, is deeply imbedded in the American character. City dwellers, living in apartments and using public transit facilities, typically own nothing at all by these standards. For many, therefore, the suburban movement replicated the essential American experience by which the dependent Easterner became the freeholding Westerner. The pioneers had also sought community. They built schools and churches, formed social and political organizations, and developed an intricate community life. The city is, by comparison, a social wasteland. New Yorkers are fond of pointing out that they have lived in the same apartment building for twenty years without ever getting to know their neighbors. Dedicated urbanites are horrified at the thought of living in the open, as it were, and of knowing everything about their neighbors while their neighbors know everything about them. But for many people this was a principal virtue of the tracts. Here too the pioneer social experience could be imitated, schools and churches built, neighborly ties formed, and the dense infrastructure of small American communities reproduced. The social life of suburbia became, in fact, much more complex and demanding (or rewarding) than urban life. The PTA flourished, as did volunteer political organizations like the League of Women Voters, the Americans for Democratic Action, and the John Birch Society.

The search for community probably also accounts for another baffling aspect of the fifties, the religious revival. Through the first half of the twentieth century religion was on the defensive almost everywhere in America. Science had, it seemed, discredited the church's claim to truth, while the school, the welfare agency, and other public institutions had usurped many of its traditional functions. In the postwar era, however, church membership increased strikingly, and, in consequence of it, religion gained a new dignity and importance. A variety of reasons were advanced to explain this surprising development. The horrors of war and the strains of a nuclear peace undermined men's faith in science and reason as the sole guides of conduct and the only conduits of knowledge. In these terms the religious revival was an emotional reaction against a world suddenly grown too terrible for solitary man to bear. Considering that most church growth took place in the suburbs, whose pleasures we have just described, this explanation somehow lacks authority. Other explanations concerned doctrine: for example, that the neo-orthodoxy of Reinhold Niebuhr was more intellectually satisfying to Protestants than the theologies it displaced. But the most striking feature of postwar Christianity was the ecumenical movement and the suppression of doctrine which it entailed.

This suggests that the new institutional strength of the churches *was* a function of suburbia; that it was produced by the same drives which built the schools. Church membership was a mark of community solidarity and stability. At a time when there was so much talk of "atheistic" communism, it was also a badge of good citizenship. Religion was good for children too. It strengthened their character and helped them resist the temptations of a materialistic age. The churches may sometimes have seemed irrelevant in an urban context, but in suburbia they had several useful functions, and it made perfectly good sense to support them. The churches, it must be said, made excellent use of their opportunities. Although it was awkward for them to preach against the very affluence that created them, they did so all the same. They provided much of the institutional support for the civil rights movement that emerged in the late fifties. And by joining together in all those cooperative ventures that flowed out of the ecumenical spirit, they helped heal many old wounds from the sectarian past. It was, in fact, just this new spirit that made possible the election of a Roman Catholic President in 1960.

One of the most extraordinary features of the postwar era was the degree to which young people accepted the values of their elders. The dedication of bourgeois America to personal security and sociability produced a generation with strongly middle-aged attitudes. In high school the emphasis was on successful peer relations and becoming, as it was said, "educated for life." The life to which young people were educated was generally one of docile citizenship and earnest consumption. In college the physical sciences and humanities declined, while practical fields like business and engineering rose. About half of the male college graduates went into business, mainly big business. When William H. Whyte investigated this situation he discovered that the appeal of big business derived from the student's perception of it as a kind of private welfare state. Students did not look forward to a life of challenge, high adventure, and great profits, but rather to one of modest advancement, numerous fringe benefits, and a reasonable security. The functional hero of *The Man in the Gray Flannel Suit* perfectly represented their aspirations when he turned down an important promotion because it would interfere too much with his family life. By all accounts, college men looked forward to the same comforts and moderate prosperity that their fathers enjoyed, while college women aspired only to relive their mothers' lives.

The young were not, of course, wholly contented. From time to time the placid campus suffered "panty raids," as attacks on female dormitories by young men in pursuit of underwear were called. Such acts usually were viewed indulgently by the authorities, who regarded them as mere pranks. Once in a while indignation was voiced at the racial and religious prejudices of fraternities and sororities. On the whole, however, most complaints concerned what student editors always called the "apathy" of what had become known as the "silent generation." The protests and demonstrations of yesteryear were nostalgically recalled by professors and administrators who would later have to eat their words. Even when the young were visibly disturbed, however, they found it impossible to say why. The silent generation's most significant folk hero was James Dean, who starred in a motion picture called *Rebel Without a Cause*. In it he played an unhappy young man who expressed himself by driving his automobile in a dangerous manner. The film intimated that society had failed him in some undisclosed way, but the message was vague and without point. So was Dean's premature death in a sports car accident. In death as in life, James Dean symbolized the aimless resentments of submerged youth during what was, after all, a very boring time.

The Nineteen Sixties

This last decade has been so different from the one which preceded it that we often have trouble recalling what it was like in the Eisenhower years. To students today the names of Alger Hiss, Joe McCarthy, and John Foster Dulles mean practically nothing. The events which took place in Little Rock, Arkansas, and Montgomery, Alabama, are equally forgotten. No one any longer frets about conformity or condemns the young for adapting so readily to corporate demands. Instead, a whole new set of anxieties has developed and a variety of unexpected satisfactions has been generated. Many of the best essays in this volume deal with current issues, and there is no need here to dwell on themes the reader will soon encounter. But a word of explanation is probably in order. We can see now that the postwar era came to an end sometime in the early sixties. Its domesticity and general conservatism, its hysterical fear of subversion and the Russian menace, its preoccupation with the moral consequences of affluence are behind us. Less clear are the reasons for these momentous changes.

One cause seems to have been the election of John F. Kennedy as President. On the face of it there was little reason to expect much from his administration. He had been a successful politician but an undistinguished member of both houses of Congress. Moreover, he belonged to, and drew his support from, the very generation which had settled down after World War II to a life of quiet security. Yet, Norman Mailer, whose prescient essays in the 1950's frequently illuminated that dark time, saw in Kennedy unimagined possibilities. In 1960 Mailer wrote an essay, "Superman Comes to the Supermarket," for the express purpose of getting Kennedy elected. Recalling it later he wrote:

> I knew if he became President, it would be an existential event: he would touch depths in American life which were uncharted. . . . America's tortured psychotic search for security would finally be torn loose from the feverish ghosts of its old generals, its MacArthurs and Eisenhowers—ghosts which Nixon would cling to—and we as a nation would finally be loose again in the historic seas of a national psyche which was willy-nilly and at last, again, adventurous.

So it happened that Kennedy became President and the existential event that Mailer had foretold came to pass.

The country did, indeed, get moving again, just as the candidate had promised. It did not, however, always move in the desired direction. The Cold War heated up, and we endured a harrowing series of trials—notably the Bay of Pigs and the Cuban missile crisis—before an accommodation with the Soviets was reached and the long-awaited Test Ban Treaty signed. The civil rights movement swelled rapidly, staging confrontations in Birmingham and elsewhere which culminated in the great March on Washington of 1963. Students, in particular, were affected by these events. Many joined the newly organized Peace Corps, or its domestic counterpart VISTA. More were drawn into what became known simply as the Movement. As friends of Snick they supported the Student Non-Violent Coordinating Committee in the South. In the North they joined the Congress of Racial Equality. Everywhere they marched and picketed, sat-in, prayed-in, slept-in, and swam-in to secure justice for the Negro.

Few areas of American life remained untouched by the liberating ferment of those happy, if dangerous, years. The cool, detached, ironic social criticism of the fifties gave way to passionate tracts like Michael Harrington's *The Other America,* which launched the War on Poverty. The movie industry, producer of a thousand dismal epics and family comedies in the fifties, began to turn out pictures of value again. Creative forces were released that in a few years led to such extraordinary and diverse films as *Dr. Strangelove* and the memorable *Bonnie and Clyde.* The sterile censorship which had forced moviemakers to end their pictures on a high moral note, and barred vast areas of human experience and the feminine anatomy from exposure, was finally broken. Books too became more candid. In the fifties it was all but impossible to distribute an admitted work of art such as *Lady Chatterly's Lover.* In the sixties pornography itself became admissible, enabling farsighted publishers like Grove Press to wax deservedly rich. Women's fashions followed a similar pattern. The "New Look" of the postwar era, with its low hemline, gave way to the "mini-skirt." Even more gratifying was the appearance on American beaches of the abbreviated "bikini" bathing suit, a feature of the European scene long before it won approval here.

All this amounted to an American equivalent of the Russian thaw. As in Russia, repression had silenced but had not destroyed the desire for change. The poor were invisible only because they cooperated with the public's desire that they remain so. Students were complacent or apathetic because no one, least of all themselves, expected anything more. Housewives dreamed the small dreams society thought appropriate for them. But the American people were better, and America's problems more severe, than either seemed to be in the fifties. For all the talk about affluence and success in the Eisenhower years, poverty, racial injustice, and urban decay were becoming intolerable. Martin Luther King, Jr., and his Movement compelled the nation to begin facing its problems, but it was not until Kennedy was elected President that renewal became a national policy. The New Frontier, as his administration was absurdly misnamed, produced little in the way of important legislation, but it performed the indispensable function of liberating the suppressed hopes and ambitions of the very best Americans. A kind of de-Stalinization began which generated its own momentum. It spilled over into all sorts of unexpected areas with surprising and unpredictable consequences. Finally, of course, it produced a counterrevolution.

The renewal had hardly begun when President Kennedy was assassinated. Less than a year later the civil rights movement was fatally wounded in the terrible Mississippi Summer of 1964. A small army of rights workers moved into that state and were bloodily repulsed. Although whites as well as blacks were martyred, the experience was more divisive than unifying. Negro militants in growing numbers turned against nonviolence. "Black and white together, we shall overcome" gave way to "Black Power." At the same time ghetto uprisings erupted, first in Los Angeles, then in Newark, Detroit, and other cities. In Asia, President Johnson, convinced that only massive intervention would prevent a rebel victory, poured American troops and munitions into South Vietnam and launched an air war against the North. Thus the tide of violence rose. Detroit burned, but so did Saigon and Hanoi. The mood on college campuses became progressively uglier. Militant white students, banished from the Movement by black segregationists, brothers no longer, began concentrating on what they saw as the oppressive institution closest at hand—the university.

The life of a student generation is only four years. This fact alone impels young activists to take a short-range view of events and to demand immediate results. Thus, when it became clear that the great expectations regarding racial justice and social change aroused in the early sixties were not to be fulfilled, when renewal gave way to repression in the turbulent Northern ghettos, when escalation in Vietnam revived the flagging Cold War spirit, when the efforts of radical groups like Students for a Democratic Society to build organizations in the slums through "participatory democracy" failed, the romantic revolutionaries of the "New Left" became rapidly less romantic and more revolutionary. It is easy to understand why the deterioration which set in after 1964 hardened the spirit of radical students. More difficult to understand, however, were the reasons why their desperate energies were increasingly devoted to assaults on the university which, whatever its faults, is surely one of the better American institutions. The militant students have developed a rather sophisticated explanation that involves, on the one hand, the university's role as an adjunct of the military-industrial complex, and, on the other, its authoritarian disregard for student needs. A more plausible reason for these attacks, however, would seem to be that the university is the only important agency that young radicals are in a position to hurt. The Pentagon, IBM, and their like are invulnerable to the pressures students can generate. But at Columbia in 1968 it was demonstrated that a university can, in fact, be shut down by a handful of insurgents. If the country at large refuses to change, students, who are willing to risk the beatings and arrests with which the university tries clumsily to defend itself, can nonetheless make the campus pay for the shortcomings of our whole society.

As of this writing the American situation defies analysis. The nation seems to be at one of those great turning points which will decide its course for years to come. In the winter of our discontent Senator Eugene McCarthy showed what a man can do by entering the Democratic primaries, forcing President Johnson to withdraw from the race and inaugurate diplomatic contacts with the North Vietnamese. Senator Robert Kennedy, with his great personal following and immense human and material resources, therefore declared his candidacy, promising to revive the spirit that had begun with his brother's election in 1960. Then, in short order, Martin Luther King, Jr., probably the most important figure in American life, was murdered, and after him Senator Kennedy too was slain. The violent years that began with the President's assassination in 1963 have obviously not yet ended. Now that the Democratic party has fulfilled its death wish and made Richard Nixon President by denying the nomination to Senator Eugene McCarthy, its chief surviving proponent of reconciliation and renewal in 1968, the future seems more uncertain than ever. Will President Nixon end the war in Vietnam and use the money thus released to save our cities, or will he simply give us more of the same old politics that brought America to the edge of despair before his election?

Yet, even if further disasters await us, it would be foolish to give up hope for this country and its people. While politics strongly influence us, politicians cannot dictate the shape of our lives. American society, despite the tragedies of these last few years, has never been more various and exciting than now. Our movies were never better, our writers more fertile and inventive, our universities more stimulating, our popular culture richer, and our garments more surprising. Scarcely a decade has passed since those tired years when it seemed as if the vitality had somehow leaked out of American life. But in that short time the country has been turned upside down and the talk of complacency and conformity proved irrelevant. For all its terror and danger, and even with the possibility of fresh horrors before us, this is a wonderful, wild, exasperating era. Perhaps the country will destroy itself, and perhaps it should for its sins against Asian peasants and American Negroes. Maybe, as Norman Mailer often thinks, we are all going mad and some incredible, insane apocalypse is just around the corner. Even so, who would turn the clock back and erase the sixties? Nothing turned out as it was supposed to. Our friends and enemies alike were disappointed. And yet we became, if not the best, at least the most disturbed and unsettling people on the face of this earth. Who knows, that just may be enough.

Part 1

A VARIETY OF CONCERNS

THIS FIRST GROUP of articles suggests the range of developments which took the country by surprise in the postwar era. The religious revival was one of the earliest, and its significance is hardly more apparent today than it was when Reinhold Niebuhr wrote the first of these essays. We can, however, speak with more confidence on the subject of tract housing. In one sense the subdivisions were a success. The postwar housing shortage was ended and the domestic life of a substantial percentage of the population improved. The builders got rich. On the other hand, the aesthetic poverty and social short-comings of the new suburbia are no longer in doubt. Even when the builders were honest men giving good value for the customer's money, like the Levitts discussed in Penn Kimball's article, the results were not very impressive. Lately, developers in Reston, Virginia, Irvine, California, and elsewhere have shown that private housing need not be monotonous, that people do not insist on little boxes in the middle of little lots, and that town houses, village greens, and the like can be mingled with conventional structures to provide a handsome and stimulating environment. It seems clear now that a great chance was missed in the late forties and fifties to house the American people in a manner befitting their assets and aspirations.

In the fifties, as the old anxieties faded, new ones took their place.

People worried less about getting and keeping jobs, and more about the spiritual hazards of success. A special type of muckraking exploited the period's malaise. Its most characteristic practitioner was Vance Packard. Not so scholarly as William Whyte, not so angry as Fred J. Cook, a poorer writer than John Keats, he had something in common with all of them. His short piece reprinted here is a virtual compendium of the period's fears—excessive consumption, materialism, Russian technical achievements, motivational research, and the current recession—all in one package. Nothing else in this book demonstrates better the odd, sometimes unreal, flavor of American life in the fifties.

The sixties bred a tougher strain of social critics, which Victor Navasky here calls "The Intellectual Establishment." This is not to say that all, or even most, of its members are products of this decade; quite the contrary, however, things did not fall into place until the *New York Review of Books* was established a few years ago. It then became clear, as, perhaps, readers of *Partisan Review* and *Commentary* knew all along, that the country had finally come of age intellectually. Not only was there in being an entire company of essayists, critics, and assorted literary artists of wit and brilliance, but, even more important, there was an audience for their work. The *New York Review* deserves to be successful, yet many periodicals have deserved success without getting it, and the *New York Review* has an especially demanding character. Every reviewer seems to assume that his readers are thoroughly familiar with French poetry, medieval history, classical sociology, or whatever else may be under discussion. Even more remarkable is the subscribers' tolerance of the magazine's occasional bitchiness, persistent inbreeding, and obsessive partisanship. Still, it may be exactly this mixture of spice, venom, and elegance that makes the sheet attractive. In any event, both the Establishment's flowering and its popular acceptance are encouraging signs that, whatever else is lacking, the country has the critical intelligence required for a new start.

Of the items in this miscellany, the hardest to assess is Martha Weinman Lear's study of the new feminists. This is because it is still unclear whether the "Second Feminist Wave" is going to amount to much. Most Americans have never heard of it. More disturbing is the resemblance between the new feminists and the old. There is much to be said for the earlier generation of women's rights leaders, but the first thing to be admitted is that they failed, which is what made a new feminism necessary. Perhaps the new feminists are right to continue in the traditional ways, and perhaps the existing body of feminist thought is adequate to their needs. But even if they are wrong, they have at least broken with the clichés of the forties and fifties, and that is a comfort to everyone who believes that women are our most neglected national resource.

Is There a Revival of Religion?

by Reinhold Niebuhr

THE EVIDENCES of a contemporary revival of religion are not conclusive. There are certain marked tendencies in both the cultural and
the popular interests of our day which would seem to prove the
reality of such a revival. But it is not possible for a contemporary
observer of any "tendency," whether in politics or religion, to offer
conclusive proof of the reality of any "movement." There is always
the danger of regarding a single swallow as evidence of the summer's advent; and, on the other hand, there is the temptation to
reject the evidence of any number of swallows as conclusive proof
that the summer is here. Our own commitments and sympathies,
whether for or against particular movements, color our judgments
and tip the scales on which we weigh the evidence.

The evidences for a revival of religion, for those who care to weigh
them, are, in brief, of two types. In the realm of popular religion
there is the evidence of "mass" conversions under the ministrations
of popular evangelists who arouse religious emotions and elicit religious commitments with greater success than at any time since the
days of "Billy Sunday." On the other end of the scale there is
evidence that in the world of culture there is, at least, a receptivity
toward the message of the historic faiths which is in marked contrast
to the indifference or hostility of past decades.

The "conversion" of some significant writers, artists and cultural
leaders is the most obvious evidence of this new mood. More solid

From the *New York Times Magazine,* November 19, 1950.

evidence is the increase of interest in religious problems in the academic communities of the nation, in which for obvious reasons the "secular" spirit of the age was more pronounced than in any other part of the culture. There is scarcely a college or university which has not recently either created a department of religious studies or substantially enlarged existing departments. I know of more than one college campus in which young men are just beginning their teaching careers in these departments, after finishing studies in religion, upon which they were launched by religious experiences and commitments made while serving in the armed forces of our country.

The qualitative difference in these college courses is perhaps even more significant than the quantitative ones. Until very recently religious studies in our colleges were very much on the defensive. Frequently the one surviving course was entitled "The Bible as Literature." The title was meant to suggest that no one need take the religious content of the Bible seriously, but that a well-rounded education demanded that one know something about the literary treasures of the Bible, more particularly since one could hardly understand some of the great literary figures, Milton for instance, without a knowledge of the Bible. This defensive attitude has been replaced by a type of teaching which avails itself of all the instruments of modern historical scholarship but is guided by a conviction of the importance and relevance of the "message" of the Bible, as distinguished from the message of, say, Plato on the one hand or Herbert Spencer on the other.

The interest of the cultured classes in the historic faiths may be even more marked in Europe than in America, particularly in France and in Germany. One of the most significant intellectual journals in Germany is the Catholic Frankfurter Hefte. In France Catholic thought has a prestige in the arts and in philosophy much broader than the influence of the two Catholic philosophers Gilson and Maritain, who are the sole symbols of this movement to the average American. There are some apprehensions in non-Catholic circles about the effect of the recent papal encyclical upon the creative movements in European Catholicism. These apprehensions may or may not be shared in Catholic circles. From the outside it would appear that the encyclical is intended to discourage Biblical, philosophical and historical studies which seem to have strayed from the presuppositions of a strict "Thomism." Be that as it may, the influence of the Catholic faith upon culture in Europe is wider and deeper than either Protestant or secular leaders of thought in this country are able to understand or are inclined to admit. That influence has waxed rather than waned in the past decade.

The evidences of a religious revival thus far adduced are taken from the popular manifestations of mass evangelism and the religious interests of the cultured classes. In between is the broad life of organized religion with its devotees of various shades of conventionality and piety and of various degrees of commitment. It would be hazardous to make any generalizations about how the temper of our time has affected this life. The evidence is too varied and the criteria of measurement too dubious to justify any confident generalizations. It is apparent, however, that organized religion has not lost strength in recent decades; but beyond that one cannot go. The evidence for a revival of religion, such as it is, must be drawn from the explicit manifestations of religious interest as seen either in popular evangelism or in the color and the mood of the thought of the more articulate portion of our culture.

Perhaps the belief that there is a revival of religion rests primarily upon *a priori* judgment. It is generally assumed that periods of crisis are conducive to a revival of religion; and this assumption encourages the conviction that an age of crisis, such as our own, must therefore be more interested in religion. If the assumption is valid, as it probably is, it probably does not color empirical evidence any more than any other assumption which lies at the foundation of any historical analysis. In this case both the religious and the irreligious frequently join in common assumptions and conclusions because they are able to attribute the coincidence to different causes.

The critics of religion attribute the revival of religion in times of crisis to a "failure of nerve." Sometimes they equate it with the general "hysteria" manifest in times of great insecurity. Or they regard religious experience as an escape from the hard realities of a tragic period of history. Even religious devotees cannot deny some manifestations of escapism in the present religious mood. One of the most popular of the current evangelists, for instance, aroused a New England audience recently by assertions that he had sub rosa information from Washington to the effect that in the event of war the first atomic bombs would be delivered by the enemy in Boston harbor.

He drew no conclusions from these alarms which had any relevance to the responsibilities we face as Americans to work for the avoidance of war by strengthening the whole system of justice and unity in the free world, in which America has so precarious an eminence. He sought, rather, to persuade his hearers to "get right with God" under the compulsion of mass annihilation. This might be termed an escape from public into private perplexities. It could not be maintained that there is anything very creative in this type of religious emotion.

On the other hand, the secular world probably speaks a little too simply of religion as an "escape" from tragic realities. These criticisms may come with poor grace from a culture which has falsely promised man every type of fulfillment in the historical scene and is now unable to keep these promises. There are experiences which seem to be "escape" from the standpoint of a highly prudential culture which are actually the attainment of serenity within historical frustration, and the achievement of a sense of life's meaning above and beyond the chaos of the day. Such serenity and such faith may become resources for doing our social and historic duties, rather than a mode of escape from them.

Thus we arrive inevitably at the interpretation of the coincidence between religious faith and historic crises which those of us make who are committed to one of the historic faiths. We would question, in the first instance, the distinction which both some secularists and some Christians are inclined to make between religion and irreligion. In one sense there are no irreligious ages or individuals. Every age and every person has some sense of the meaning of life. That is its or his religion. The stable and expanding culture of the nineteenth century was not less religious than our own. It had a different religion. It rejected religions which talked about sin and grace. The perplexities about human nature comprehended by the word "sin" in the historic faiths gave way to an unperplexed belief that human wrongdoing was due either to ignorance or to faulty social organization. It would be eliminated by a growing intelligence and by a reorganization of our political and economic life in either revolutionary or evolutionary terms.

A religion which spoke of revelation and faith gave way to a religion which required no apprehension by faith of the final source and end of life. For there was no mystery to be clarified and no meaning which was not identical with the observable structures of nature, history or reason. Life was meaningful because it was rational. A religion which spoke of "rebirth" and repentance or of "dying to self" gave way to a religion which equated life with growth. Was there anything the matter with life which growth would not cure? Would not technical development cure us of poverty? And educational progress cure us of ignorance? And political development establish a universal society? The historic faiths, with their insistence upon repentance and rebirth, assumed that there was something "wrong" with human nature: that the human self was inclined to destroy itself because it was too intent upon itself; that it was in perpetual need of reversing the process and "dying to self" that it might truly live.

The historic faiths believed that the "dignity" of man and the "misery" of man had a common source in the unique character of man's spiritual freedom, since that freedom made both human creativity and destructiveness possible. Since the seventeenth century our culture has talked much of the "dignity of man"; but as Pascal complained, it knew nothing of the misery of man. Nor was it able to embody tragedy, discontinuity and historic frustration in its sense of the meaning of life.

From the standpoint of the historic faiths, an age of crisis is more explicitly "religious" in the sense that it tends to refute the quasi-religious schemes of meaning by which men have lived in times of stability and ease. The quasi-religious schemes of meaning assumed life to be more simply rational than it is. They regarded historical progress as morally more unambiguous than it proved to be. They found the root of human selfishness too simply in the ignorance of the mind and not in the self. For that matter they frequently obscured the curious human self in all the height of its dreams and the depth of its anxieties in their conception of the "mind." They saw the fulfillment of human hopes too simply in the social-historical process and were covered with confusion when men faced the kind of historic perplexities and frustrations as is now our lot.

The so-called "credulities" of the great historic faiths are really quite sophisticated compared with the credulities of an "age of reason" which seeks to reduce the dimensions of life to proportions which cannot contain its full meaning, particularly not its tragic mixture of beauty and terror. Sometimes the credulities of an age of science sink to the level of the assumption that the same techniques by which we mastered "nature" will also master human nature. Thus we have projects for curing the German people of their aggression by teaching German mothers to be less rigorous in the toilet training of their infants. There are also projects for eliminating the aggressiveness of all nations by establishing mothers' clinics which will teach mothers how to give their children "absolute" security so that no anxiety will tempt them into aggressive behavior. These examples are not a fair sample of the best thought of our age. But they do represent particularly vapid versions of general credulities about the nature of man and the problems of human destiny.

The reasons these "surrogates" for the Christian faith break down in times of historic crises are because they base the meaning of existence upon some assumed stability of human virtue or reason, some pattern of history or some societal security which is swept away by the great upheavals of history.

The examples cited have been taken from the so-called "liberal" or democratic world. We would not do justice to the radical religious reorientation of our day without also citing the tragic refutation of the Marxist surrogate for our historic faiths. My own contact with American colleges began three decades ago when one could assume that the socially sensitive members of the college generation were Marxists. Many of them had acquired their moral sensitivity in religious homes, but they were more or less convinced that Marxism was a receiver in bankruptcy for a moribund religion. They were rightly in revolt against the social irrelevance of the religious faith of their fathers. But they wrongly raised a political and economic program, which may have considerable justification as purely an economic program, into a scheme of salvation.

Most of them were not Communists. But it would be wrong to suppose that present communism is merely a fortuitous corruption of the Marxist dream of utopia. Not all Marxists become Communists. Europe is full of Democratic Socialists, whose devotion to freedom we Americans do not sufficiently appreciate. But they are apostates from the true Marxist faith; and the Communists are the true exponents of the faith and the corrupters of the dream.

The corruption of the Marxist dream of utopia on earth is implicit in the exposition of the Marxist faith. For Marxism in its pure form ascribes all human evil to a social institution: property. It therefore promises mankind redemption from every ill through the project of the socialization of property. In this mistaken belief it creates an omnipotent oligarchy which has all political and economic power in its hands. It places no political checks upon the oligarchy, for in theory the reigning group has identical interests with the total community since it "possesses" no property, the alleged sole cause of divergent interests.

We are all aware of the cruelties and fanaticisms which have sprung from these illusions. They threaten to bring disaster upon the whole world. But we are not fully aware of the religious implications of this development. It is significant that a culture which disposed of God, heaven and hell and tried to reduce life to a cool rationality should have substituted an improbable utopia for an improbable heaven. It is even more significant that this utopia turned into a real hell—on earth. Our own liberal utopian illusions are not as dangerous as the Marxist ones. They have not brought as much pain upon our fellowmen. But they have brought disillusionment upon ourselves. And they have ill prepared us for dealing with the menace of the hard utopian fanatics.

The fact is that man is a "self-surpassing" creature of great creativity and destructiveness who cannot easily find a home in either "nature," reason or history. Every period of social stability tempts him to deny the perplexities of his existence; and to find some easier scheme of redemption than one which challenges him at the very center of his life. The recent period of social stability and technical progress was particularly fertile of such schemes. The refutation of these schemes by contemporary history constitutes the religious dimension of the present crisis.

Some aspects of the current religious "revival" will be no more than manifestations of the general hysteria and disillusionment. Some of them will be quite irrelevant to our present perplexities, though they may be no more irrelevant than, let us say, the secular dream of beguiling the Russians into a world government. But those of us who are devotees of the great historic faiths have the right to hope and believe that there will be aspects of the revival which will represent a profounder awareness of the depth and height of our human existence, of the mystery and meaning of the divine power which bears it, and of the renewals of life which are possible if destructions and frustrations are appropriated with contrition rather than bitterness. Such a religious faith could contribute to the "healing of the nations."

"Dream Town" – Large Economy Size

by Penn Kimball

LEVITTOWN, PA.

THE SPARKLING VISION of new towns in America, graceful and spacious cities with attractive homes and progressive civic planning, has danced on the drafting boards of idealistic young architects for years immemorial. A few tentative experiments in greenbelt living actually advanced beyond the blueprint stage prior to World War II. Some were an esthetic success; most were financial failures. In today's environment of urban catacombs and suburban cell-blocks mankind's inner yearning for reasonable shelter plus tolerable elbow-room flames more fiercely than ever.

How to build the ideal town—on paper—no longer stumps the experts, although individual ideas may clash. How to build a dream town with hard brick and mortar, on the other hand, becomes a knotty question: first of finding economic incentives to bring it to life; then of working out practical ways to amortize twentieth-century luxuries like grass, trees and playgrounds in addition to absolute necessities like asphalt parking lots. Initial cost is the great compromiser of planners' dreams; upkeep is their destroyer.

Yet forces are now being turned loose by an explosive American technology which—potentially, at least—are capable of transforming yesterday's wild dream into tomorrow's commonplace. Building is being revolutionized by assembly-line construction with standardized

From the *New York Times Magazine*, December 14, 1952.

materials. Geography is being upset by the movement and growth of mammoth new facilities for making aluminum, steel, power, atomic weapons.

The vital ingredient for the planners' brave new world is finally within reach. Industry, bursting at the seams, is not only creating the demand for new plant sites and new homes for shifting thousands of factory workers; relocated industry, more than that, promises new sources of stable and taxable wealth to support the planners' schemes, an indispenable artery to pump life into the phantom carcass of a model town.

Thus it is that on the Pennsylvania bank of the Delaware River, not far from where Washington crossed to surprise the Hessians at Trenton, an astonishing pattern begins these days to unfold. A fabulous new skyline of masonry and metal soars from the river flats—a half-billion dollars in blast furnaces, stacks, coke ovens, rolling mills for United States Steel's giant new Fairless Works, which last week poured its first molten iron from its first open-hearth. Conveniently close to thousands of new jobs and already starting to fill with married couples, baby carriages, respectability and hopes (3,250 families will be moved in by Christmas), is the pre-planned new town of the pre-planned frontier.

The paper dreams of planners here stir into reality above the reddish-brown loam of the Bucks County landscape. If a little rubs off on the planners' purity of concept, the process is perhaps less drastic than usual wherever shiny hopes rub against the drab facts of life. Here mass production is joined to mass housing by the cord of mutual advantage. Here also mass housing at irresistible unit prices bowls over the old-fashioned values from a more laggard culture—such as the outmatched urge to be original or the stifled passion for privacy.

Here most any day can be found William Levitt of Levitt & Sons, Inc., builders and merchandisers of new houses in bulk, sitting, quite likely, in the expansive living room of a lovely, old, non-mass-produced Bucks County farmhouse. The thick stone walls and stout beams of the ancient house were painstakingly fashioned by the loving hands of some highly skilled craftsman—built to outlast the ages. Standing alone here, a splendid sentinel on the crest of a wooded hill, the house has both majesty and charm. The house has character. The house is, in fact, obsolete.

"It isn't fair," Mr. Levitt explained, pointing to the old room's ornate moldings and broad baseboards, "to ask the public to pay for things they don't need and can't afford. Imagine asking a modern housewife to clean this place." Mr. Levitt's lawyer and public relations man nodded quick confirmation. "Imagine sticking your own wife way off in the country like this, all by herself. People like people. That's been our experience."

As long as people continue to like people, Levitt & Sons are prepared to accommodate them. Through the wide window of Bill Levitt's farmhouse headquarters are plainly visible the first rooftops and light poles of a booming new Levittown—the first batch of 16,000 houses to go up on 1,100 streets cut through acreage where but a few months ago local farmers raised only spinach. The view from this farmhouse window three years from now will have erupted into the tenth largest city in the State of Pennsylvania.

Starting from scratch, the Levitts will have converted eight square miles of open farm country into a densely populated community of 70,000. Paved streets, sewer lines, school sites, baseball diamonds, shopping center, parking lots, new railroad station, factory sidings, churches, trunk arteries, newspapers, garden clubs, swimming pools, doctors, dentists and town hall—all conceived in advance, all previously planned in one of the most colossal acts ever of mortal creation.

"The most perfectly planned community in America," the Levitts say.

Confidence in this ambitious undertaking and its far-reaching results positively radiates from the counteance of Bill Levitt. The 45-year-old builder, organizer and salesman scarcely looks like a planner as he strides about in a royal blue sports coat, light slacks and fawn-colored oxfords. He doesn't talk exactly like a planner either.

"Personally, I don't put much stock in theories or the book. In this business that market research stuff is the bunk, too. People need to be shown. Ask a woman if she wants a door on the kitchen, she says she wants a door on the kitchen. Then you build a kitchen the size she can afford and she complains of claustrophobia. We know that by experience, the hard way. We don't have to take the door off because she complains. We don't put it on in the first place."

Self-confidence is one of the by-products of the fact that customers have been registering faith in Levitt decisions for a quarter of a century, and spectacularly so during the mass migration to Levittown, L. I., after the war. William, his brother Alfred and father Abraham designed, built and sold 17,500 homes there in five and one-half years. The four-room Levitt house, appearing on the market in the midst of a shortage, offered light, air, convenience and value—selling for substantially less than $10,000 with closing fees, landscaping and kitchen appliances thrown in.

Mass production methods right on the building site (Levitt carpenters never touch a hand saw; paint speckled in two colors comes out of one spray gun) made the Levitt price feasible. But they also defined the massive contours of a rather formidable looking city. Like Topsy, Levittown, L. I., just grow'd—and grow'd.

Late commuters, lost among identical rows of houses along identical street blocks, sometimes reported a sense of panic like bewildered children suddenly turned loose in a house of mirrors. "I got lost there myself looking for street names I never heard of," Bill Levitt recalls. When the lady of the house hung out the wash, the awesome result was 17,500 pairs of shorts flapping in 17,500 backyards. The struggle for identity in these prefabricated circumstances reduced itself occasionally to a pretty fine point—like the tone of a door-chime or a novel idea for a wastebasket.

People liked it, anyhow, were grateful for it, got used to it, grew fond of it. People, it turned out, liked people.

Levittowners, mostly young ex-G. I.'s just getting started, acquired a certain esprit de corps. The crime rate was phenomenally low. By some mysterious process (perhaps some form of mass immunization via mass infection) Levittowners seemed to grow progressively healthier.

The Levitts learned as they built. When a rash of head lacerations swept over the community, they solved the epidemic by removing a swinging window pane from their original design. They found out, contrary to some social theorists, that their customers resisted a chance to acquire extra-sized lots around their houses at no extra expense. The man of the family proved allergic to mowing more lawn and clipping more hedge.

Levittown lawns must be mowed once a week nowadays and the wash never flaps on Sunday. It's all in the deed.

Luckily, Levittown, L. I., sprang up in a previously settled suburban district where such essentials as fire departments, garbage collection and snow plows were already in supply. But the problem of providing and paying for sudden additions to overtaxed facilities quickly had to be faced. One Levittown school district had thirty-one pupils in its two-room school in 1947. Three thousand school kids inundated the same district three years later.

The experience, the pain, the knowledge, the frustrations of their pioneering venture in the potato fields of Long Island—all these are being plowed back into the Levitts' latest project on the banks of the Delaware. "Sure, there's a thrill in meeting a demand with a product no one else can meet," Bill Levitt said. "But I'm not here just to build and sell houses. To be perfectly frank, I'm looking for a little glory, too. It's only human. I want to build a town to be proud of."

The Levitts can, for example, put down water mains and sewer pipes just about where they choose to. They have chosen to put them beneath the backyards of houses instead of under the streets— a simple idea which will save Levittowners the future expense of digging up the pavements every time repairs are needed. A town hall, containing meeting rooms and an 800-seat auditorium, is built where the same parking lots which service a shopping center by day can service community activities in the town hall at night.

Nearly everything does double duty at Levittown. A growing gravel pit adjacent to the concrete plant eventually turns into a community lake. It's all in the plans.

"Intelligent planning is just plain common sense," brother Alfred maintains.

The Levitts discovered on Long Island that 2,000 families can make use of a swimming pool, which occupies no more land than an ordinary tennis court, which at most can accommodate only four persons at a time. There will be eight swimming pools and no tennis courts in Levittown, Pa. Growing trees enhance the value of property as the buildings deteriorate. Trees are being planted at the rate of one every twenty-eight feet—two and one-half trees per home.

In the struggle against monotony the same floor plan has been enclosed by four different types of exteriors, painted in seven varieties of color—so that your shape of Levittown house occurs in the same color only once every twenty-eight times. Streets are curved gently for further esthetic effect, and to slow down auto traffic.

Most ambitious of all is the mass builders' solution for what Lewis Mumford has called the need for "a return to the human scale"—a scale small enough to be recognizable, intimate enough to be neigh-borly, cohesive enough to function.

Levittown, Pa., will be subdivided into sixteen separate "neighborhoods," each bearing distinctive place names like Stonybrook, Lakeside, Birch Valley. (Every street in Stonybrook, for example, begins with "S"—a big help to the postman and late celebrants.) "Birch Valley lies in a little valley where hundreds of birch trees grow," a publicity release idyllizes.

Sociologically speaking, the 300 to 600 families in each of these distinguishable communities will be encouraged to think of themselves as Lakesiders rather than Levittowners, to create their own garden clubs, Little League baseball teams, veterans' organizations, and neighborhood idiosyncrasies. Thus, it is hoped, tender shoots of friendship, kindness and goodwill can push through the chaos and blight of our machine society.

Two or three of these integrated neighborhoods center upon a single school site, with adjacent recreational and athletic facilities. Children can walk to each hub, away from the circumferential boulevards enclosing each community unit, without ever crossing a through street. No school buses will be necessary, another money-saver.

How does all this stack up against professional theory about the ideal town?

Lewis Mumford, a demanding critic of many recent housing developments, has conceded that the Levitt house by itself has a "superior interior design" and offers the public "a great deal of value for the price." After a recent trip to Bucks County, however, he observed that, outside, the Levitts appeared to be using "new-fashioned methods to compound old-fashioned mistakes."

"Most of the open space is in the form of streets instead of gardens," Mumford said. "Endless roads and lengthy sewer lines cost money that might better be spent on reducing the number of houses per acre."

The most pressing requirement of the ideally planned town, Mumford believes, is diversity. "Levittown offers a very narrow range of house type to a narrow income range. It is a one-class community on a great scale—too congested for effective variety and too spread out for social relationships necessary among high school children, old folks and families who can't afford outside help. Mechanically, it is admirably done. Socially, the design is backward."

"What would you call the places our house owners left to move out here?" Bill Levitt replied. "We give them something better and something they can pay for."

Mumford and other experts agree that the Levitts are aimed in the right direction with their plans for identifiable neighborhoods, interior school locations, shade trees, swimming pools and built-in community services. These are ideas which have been set down for years in planning textbooks. The sight of actual earth-moving machines, actual warehouses jammed with crates of home appliances, the sawmills sawing, the trenchdiggers digging, the miles of sewer pipe, the miles of brick, the cement plant (worth $165,000), the pumping stations, the forty-eight carloads of material arriving in the rail yards each morning—all this only suggests the immensity of the investment required, the enormousness of the gamble.

"You have to have nerve," Bill Levitt said. "You have to think big."

Experts are also agreed on the difficulties of creating new communities that can be both self-supporting and self-respecting—that is, neither "company towns" nor "government towns" and still boasting all the modern conveniences. There never was an acute need for industrial acreage in the settled suburban tract over which the Levitts first expanded in Nassau County. With U. S. Steel's giant plant only two miles away, however, the demand of suppliers and satellites for industrial sites in the unsettled Levittown, Pa., area is expected to be tremendous.

New industry is important to independent communities because factories add to the tax list needed to support municipal services. The Levitts estimate that there is already nearly $1,500 worth of community facilities in the $10,500 price they are asking for their 1953 house. Even so, their plans fall short of the ideal. For instance, to remove one eyesore—row upon row of overhead wires and light poles—would add $500 to the cost of each house, Bill Levitt calculates. Although the builders turn over streets, swimming pools, water mains, sewage lines, and town hall free and clear to civic authorities, local residents are going to have to solve the problem of maintaining them.

The dilemma was graphically illustrated when it came time to turn on the street lights for Pennsylvania Levittown's first completed and occupied neighborhood. The stout farmers of Tullytown, one of the four boroughs in which Levittown's 5,000 acres happen to fall, simply refused to switch on any juice for those city fellows over the hill. There never had been any street lights in Tullytown before. Besides, who was going to put up $4,200 a year to pay for them? The Levitt lawyers stepped in and the lights were lit.

As far as local government is concerned, Levittown, Pa., doesn't really exist—just Tullytown, Falls Township, Middletown and Bristol. Politically, the new arrivals have thus been gerrymandered in advance. Traditionally, this has been Republican territory, the home bailiwick of Pennsylvania's famous old Joe Grundy. Part-time road commissioners in these places used to handle most of the public issues which ever popped up prior to the arrival of Bill Levitt's bulldozers. Levitt's dream is to incorporate all of his pre-planned town under one political roof. "It would cost me a million in capital assets," Levitt sighed. "But what a town we could make then, what a town!"

Resurvey of "Hidden Persuaders"

by Vance Packard

"THE HIDDEN PERSUADERS" was a protest against the growing interest professional persuaders are taking in techniques which promise to manipulate the public. Increasingly, they are eschewing rational appeals to us in favor of appeals carefully baited to trigger desired responses at the subconscious level. To this end, they are drawing upon the insights of social scientists and psychiatrists who, in a great many cases, have cooperated with the persuaders in pinpointing subconscious motives which can be tapped. Many of these efforts at motive-tapping are being made beneath the level of our awareness.

The greatest use of depth techniques is being made in the field of commerce, to influence our consuming habits. Although this so-called scientific approach to the consumer at his emotional level is still in the groping stage, it already has been used in campaigns where, in total, billions of dollars' worth of goods have been involved. Many of the nation's largest marketers of consumer goods have been involved in these attempts.

On a more modest scale (because of more limited budgets) publicists, fund-raisers and political campaign managers have been exploring possible ways—through a dredging of our motives—to engineer our consent to their projects or to engineer our enthusiasm for their candidates. We see political candidates being groomed as father images, and political managers seeking to condition the public with

From the *New York Times Magazine*, May 11, 1958.

techniques inspired by Pavlov's famous experiments in conditioning dogs to respond to given stimuli.

In the field of marketing the following techniques for subconscious selling are, I wrote, most commonly used:

(1) Create an image for a product that triggers a favorable response with the consumer because it has an "affinity" for an important aspect of his own personality.

(2) Present a product in such a way that it offers to satisfy a hidden need of the consumer, such as need for security or power.

(3) Offer the consumer relief from his feelings of guilt or anxiety concerning a product. The problem of calming these hidden reservations is said to be an important consideration in marketing billions of dollars' worth of self-indulgence and labor-saving products today.

(4) Present a product in such a way that it seems especially appropriate for the consumer's particular social class, sex or ethnic group.

(5) Offer the consumer status enhancement if he buys the product (i.e. the long car, the costliest perfume, the suburban home).

(6) Create dissatisfaction in the consumer's mind with a product he already owns (which may still be completely satisfactory from a functioning standpoint) so that he will feel a "need" to buy a new model.

(7) Finally, create a mood on the part of the public that encourages people to give vent to their whims and mollify their ids. Techniques for promoting impulse buying in supermarkets are being perfected. Marketers are being admonished to reassure consumers that the hedonistic approach to life is the moral one and that frugality and personal austerity are outdated hangovers of Puritanism.

These techniques are subject to scrutiny first of all on the ground of validity. There has been a great deal of overacceptance on the part of marketing enthusiasts of "motivation research." The clients often fail to examine the research tools being used in their behalf or the caliber of the staffs of the professional firms doing the research. Furthermore they often have failed to subject the findings of motivational analysis to conventional testing for confirmation.

More important, the techniques are subject to scrutiny on the ground of morality. Some of the techniques, certainly, have constructive or relatively harmless application. Many, however, do raise ethical questions of a most disturbing nature.

I referred to those that invade the privacy of our minds by playing upon our frailties, those that deliberately encourage irrational behavior, and those that seek to reshape our national character in the direction of self-indulgent materialism. Both the professional persuaders (advertising men, publicists, etc.) and the cooperating scientists need, I felt, to develop codes of ethics which would cover the kinds of projects that can be condoned and those that cannot be condoned.

That, in gist, is what I conceived my book to be about.

The response to "The Hidden Persuaders" apparently reflects an increasing uneasiness on the part of the public concerning the growing role and influence of these professional persuaders in American life.

An analysis of criticisms of the book by advertising and marketing people reveals these as their major objections:

(1) The book was "malicious." (I wasn't aware of any malice but won't argue the point.)

(2) The book contained nothing new to advertising men. One critic pointed to such pre-Madison Avenue "manipulators" as Tom Paine, Harriet Beecher Stowe, Voltaire and Demosthenes. Another stated: "This psychology stuff is nothing new." (The "newness" of what is going on is the massive recruitment of social scientists to guide the manipulators.)

(3) I had been oversold on the effectiveness and potency of motivational research. A market researcher charged that I had "tumbled unsuspectingly" into the more "lurid" wing of market research and said I had recited with too much trust the "tricks, devices and formulas" of the motivational analysts.

My main defense is that the efficacy of the techniques described was not, frankly, my principal concern. Techniques can be perfected, and these, I repeatedly stressed, were in their infancy. My concern was with the fact that these techniques, whatever their present validity, were *even being attempted* on the public. The public, I felt, should be put on notice. I still feel so and, were I writing the book today, would go further.

Since the book appeared the economic climate in America has changed in some unsettling ways. Several months ago we began experiencing an economic recession despite the best efforts of the industrial persuaders, hidden or otherwise, to move our goods as fast as our economy could produce them. Warehouses became uncomfortably crowded with the products of our excess capacity. The long, fat, chrome-crusted automobile, our prime status symbol, became the victim of rather widespread disenchantment.

Approximately simultaneously Russian satellites began streaking overhead and inspired a great many Americans to begin re-examining the materialistic values by which our society has increasingly been living.

In the field of marketing, meanwhile, the trend toward subconscious selling reached something of a nadir with the unveiling, as I had predicted, of so-called subliminal projection. That is the technique designed to flash messages past our conscious guard.

These developments, plus my own further reflections, have caused me to shift my main area of concern from the manipulators to the climate that has produced them. Today I see their efforts as symptoms of the strain our system is undergoing. Our system itself, which has been impelling us more and more to conform to a materialistic set of values, needs examining, I now see, along with the symptoms.

Our leaders, from the President down, are admonishing us to "buy" more. What we buy is not as important, seemingly, as the mere fact that we buy. A New York newspaper recently headlined the fact that a "rise in thrift" was "disturbing" the Administration. In one United States city a forty-five-voice choir has been admonishing the public over the airways, seventy times a day, with a jingle which ends: "Buy, buy something that you need today."

The really critical problem, as I now perceive it, is this: We as a nation face a set of conditions unique in the history of mankind. In the past man has always had to learn to live with his wants. His world was geared to scarcity. Today the challenge is for man to develop and expand his wants. He is being urged and admonished, here in America, to become more and more self-indulgent in order that he may live comfortably with the ever-greater abundance provided by the fantastic, and constantly soaring, productivity of our automated factories and mechanized farms. We all face not merely the opportunity but the necessity of learning to live like sultans or our system, as presently geared, will languish.

Our gross national product has soared more than 400 per cent since 1940. It shot past $400,000,000,000 in 1956 and some economists have predicted it may reach $600,000,000,000 by the mid-Sixties if our economy remains reasonably healthy.

In order to consume the greatly stepped up output indicated by such a growth our population must, according to the estimate of one leading advertising executive, increase its consumption by an amount "nearly equal to the entire growth of the country in the 200 years from colonial days up to 1940." Consequently, he warned, the American people must be persuaded to expand much further their wants and needs, and quickly.

The relentless, if wondrous, growth of productivity in America is forcing a change in the major preoccupation of the men in America's executive suites, from producing the goods to selling them. The problem of selling all the goods our rapidly expanding economy can turn out when working near its ever-expanding capacity is each year becoming more challenging. It is producing signs not only of indigestion on the part of the public but unhealthy signs of straining on the part of the professional persuaders charged with moving the goods.

I should stress that the overwhelming majority of advertisements we see today are still simply informative, and often charmingly so. Nevertheless, there has been in the past five years a growing fascination in marketing circles with strategies for subconscious selling through national mass media such as television. The straining shows itself in the willingness to adopt strategies which would play upon hidden weaknesses or encourage people to behave in non-rational ways.

Perhaps the most frightening manifestation of this straining is the widespread adoption of marketing strategies based on the creation of "psychological obsolescence" or "planned obsolescence" of adequately functioning products we already own (cars, refrigerators, home furnishings, etc.).

A few weeks ago The Associated Press carried an article citing a number of industries in which this marketing strategy has been attempted and stated: "Advocates of planned obsolescence say it is basic to the modern American economy." It quoted others who disagreed. Financial columnist Sylvia F. Porter cites a leading industrial designer as charging: "One of the causes of recession is the refusal of our people to be seduced any longer by planned obsolescence. . . . Legitimate improvements yes, but this Roman orgy of obsolescence merchandising must come to an end. . . ." Could it be that the public wants improved function more than "style"?

All this straining to keep the sales charts rising is responsible, too, for proposals in marketing circles that Americans should be constantly encouraged to modify their moral reservations toward a hedonistic (or "live it up") attitude toward life.

America has indeed become a nation on a tiger. We are being urged to consume simply to meet the needs of the productive process. That process, as theologian Reinhold Niebuhr has pointed out, threatens to enslave our culture, and force us toward an ever more luxurious style of living. What does our growing absorption with the consumption of goods—and our constant enticement at every turn by sales messages—do to the quality of life?

This necessity of learning to live with a prodigious economic plant presents us with a problem of enormous complexity. I suspect it will increasingly absorb our attention in coming decades. Certainly any acceptable solution must assure reasonably full employment of our people. And we certainly need a stable economy. But the non-material well-being of the consumer-citizen deserves thoughtful consideration, too.

Americans, certainly, should all pitch in and help consume their way out of this recession, as governmental and industrial leaders are urging. They are offering no other alternatives. But the leaders should be urged to start some long-range thinking on this problem.

Our nation, perhaps, will need to find constructive outlets for our productivity if we are to escape the fate of consuming for consumption's sake. We may, for example, find it advisable to attempt finally to expand in a dramatic way our badly neglected and overcrowded health and educational facilities, and to eliminate our hundreds of square miles of urban blight.

Meanwhile, we should look to the non-material well-being of our people. Perhaps young Americans can be encouraged to gain a better perspective on possessions in relation to other life satisfactions. Perhaps they can be encouraged, through education, to develop coherent philosophies of life, philosophies which do not begin and end with self-indulgence.

Finally, if marketers persist in devising strategies to invade the privacy of our minds, we should begin training our younger people to protect their privacy. An awareness of the techniques being attempted is itself a defense.

To sum up, the monumental problem we seem to face is that of working out a spiritually tolerable relationship between our fabulous, dynamic economy and our free people.

Notes on Cult; or, How to Join the Intellectual Establishment

by Victor S. Navasky

IF I HAD any doubts about the existence of the New York intellectual establishment, they were dispelled when Random House editor Jason Epstein told me: "There is no such thing as a New York intellectual establishment. It just looks that way from the outside." As any student of establishments knows, and as Richard Rovere, the Columbus of American establishment studies, has written, the leaders of any establishment will always deny its existence. Epstein is reputed to be on the presidium of the New York intellectual establishment.

I first became aware of this establishment last July when I read an article by Renata Adler in The New Yorker noting the emergence of "a group, a program and perhaps even . . . a new critical school." Miss Adler went on to define the group as a "clique" if not a "cartel." Miss Adler named names. My interest quickened when economist Robert Lekachman reported in the summer volume of a magazine called Social Research that there is a group of "highly articulate men and women," centering mostly around New York, who write out of a "common frame of reference on topics of common interest for *one another's* primary attention." Professor Lekachman named names, too, and he had all of Miss Adler's names and lots more—149, to be precise.

Then along came my autumn issue of The Hudson Review and

there was critic Richard Kostelanetz, who not only named names but named whole races and minority groups, contending that "if one were to investigate the social history of the American literary scene since 1920, he would notice that numerous groups, all, in effect, minorities, have made claims either to represent the mainstream of American culture or its most viable tendency." Mr. Kostalenetz charged Jewish critics with inflating the reputations of Jewish novelists like Saul Bellow, Joseph Heller, Bernard Malamud and Norman Mailer.

Since that time I have seen these same names and races and faces in numerous places, most recently in an account of a forum on Vietnam held in a West 21st Street loft where, according to the papers, Dwight Macdonald identified Yale professor and radical activist Staughton Lynd and historian Arthur Schlesinger, Jr., as "the only nonmembers of the New York intellectual establishment" among the 60 scholars, critics and artists present.

The first thing to understand about the New York intellectual establishment is that to get in, it is desirable to be an intellectual, but one needn't be a New Yorker. In fact, the ideal New York intellectual either hails from, has taught in or currently resides in England. Thus, prominent members include poet W. H. Auden, satirist Jonathan Miller and critic Frank Kermode. Experts estimate that 30 per cent of New York's intellectuals are Englishmen.

And rumors to the contrary notwithstanding, you don't have to be Jewish to be an intellectual. One of the problems Mr. Kostelanetz has with his thesis that Jewish critics have invaded American culture to promote other Jewish critics and Jewish novelists is that it fails adequately to account for such eminent New York "Jews" as Dwight Macdonald, Gore Vidal, Edmund Wilson, Elizabeth Hardwick, James Baldwin, John Phillips (Marquand), Mary McCarthy, and F. W. Dupee. Mr. Kostelanetz doesn't exactly ignore these figures, but to establish his conspiracy theory he must claim that Negro novelist James Baldwin, for instance, was discovered "by largely Jewish magazines" and has "lived his adult life more among Jews than Negroes" because he has "cast his 'alienation' in Jewish terms. . . ."

Despite the fact that some of Mr. Baldwin's best friends may be Jewish and that for all I know he *looks* Jewish, I think it is safe to assume that Mr. Baldwin is not Jewish and that he has gained admission to the circle without regard to race, creed or color. As

George P. Elliot responded in the next issue of The Hudson Review: "Let's face it. Saul Bellow is a pretty good novelist even if a lot of his Jewish friends do praise him. Wordsworth was a pretty good poet even if Coleridge, his best friend, did say so loud and long."

The simplest way to join the establishment is to edit the right magazine. Thus, charter members include Irving Howe and Lewis Coser (editors of Dissent), William Phillips, Richard Poirier, Philip Rahv and Steven Marcus (editors of Partisan Review), Daniel Bell and Irving Kristol (editors of The Public Interest), Barbara Epstein —Jason's wife—and Robert Silvers (editors of The New York Review of Books), and Norman Podhoretz, Theodore Solotaroff and Marion Magid (editors of Commentary).

It also helps to have attended Columbia University or City College, the Oxford and Cambridge of the establishment, and to have been a protégé of, say, Columbia English Prof. Lionel Trilling, but these are not firm requirements. Critic Alfred Kazin, who received a B.A. from City and an M.A. from Columbia, has such impeccable credentials that he was even able to teach at Harvard without incurring disfavor among his New York peers.

That you may never have heard of a majority of these people is not surprising, because members of this establishment traditionally talk only to each other and publish in journals which are prepared primarily for each other's consumption. Nevertheless, occasionally an establishment figure will write an article for Life or some other high-paying market, confident that none of his colleagues will ever see it (unless the colleague happens to be researching an article on mass culture). Norman Podhoretz, one of the more prolific extracurricular establishment writers, once even wrote a caption for a picture in Esquire. And a group of middle-aged Turks, including Dwight Macdonald (also Esquire's movie reviewer), Mary McCarthy and Harold Rosenberg, write with varying degrees of regularity for The New Yorker; this is generally regarded as an aberration traceable to the profit motive, not as a defection from the ranks.

Partisan Review editor William Phillips once provided the definitive explanation for the relative anonymity of the New York intellectual establishment. "While preparing for a course I was teaching," he is reported to have said, "I suddenly realized why the New Critics like Tate and Blackmur and Ransom enjoyed such fine reputations and nobody has ever heard of us. They were always praising each other and we are always at each other's throats." It is an iron law of the establishment that it is better to be attacked by an establishment comrade than to be praised by an outsider.

If you can't edit a journal, the next best thing is to write for one. It is not true that the establishment has typewriters with special keys for words like "alienation," "ambivalence," "apocalyptic" and "middle class," but it is true that writing stories, novels and plays won't do you much good.

The tradition of discourse with which the New York group associates itself is the free-ranging eclectic essay, more profound than journalism but less circumscribed than scholarship. Voltaire and the 18th-century *philosophes* were masters of the form. Mr. Podhoretz, who serves as a kind of Boswell to the establishment (his essay "Book Reviewing and Everyone I Know" caused Amherst Prof. Benjamin DeMott to denounce the establishment as a "socialized," "coherent group" with a too-comfortable "nontoxic environment"), has for some time been writing articles defending the essay-as-art against the novel.

It is not surprising that those novelists who enjoy club privileges, like Baldwin, Mailer (who has been called the Trojan horse of the establishment), Vidal, Philip Roth and Paul Goodman, also put in time as nonfictionists. In fact, when reviewing their novels it is fashionable to mention that they really excel in the nonfiction form. If you want to join the essayists this season, a good topic might be "Understanding Menshevism: From Trotsky to McLuhan," subtitled "A study in ambivalence."

As of this week, the only certified way to gain entry to the inner circle is to write regularly for two of the big three outlets. The Pravda and Izvestia of the establishment are The New York Review of Books, a 57,000-circulation, frankly highbrow, Anglophiliac fortnightly paper founded during the New York newspaper strike of 1962-63 which is distinguished by the breadth, length, depth and width of its book reviews, and which of late has been especially eloquent in identifying the defects of American policy in Vietnam; and Commentary, which has approximately the same number of readers, a free-wheeling monthly funded by the American Jewish Committee and often analogized to the British magazine Encounter. Mr. Podhoretz, its editor, is a frequent and articulate symposiast-around-town whose political views seem closer to the "establishment" establishment than the intellectual one.

Partisan Review, the third member of the troika (with about 20,000 readers) is really the mother of the New York intellectual establishment. At the peak of its influence, in the late thirties, it was an anti-Stalinist, pre-revolutionary, pro-autonomy of culture, pro-European modernist literature journal. In its heyday Partisan was accused of "social fascism," "Trotskyism," "infantile leftism," and "white guardism" but today, as the result of articles like Susan Sontag's famous discussion of Camp, it is accused primarily of "dilettantism." The magazine has recently moved to Rutgers University where it is edited chiefly by William Phillips and Richard Poirier (Philip Rahv has moved to Brandeis University and is editing his own annual, a collection of politics, poetry, fiction and criticism); Mr. Phillips, who has survived the factionalism which has plagued Partisan down through the years, has been called by his critics the Ilya Ehrenberg of the intellectual establishment.

Magazines like The New Republic, The Nation, Commonweal and The New Leader, unlike "the triple alliance" (as Irving Kristol calls the big three) are fellow travelers of the establishment but quite distinct from it.

Mr. Kostelanetz has written in Holiday that "any reviewer who publishes primarily in the self-styled establishment threesome . . . is not a critic but a careerist." But at a recent press conference Miss Sontag pointed out that "Mr. Kostelanetz probably has trouble getting published in these magazines" and that "you can be a career-ist even if you write for The Hiccup Falls Journal. The point is that these are probably the most distinguished magazines in America and it is trivial, envious and spiteful to condemn them in that way."

Contrary to popular opinion, there is no party line except on hang-over sectarian issues of the thirties. On Partisan Review it doesn't hurt to know where you stood in the Trotskyite split between James P. Cannon and Max Schachtman over Russia's invasion of Finland in 1939. In general, though, establishment politics range from Steven-sonian Democratic on the right to Trotskyite Deviationist on the left. And Paul Goodman, who enjoys establishment favors (while violat-ing most club regulations) is an anarchist.

It may help to locate the establishment's vital center to recall that a few months ago when Irving Howe, Michael Harrington, Bay-ard Rustin, Lewis Coser and Penn Kimball chose The New York Re-view of Books to propose a non-Stalinist popular-front opposition to Vietnam policy, they were attacked from the left by Staughton Lynd, who had recently returned from Hanoi, and from the right by former A.D.A. chairman John P. Roche. When Roche resigned a teaching position at Haverford College to accept one at Brandeis University some years ago, he told his students, "I was born a Catholic and I'm a practicing Quaker but I'm going to Brandeis because at heart I'm a Jewish intellectual."

You can't have voted for Richard Nixon, however, and be a member of the New York intellectual establishment.

Of course, the real reason ideology is not controlling in establishment article-writing is that the secret purpose of establishment articles is to attract letters. Mr. Podhoretz admits that when Commentary ran an article called "Johnson and the Intellectuals," by the Englishman Henry Fairlie, attacking the intellectuals for mistaking Johnsonian style for Johnsonian achievements, he did so "as a provocative act" and that he "disagreed with almost every syllable." Letters are still coming in.

That is one of the reasons so many members of this group resent The New Yorker, which makes a policy of not printing letters. Irving Howe went so far as to publish an article in Commentary criticizing The New Yorker's no-letter policy on the occasion of Hannah Arendt's Eichmann articles. He suggested that while rebuttals, counter-rebuttals and counter-counter-rebuttals may appear "tiresome" and "grubby" they are what our intellectual life is all about, especially when the rebutters may know more than the original writer (as Mr. Howe believed to be the case in the instance under discussion).

The only immediate impact Mr. Howe's article seems to have had is that Miss Arendt has stopped speaking to him, but various New Yorker writers have taken their own potshots at Howe & Co. For instance, New Yorker staffer Calvin Trillin claims that all of the members of Mr. Howe's club (which Mr. Trillin calls "the College of Irvings") never leave the clubhouse. Their only contact with the outside world is a clipping service and every month a different member is permitted to go out and pick up the clips on the topic of the month (recent topics have included "Camp," "the so-called New Left" and "Vietnam"). When the clippings are in they are passed around and then everybody sits down and starts writing letters to everybody else.

Actually, there *are* certain simple rules for establishment letter-writing which, if followed, should guarantee publication. (1) You should attack the content of a man's article. You can do this either directly or indirectly by misstating his argument (which will force him to waste part of his rebuttal on correcting trivia); (2) you should attack his style; (3) if nothing is wrong with either content or style, you can always attack his personality; (4) if that doesn't work, you can attack his friends (as Columbia sociologist Amitai Etzioni did when he claimed that "Mr. [Jason] Epstein's criteria for reviewing . . . reflect the personal problems of a small group of antiestablishment establishmentarians rather than those either of my profession or of this country," and added: "I wish Epstein and company would be somewhat more bound by the canon of evidence and, instead of quoting each other, would learn to count"); (5) and when all else fails, you can attack the publisher. Mr. Podhoretz opened up a sixth possibility for letter writers when, in an article called "My Negro Problem—and Ours," he attacked himself.

Last year's award for the most successful *ad hominem* rebuttal went unanimously to the establishment's Girl of Last Year, Susan Sontag, for her campy attack in Partisan Review on antiestablishment critic John Simon's "bodily juices." Mr. Simon had attacked her article on Camp. Actually, what Miss Sontag did was to assure Mr. Simon, known in the trade as John Simon the Bad (as distinguished from a Random House editor of the same name known as John Simon the Good), that nobody was "contaminating" his bodily juices; but in the correspondence game such a denial is equivalent to a veiled accusation.

Honorable mention for the most subtle *ad hominem* attack went to Lionel Abel for attacking the reviewer of his play by forgetting the reviewer's name: ". . . many of us had come to think that in The New York Review of Books, at least, ignorance and arrogance could not pass for criticism. Were we wrong? . . . I have in mind the hapless review of my play, 'The Wives,' by some person unknown to me. What is his name? I shall have to look—I don't want to misspell it. . . ." And while it is an old trick to suggest to a reviewer that he read the book being reviewed, a special education award goes to the signers of the letter which invited George Lichtheim, the reviewer of Herbert Marcuse's "One-Dimensional Man," to *re*-read Marx, Mills, Hegel and Freud, not to mention Marcuse.

Negro playwright LeRoi Jones, who used to be an establishment pet until he started biting his masters, won the all-purpose libel award when he wrote to Philip Roth, who had reviewed his play,

"Dutchman": "Sir, it is not my fault that you are so feeble-minded you refuse to see any Negro as a man, but rather as the narrow product of your own sterile response. . . . The main rot in the minds of 'academic' liberals like yourself is that you take your own distortion of the world to be somehow more profound than the cracker's. . . . Mr. Roth, you are no brighter than the rest of America, sicker perhaps."

Occasionally, to reach the establishment it is necessary to go beyond its borders and parachute in from alien territory. Thus when Hans J. Morgenthau had a falling out with Commentary editor Podhoretz over the editing of a Morgenthau article on Barry Goldwater, he elected to air his grievance as an open letter in the counter-establishment Hudson Review. Taking his cue, Mr. Podhoretz published a reply in another non-establishment periodical, Harper's, arguing in the course of a piece called "In Defense of Editing" that Mr. Morgenthau didn't appreciate the editor's role.

This proved to be a mistake because it left the versatile Mr. Podhoretz's flank open to an attack some weeks later by New Republic theater critic Robert Brustein, an establishment alumnus (he has since accepted an appointment as Dean of the Yale School of Drama), who recalled that the last time out Mr. Podhoretz had been defending the article-*writer's* role. "I am certain," wrote Mr. Brustein, "that if Mr. Podhoretz ever went into the plumbing business, we would soon have an essay on how the toilet bowl is replacing the book." Mr. Podhoretz ended the exchange with a brief letter which in effect stated that Mr. Brustein's charge didn't *deserve* a letter.

According to Paul Goodman, it is not enough simply to be published in the right places. If you want to enjoy the fringe benefits, you have to adapt to establishment folkways. "If you play the game," he says, "go to the right parties, talk to the right people and review books in the right way, then you get the patronage—the literary plums. It's worse than Surrogate's Court. You get $2,000 for collecting the short novels of Henry James and pasting together an introduction from stuff somebody else has written. I don't want to collect the short novels of Henry James."

Irving Howe disagrees, saying: "There's a lot of talk about back-scratching, but I don't see much. Change the word 'back' to the word 'eye' and maybe you've got something."

Nevertheless, veteran establishment watchers confirm that on occasion failure to "play the game" can result in massive retaliation. For instance, the current administration has been guilty on more than one occasion of Reviews Management. Thus, when establishment in-and-outer Richard Gilman's favorable review of Wallace Markfield's *roman à clef,* "To an Early Grave," was turned down by one of the big three and a less charitable review appeared in its place, the *clef* to this situation may well have been the fact that the editor of the publication in question was reportedly the model for a key character in the novel.

And when W. D. Snodgrass, imported to review his former mentor Robert Lowell's play, "The Old Glory," came up with a review which, although laudatory, failed to contain any quotable praises for advertising purposes, the editors and/or proofreaders of New York Review apparently retaliated by employing what can only be called typographical warfare. The Contributors' Notes described "Heart's Needle," Mr. Snodgrass's Pulitzer Prize-winning book of poetry, as "Heart's Noodle." Although it must be conceded that, given the average number of typos per issue, the New York Review's otherwise scrupulous editors would have a good case if they simply pleaded the law of averages.

Perhaps the most blatant instance of Managing the Reviews occurred when Jason Epstein reviewed W. H. Auden's "The Dyer's Hand" in Partisan Review. There was nothing irregular about it except that Mr. Epstein is Mr. Auden's editor at Random House. (Epstein has pointed out, in his own defense, that nobody really "edits" Auden.)

Circumstantial evidence of this sort has led some applicants to conclude that it is possible to circumvent the requirements of the establishment's admissions committee by having a man like Mr. Epstein let you in through the side door. "Jason is the broker who holds it together," says writer David Bazelon, whose book "The Paper Economy" (which Epstein edited) analogizes the literary world to a barter society where social invitation and reputation are the basic currency and a recent success is the most substantial collateral for further credit.

In such a society, having an introduction from Mr. Epstein cannot do any harm. In addition to whatever power is conferred on him by virtue of his position as an officer and editor at Random House, he helped found The New York Review of Books; he has been close friends with Commentary editor Podhoretz since their student days at Columbia (and these days, Mr. Podhoretz and his wife, Midge Decter, attend dinner parties with Jacqueline Kennedy and have even been awarded a three-hour private White House audience with President Johnson); he stands in a filial relationship to such supra-establishment figures as Lionel Trilling (his former professor) and Edmund Wilson (his one-time Cape Cod summer landlord); he has literary, social and sentimental links with Partisan Review (associate editor Marcus was a Columbia contemporary); he maintains social intercourse with George Plimpton's transcontinental Paris Review (Paris Review staffer Jill Fox is the wife of Epstein's closest Random House colleague, Truman Capote's editor, Joseph Fox); he publishes a roster of establishment authors; and, although more than a decade has passed since his days at Doubleday's Anchor Books division, he still maintains a justifiably high credit rating as the founding father, at age 24, of the quality paperback (author Martin Mayer has dubbed him "the Robespierre of the paperback revolution").

A good example of a book which benefited from this circuit is Paul Goodman's extraordinary "Growing Up Absurd." This book had been turned down by 18 publishers when it came to Commentary. Mr. Podhoretz read it, called Mr. Epstein and insisted that he come over that night. Epstein, who had heard of the book but had been unenthusiastic, spent the evening reading it in a corner of the Podhoretz living room and Goodman had a contract offer the next morning. Since that time the book has sold over 150,000 copies. When I asked an editor from a rival publishing house (which had turned it down) the secret of the book's success over and above its message, he said, without hesitation, "Jason Epstein's big mouth."

Norman O. Brown's radical reinterpretation of Freud, "Life Against Death," traveled something of the same circuit. And Mr. Eliot Fremont-Smith, a daily reviewer for The New York Times, complained, on publication day of "Against Interpretation," a collection of essays by the controversial Susan Sontag, that "she did not creep modestly and hesitantly onto the intellectual scene. . . . Instead, she burst from nowhere amid something like a tickertape parade . . . throwers being her publisher (Roger Straus, Jr.) and the somewhat brassy, assertive and valuable junior members of the Partisan Review–New York Review of Books culture coterie. . . . Instead of being announced, she had been proclaimed."

If I have given the impression that the establishment spends half its time attacking its members in public and the other half promoting their good works in private that is only partially true. It also attacks other people and institutions.

One of its chief subdivisions, the Intellectual SMERSH, is headed by Dwight Macdonald, who scours the country searching for middlebrow culture to expose and demolish. Mr. Macdonald has taken on such "masscult" (Mr. Macdonald's word for culture for the masses) and "midcult" (Mr. Macdonald's word for masscult which masquerades as high culture) institutions as the Book-of-the-Month Club, Archibald MacLeish's play, "J. B.," the dictionary, and the Bible. It is important to recognize that the mission of the Intellectual SMERSH is not to get the masses reading Freud, Marx, Kierkegaard, Dostoyevsky and Proust, but rather to protect high élite culture from contamination by the Philistines.

It is rumored that the SMERSH division has a number of researchers' positions open. Their job is to scan the latest issues of Time, Life, Look, Harper's, Atlantic, The Reader's Digest in the time left over after watching television and listening to the radio. Whatever everybody else is for, SMERSH is against.

The audience at a recent symposium on "Literature and Politics" at the 92nd Street Young Men's Hebrew Association, an athletic club which is really a front for the establishment, were privileged to witness the dynamics of this process in action. "Since it is soon going to be fashionable to attack Truman Capote's 'In Cold Blood,'" stated symposiast Podhoretz, implicitly acknowledging the reams of publicity Capote had been receiving, "I want to go on record as saying I think it's a good book . . . not a great book, but a good book." Mr. Podhoretz then eloquently proceeded to explain why it was *not* a great book and SMERSH was on its way. As novelist George P. Elliot has observed, "These people are the Diors and Schiaparellis of intellectual fashion design. What they think today, you're apt to find yourself, in a Sears, Roebuckish sort of way, thinking tomorrow."

Today's most fashionable target is, of course, Lyndon B. Johnson. Ever since he made the mistake of inviting the New York intellectuals to last season's White House Festival of the Arts, the President has had cause to regret it.

Robert Lowell, it will be recalled, made national headlines when he refused to attend and/or read his poetry on the grounds that to do so would be to condone the napalming of Vietnamese villages.

SMERSH had agents on the premises who circulated a Vietnam peace petition. Symposiasts always get a cheap hand when they attack the President and Norman Mailer recently got cheers when he told a Y.M.H.A. audience that L.B.J. "inspires nausea." With the departure from Washington of former Assistant Secretary of Labor Daniel ("Pat") Moynihan and former White House Assistant Richard Goodwin for a year's writing and research at Connecticut Wesleyan University (which is becoming something of a rehabilitation center for New York intellectuals *manqués* on their way back to civilization) communications between the President and this particular group of subjects leaves more and more to be desired.

Nobody is saying that you have to defame the President in order to publish, say, in Partisan Review. It is merely that such activity is at present a popular hobby. Other causes which have mobilized establishment support in the form of petitions, letters, advertisements, committees and direct action include appeals for clemency for Morton Sobell, protesting the arrest of Lenny Bruce as a violation of the First Amendment, intentionally failing to take cover during civil defense alerts, appealing to the Soviet Union on behalf of imprisoned Soviet writers Daniel and Sinyavsky, protesting the fingerprinting of New York cabaret performers as an invasion of privacy and demanding that the late Adlai Stevenson resign his post as Ambassador to the U.N. (In a posthumously published letter to Paul Goodman, Mr. Stevenson wrote that he did not share the intellectuals' belief in "the disastrous trend of American foreign policy.") And Susan Sontag traveled to Hollywood to speak at the unveiling of a 60-foot-high "tower of protest" symbolizing opposition to the war in Vietnam.

In the late thirties and forties political issues were thrashed out at a roving Saturday night party, but by the mid-fifties the party (which West Coast writer Paul Jacobs calls "the roving kibbutz") was on the wane and today everybody sees everybody else only on an *ad hoc* basis. Although a number of people have tried to start establishment salons, there really aren't any and so, unlike 18th-century France, it is impossible for today's young man from the provinces to rise to the top of the establishment in somebody's living room.

The reason there are no successful salons is simple. To have a salon, enemies must at least be friendly. But as Columbia English Prof. Albert Goldman has pointed out, "We don't have enough manners to constitute a salon. We don't have enough social quality.

We don't like each other enough." Mr. Podhoretz confirmed this when he told me, "We talk to each other only because respect is compelled by achievement."

And Irving Kristol theorizes, "A lot of New York intellectuals have roots in Eastern Europe where, unlike England and France, there was no tradition of civility. In England and France you operate within a framework of existing institutions. In Eastern Europe we wanted to *change* the existing institutions, to improve them. The Cossack was the existing institution. So ideas were more important than institutions. That's why if you disagree with somebody you stop talking to him and start your own magazine." (Mr. Kristol and Daniel Bell, who are more conservative than most of their establishment colleagues, have recently inaugurated The Public Interest, whose purpose is to bridge the gap between the intellectuals and working politicians and bureaucrats.)

Perhaps the point is best made by recalling what happened when, some years ago, a Partisan Review editor entered the home of Roger Straus, Jr., who does more dinner party recruiting and entertaining than most, and spied a novelist friend coming down the stairs in a dinner jacket. Before he could contain himself, he is reported to have blurted out, "What are *you* doing here?"

Everything else aside, the establishment is pretty much unanimous in insisting on one final, minor membership qualification—brilliance. As Mr. Podhoretz puts it, "On the whole, I should say these are the most intelligent people in America."

Robert Nisbet, who has astutely noted that today's intellectual is lineally descended from the medieval court jester, has written in Commentary, "No one could have accused Voltaire, D'Alembert, Diderot and Helvetius of thoroughness or depth and I am not sure that any one of them would have claimed it. But the *philosophes* would have loved the praise of brilliance applied to them. And indeed they were brilliant, as are so very many of us today."

And when I asked Irving Howe why he remains in New York despite attractive offers to teach elsewhere, he said, "It's because in New York I can talk to people like Meyer Shapiro, Daniel Bell, Harold Rosenberg and Lionel Abel. They usually disagree with me but they put me on my mettle. Outside of New York I might be a big cheese in a small town. But the trouble with big cheeses is that they're full of holes and I want to be near people who can point them out."

It is fashionable for the New York intellectual establishment not only to deny its existence but as a corollary to deny its influence. Yet the White House took the trouble to call the New York Review and request that an I. F. Stone analysis of Vietnam not go unchallenged, and when Arthur Schlesinger, Jr., was asked at the Theater for Ideas debate on Vietnam whether the intellectual opposition to our involvement had any impact, he responded, "It has had a genuine effect. I think the President's Johns Hopkins speech . . . was given when it was, partly because of that opposition."

Albert Goldman makes the point: "Of course, they wield influence. And it's probably a lot more than anyone will admit. Every time an intellectual burps, the mass media amplify it coast to coast. Susan Sontag is brilliant and profound but all she did in her 'Notes on Camp' was to casually throw a match and it turned into a forest fire."

Time magazine takes 12 subscriptions to Commentary. And a review by Irving Howe (in a non-establishment publication) converted Henry Roth's forgotten novel, "Call It Sleep," into an overnight best seller. The cult-heroes of yesterday (from Joyce and Eliot through Ionesco and Ginsberg) are taught in the classroom today. At its best, the New York establishment keeps the real establishment honest. It is fighting (even among itself) to preserve standards and refine the future quality of our culture. David Bazelon goes even further. "There's an intellectual revolution going on," he says, "and we're about to see the emergence of a New Class—a new intelligentsia. Guys like Epstein and Podhoretz are riding herd on a hurricane. They are giving direction and shape to this revolution."

The moral is, if you want to join the New York intellectual establishment you had better hurry up. Remember, all you've got to do is make the right friends and then attack them, claim that the establishment doesn't exist and that everyone in it is brilliant, and denounce the mass media while they are lionizing you.

The Second Feminist Wave

by Martha Weinman Lear

IT WAS BILLED as a black comedy, nothing elaborate. Twelve comely feminists, dressed for cocktails, would crash the hearings of the Equal Employment Opportunities Commission on sex discrimination in employment. They would make some noise, possibly get arrested, certainly get thrown out, meet the press, and all the while give prominent display to large, home-lettered signs, of which my favorite read: "A Chicken in Every Pot, A Whore in Every Home."

The feminists were members of the New York chapter of NOW (a multi-layered acronym: The National Organization for Women, which wants "full equality for all women in America, in truly equal partnership with men," *now*). To the press, they would explain that they were protesting all those prejudices and laws of the land which keep women at home and in the bottom of the job market, and exclude them from jobs that utilize intelligence in any significant way.

This makes it clear, they would say, that women are valued not for their intelligence but only for their sexuality—i.e., as wives and mothers—which, stripping the matter of its traditional sacred cows, reduces the Woman's Role to a sort of socially acceptable whoredom.

The point was delicate and not necessarily crystal clear, and certain NOW officials foresaw a disastrous misunderstanding. As one of them pointed out, how might the banner headlines look: "Prostitutes Picket E.E.O.C."?

By compromise, 12 "whores" metamorphosed into two secretaries

From the *New York Times Magazine,* March 10, 1968.

who picketed the E.E.O.C. several weeks back, literally chained to their typewriters. This made a precise point in an eminently respectable way, and the press coverage was good.

Shortly before that, NOW members had picketed The New York Times in protest against the "Help Wanted—Male" and "Help Wanted—Female" column headings in classified advertising. They maintained these designations violate Title VII of the Civil Rights Act of 1964, which prohibits sex discriminaton in employment. The E.E.O.C. permits such column headings, by a logic which seems capricious to feminists and complex to almost everyone. NOW representatives met with officials of The Times. ("We told them," one feminist said, "that those column headings perpetuate the employment ghetto." "We told them," said Monroe Green, then The Times vice president in charge of advertising, "that if we discontinued the column headings there might be fewer jobs for women because men would be applying for them. After all, men can be just as militant as women.") Nothing swayed, the NOW people recently announced that they are bringing suit against the E.E.O.C. to get a ruling on the matter.

They also are helping two stewardesses' unions to fight for the right of an airline hostess to stay on the job after she dodders past her 32nd birthday. In New York, they are pushing for the repeal of all state abortion laws. In Washington, they are lobbying for passage of a civil-rights amendment for women, which has been getting tossed out of every Congress since 1923. In various states they have pending court cases which will test the validity of so-called "protective laws" (i.e., women may work only so many hours; women may lift only so many pounds). NOW says these laws are obsolescent and keep women from earning more money and getting better jobs.

What NOW wants, by way of immediate implementation of its goals, is total enforcement of Title VII; a nationwide network of child-care centers, operating as optional community facilities; revision of the tax laws to permit full deduction of housekeeping and child-care expenses for working parents; maternity benefits which would allow some period of paid maternity leave and guarantee a woman's right to return to her job after childbirth; revision of divorce and alimony laws ("so that unsuccessful marriages may be terminated without hypocrisy, and new ones contracted without undue financial hardship to either man or woman"), and a constitutional amendment withholding Federal funds from any agency, institution or organization discriminating against women.

In short, feminism, which one might have supposed as dead as the Polish Question, is again an issue. Proponents call it the Second Feminist Wave, the first having ebbed after the glorious victory of suffrage and disappeared, finally, into the great sandbar of Togetherness. When I prepared to do an article on this new tide, I prepared also to be entertained; it is the feminist burden that theirs is the only civil-rights movement in history which has been put down, consistently, by the cruelest weapon of them all—ridicule.

"We must not be afraid of ridicule," they say to one another. And, indeed, when pink refrigerators abound, when women (51 per cent of the population) hold unparalleled consumer power, when women control most of the corporate stocks, when women have ready access to higher education and to the professions, when millions of women are gainfully employed, when all the nation is telling American women, all the time, that they are the most privileged female population on earth, the insistence on a civil-rights movement for women does seem a trifle stubborn. "Oh, come off it; why ruin it for the rest of us?" a New York matron recently commented to a NOW member, and she wasn't half kidding.

But the feminists, in answer, pose a question: Ruin *what?* In the anti-feminist view, the status quo is plenty good enough. In the feminist view, it is a sellout: American women have traded their rights for their comfort, and now are too comfortable to care.

Economic power is a fraud, the feminists say, when it devolves ultimately upon the power to decide which breakfast food to buy; that is not what *men* mean when they speak of power. The corporate power is a myth. "What it means generally," says NOW's president, Betty Friedan, whose book, "The Feminine Mystique," provided a powerful undercurrent to this second wave, "is that wives and widows own the stocks and men vote them."

Equal opportunity in education is seen as similarly mythical. "By the time a girl is ready for medical school, she doesn't want to go any more," says Kate Millet of NOW's New York chapter, an artist and English instructor at Barnard. "She never really had a choice. She's been conditioned to her role ever since she got the doll to play with, and her brother got the gun." Seven per cent of the nation's doctors are women, 3 per cent of its lawyers, 1 per cent of its engineers. Nor does this represent progress; the figures have been moving downward quite steadily since World War II, when that first feminist wave receded entirely.

As to the job market: 28 million women are in it and three-quarters of them are in the rock-bottom of it. Ninety per cent earn less than $5,000 a year. John F. Kennedy's Commission on the Status of Women reported in 1963 that women earn up to 40 per cent less than men, on the same jobs. It further noted:

"The subtle limitations imposed by custom are, upon occasion, reinforced by specific barriers. . . . Some of these discriminatory provisions are contained in the common law. Some are written into statute. Some are upheld by court decisions. Others take the form of practices of industrial, labor, professional or governmental organizations that discriminate against women in apprenticeship, training, hiring, wages and promotion."

In a paper called "Jane Crow and the Law," written by New York lawyer Pauli Murray and Mary O. Eastwood, a lawyer with the Justice Department, the pivotal point was made that the doctrine of legislative classification by sex, which generally has been upheld in the courts, "totally defeats the meaning of equal protection of the law for women."

It's all there, but most women seem not to consider it a burning issue of the day. What, then, makes the feminist? One kind of answer is provided by Jean Faust of New York's NOW: 37, married, attractive, a research assistant to Congressman William F. Ryan. Of her marriage, she says: "I do not agree with the concept of marriage; but I must live in our society, and this is still the most convenient way for a man and a woman to remain together." Further:

"I grew up in North Carolina, a sharecropper's daughter. In a farm surrounding, muscle counts. I had eight brothers and sisters, and it was constantly drummed into me that the men rule, that they are smarter and more important and may live a freer life.

"In school, I was always way ahead of the boys. So I began to ask myself: 'How can they say boys are smarter?' As I grew older, I realized more and more that girls had no real part in forming the lives they would lead, or their roles or aspirations. The boys could go as far as their talents would allow, but the girls had it all planned out for them.

"I managed to get to college. I would try to express my ideas, and the men would laugh. They'd say, 'That's funny; you don't *look* like a feminist.' You know—if you're a feminist, you're not feminine.

"When I got married, it was worse. I had worked myself into an executive position with a cosmetics firm, and there were two men working for me who made more money than I did. When I asked for a raise, my employer said: 'You're a married woman. You don't need a raise. Your husband will support you.' So I quit.

"I joined NOW as soon as I heard of it, and I believe we will be historic. Men all along have determined what part we should take in society. And for the first time, we are saying: 'NO!' "

In point of fact, it has been getting said for centuries, and men have said it. Socrates said that the state shortchanged itself and its women by confining them to the domestic role. Auguste Comte spoke of "the feminine revolution" that "must now complete the proletarian revolution. . . ." John Stuart Mill wrote that "the legal subordination of one sex to the other . . . ought to be replaced by a principle of perfect equality." In our own decades, Gunnar Myrdal has written: "As the Negro was awarded his 'place' in society, so there was a 'woman's place.' . . . The myth of the 'contented woman,' who did not want to have suffrage or other civil rights and equal opportunities, had the same social function as the myth of the 'contented Negro.' "

NOW often makes this analogy between the Negro and the woman in society, calling itself, in fact, a sort of N.A.A.C.P. for women. (Not that there is unanimity on this point; predictably, there are feminist evolutionaries and feminist revolutionaries, and the revolutionaries prefer an analogy to the early CORE.)

The women who formed NOW, in 1966, had no need individually of a civil-rights organization. They wanted, they say, to reach those masses of women who stand outside the mainstream of society, and help them swim. Among the charter members were Dr. Kathryn Clarenbach, a Wisconsin educator; Alice Rossi, a Chicago sociologist; Eileen Hernandez, a California lawyer and former member of the E.E.O.C.; Caroline Davis, a Detroit U.A.W. executive, and Betty Friedan.

"For years feminism has been an apology," says Mrs. Friedan. "All those ladies' auxiliaries like the League of Women Voters, saying, 'Don't get us wrong; *we're* not feminists.' What self-denigration! I call them Aunt Toms. Aunt Toms think there are three kinds of people—men, women and themselves.

"Once I was interviewed on television and said something about getting more satisfaction out of having a byline than out of washing dishes. And the hostess, a big, tough battleaxe who has worked ruthlessly for her success, smiled tenderly at the studio audience and said, 'Oh, girls . . . what does a byline *mean?* Don't we all know that being home washing the dishes and caring for her loved ones is the most satisfying work a woman can do?' That's a real Aunt Tom.

"A group of us met in Washington with the head of the E.E.O.C. We said one of our complaints was that women were employed only in the most menial jobs in his department. He said, 'I'm interviewing girls right now for important jobs.' I said, 'Mr. Chairman, I would hope you're interviewing *women.*' It's like calling a 50-year-old Negro 'boy.' He got the point."

Today NOW has 1,200 members, with a heavy concentration of lawyers, sociologists and educators. Among these 1,200 are some hundred men, many of them also lawyers. For all of them the central issue is civil rights, as purely defined as in the Negro civil-rights movement.

"There are striking parallels," says New York attorney Florynce Henderson, an ebullient revolutionary spirit who represents H. Rap Brown. "In court, you often get a more patronizing attitude to blacks and women than to white men: 'Your Honor, I've known this boy since he was a child, his mother worked for my family. . . .' 'Your Honor, she is just a woman, she has three small children. . . .' And I think white male society often takes the same attitude toward both: 'If we want to *give* power to you, O.K. But don't act as if you're *entitled* to it.' That's too manly, too . . . white."

Not all of the new feminist activity is centered within NOW. To its left is a small group called Radical Women—young, bright-eyed, cheerfully militant—which recently splintered off from Students for a Democratic Society. "One of our main problems in the liberal left," says Anna Koedt, a New York commercial artist, "was that we were considered a sort of sex pool. The so-called 'emancipated male' wants women to be free because he thinks that means free love. It's the Playboy image, the same old adolescent sex hang-up. We want to get *away* from relating to men merely as sex objects. We believe in a total change in the social structure to achieve total equality of the sexes, so that men and women will be free to come together in more humane, meaningful relationships." So go the Radical Women. Some of them recently joined—infiltrated?—NOW, whose conservative faction ponders the alliance with a certain ambivalence.

There is also the Quid Pro Quo in New Orleans. It is a one-member civil-rights organization for women, and the member is a man: Richard N. Matthews, an attorney, who currently represents 16 women in a suit to challenge the state protective laws. "Some of these women support their families and have to moonlight," Mr. Matthews says. "They can't work more than eight hours for one employer, but they can work eight hours each for two employers. Women always have gotten the short end of the industrial stick. It's archaic. It's absurd. If women stopped working, they could shut down the country."

The evolutionaries attack concrete issues, tied primarily to employment. They are NOW's pragmaticians, and its overwhelming majority. The militants are its theoreticians—atypical, but they are interesting, because they are the movement's intellectual hip, the female version of Black Power.

Mostly they are young, incipiently successful, unmarried. (Married feminists tend to retain their maiden names, as with Suzanne Schad-Somers, a sociologist named Schad married to a sociologist named Somers, who says: "My husband urged me to join NOW. Neither of us believes you can have a good marriage on the basis of a traditional division of labor." Philosophically they are by Comte out of Simone de Beauvoir, whose book "The Second Sex" shattered the serenity of a postwar generation of sociology majors raised on *Kirche, Küche und Kinder*. Their thesis is that true equality for women can come only with profound social revolution. Their *haute* thinker, and thus the key to their spirit and style, is Ti-Grace Atkinson (in the *patois* of Louisiana, where she was born, "Ti" designates a namesake), president of the New York chapter.

Miss Atkinson is 29, unmarried, good-looking (in The Times, she has been described as "softly sexy," which is not *necessarily* a compliment to a feminist). She is an analytic philosopher, working for her doctorate at Columbia.

I saw her at a recent American Philosophical Association convention in Boston, standing toe-to-toe with a social philosopher, his nose pointed belligerently up at her chin, as he insisted angrily upon the biological superiority of men. He was perhaps 5 foot 5, and Miss Atkinson is 5 foot 9, and it really wasn't fair. Later, she sparred lightly with another philosopher, noting: "We seem to have a chary attitude toward one another." And he, sparring less lightly, replied, "Yes, but mine is much charier than yours." To a third, she said, "You mean, you don't believe women should have equal rights?" And he answered: "I don't believe they exist, so how can they have rights?" Philosophers.

Later, she said: "He wasn't kidding. Why should men think women are equal, when so many women don't?

"Most women don't really see themselves as human beings with potential. They live through their husbands and children. They see themselves vicariously as the men they're married to. They achieve their status through 'the other' [a de Beauvoir concept].

"The institution of marriage has the same effect the institution of slavery had. It separates people in the same category, disperses them, keeps them from identifying as a class. The masses of slaves didn't recognize their condition, either. To say that a woman is really 'happy' with her home and kids is as irrelevant as saying that the blacks were 'happy' being taken care of by Ol' Massa. She is defined by her maintenance role. Her husband is defined by his productive role. We're saying that *all* human beings should have a productive role in society.

"We've always been so defensive. 'Oh, no, *we're* not feminists, but can we just have a little more, huh? Please? Huh?' I think it's time for us to go on the offensive. I think we ought to say, 'Listen, you, you dumb broad, you look funny. You stay home, you're kind of empty, you're bored, you take your frustrations out on your husband, you dominate your kids, and when you get older you disintegrate. You fill the doctors' offices with headaches and backaches and depression, you tell the psychiatrists you don't feel 'fulfilled,' you get menopausal breakdown. . . . What good are you? *Who* are you? *Get with it.*' "

Miss Atkinson herself was a late starter, as feminists go. She was married at 17, with the blessing of social and conservative parents who felt that marriage would soothe their daughter's rebellious (not feminist, simply rebellious) spirit. For a time, she lived with her student husband in a campus community where, as she recalls, "I went to little tea parties given by faculty wives and sat there feeling that life was over. At 17."

When her husband went into the service, she enrolled at the University of Pennsylvania, got a fine arts degree, later got a divorce, and spent several years commuting between New York, where she was writing criticism for Art News, and Philadelphia, where she helped found the Institute of Contemporary Art. She was its first director, in 1963.

"I felt I was budding, growing, but I had no clear idea of my direction. I still knew nothing of feminist concepts." Then friends recommended that she read de Beauvoir's "The Second Sex." Whammo. "It changed everything for me. It changed my life." She enrolled at Columbia as a graduate student in philosophy and embarked upon a correspondence with de Beauvoir, who suggested that Miss Atkinson put herself in touch with some women's civil-rights group in the United States. Thus she came to the infant NOW, and was put to work as a national fund raiser; her social connections were good, and it may have occurred to some NOW officials that her appearance might help dissipate the traditional image of the feminist as a castrating crow in bloomers.

"I think, in the beginning, they thought that with my kind of genteel Republican background I might be too conservative for them," says Miss Atkinson. "Ho, ho."

She was elected president of the New York chapter last summer, and promptly drafted the position paper on abortion, which claims as a civil right a woman's control of her own reproductive process up to the time of birth. "I'm a little bored with the abortion issue now," she says. "I'd rather talk about the demise of marriage.

"I'm afraid the women's movement in this country is still pretty low-class, intellectually. Practically all we talk about is equal rights in employment. That's not opportunity; it's *opportunism*. Who the hell can say that getting a woman's job changed from a stewardess to a typist is a breakthrough? [She is referring to the case of Pauline Dziob, a ship's stewardess who recently fought for the traditionally male rating of yeoman. Miss Dziob was upheld by the New York State Human Rights Commission.] The breakthrough can come only with a change in the social institutions.

"We're afraid of the truth. To say that you can be both a career woman and a wife and mother, and that the institutions won't change and won't be threatened—that's a cop-out. De Beauvoir says that some men may be limited by marriage, but few women fail to be annihilated by it. Any real change in the status of women would be a fundamental assault on marriage and the family. People would be tied together by love, not legal contraptions. Children would be raised communally; it's just not honest to talk about freedom for women unless you get the child-rearing off their backs. We may not be ready for any of this yet, but if we're going to be honest, we've got to talk about it. Face it, raise the questions."

The trouble is, hardly anybody wants to. Even feminists who take a most cavalier attitude toward marriage turn cautious when the question of children arises. Miss Atkinson's own view is that the concept of the nuclear family must be abolished entirely, giving way to a society in which the bonds between generations would be maintained communally instead of by the one-to-one parent-child relationship—a society, she says, in which "all children would be loved by all adults. They would form close relationships within their own age groups, rather than needing to get approval and value from authority figures. Of course, close human contact is essential, but there is no reason to believe that it must come from a mother. Children can get it from one another, as adults do."

In Miss Atkinson's view, the early communal experiments in Russia and Israel, and those which pertain in many Communist countries today, are bound to fail because they don't go far enough—in other words, parents still identify with individual children. "The continuance of the inheritance idea—the idea of living on through things, property, children—subverts any possibility of the communal society succeeding. For people to live communally instead of competitively, the bonds of inheritance must be completely broken." The question then arises: Why bother to have children at all? And Miss Atkinson answers: "Because of a rational decision to continue the human race."

Well, this is where the shouting starts. As regards communal child-raising experiments in our time (none of which, by the way, has gone nearly so far as Miss Atkinson proposes, nor is likely to), no one can call them a failure, and no one can call them a roaring success, either. Sociologist Schad-Somers, who teaches at Rutgers, says: "My own conclusion, based on the empirical evidence, is that children raised collectively are more independent, more cooperative, with fewer psycho-sexual problems than kids raised in the United States." Mrs. Schad-Somers would not for a moment, however, advocate a complete break of the family ties. "We would be giving up something precious, needlessly," she says. "I surely want children, and I would hope to raise them in a good day-care center. The day-care supervisors and the natural parents would provide alternate models and love objects for the child, which probably would be much better for him than the exclusive and highly interdependent relationship with his mother."

On the other hand, Dr. Selma Fraiberg, director of the Child Development Project at the University of Michigan's Child Psychiatric Hospital, says some research on the early kibbutz children suggests that they turned out to be "a bunch of cool cookies who wouldn't give one the feeling of knowing them awfully well. Certainly, they seem in no way superior to children raised in our family system."

And a third view comes from the director of a leading child-research clinic in New York, who says that, on the basis of current evidence, no one can say much about communally raised children except that, like all children, they have problems. Besides, he says, this is not the point. "The point is that we are moving in this direction, inevitably. In the next few years, the interrelationship between family and communal care of children will be a major topic on the American scene. We are not talking, of course, about *destroying* the parent-child relationship, but *supplementing* it, and the findings from other countries give us no reason to feel apprehensive."

Dr. Fraiberg takes the most conservative position. In her view, even a day-care system would have its hazards.

"It is almost impossible in such a system to maintain true intimacy, continuity, a continuous dialogue," she says. "Whatever problems may emerge from the intimacy between mother and child, the things we value most also emerge from just this intimacy. It needn't be a crushing intimacy. Sometimes it is. But because human ties sometimes produce neurosis doesn't mean we should throw out the ties." And as to Miss Atkinson's vision, she says: "It is at least comforting to know that such women are not going to reproduce their own kind."

Within NOW, there is an altogether understandable reluctance to pursue the matter. Here are the radicals, wanting to be heard. Out there are the mothers' clubbers, waiting to be alienated. The feminists are not anxious to alienate anyone, and even mild threats to the abiding institutions do tend to frighten most women to death.

I remember the extraordinary response to an article Marya Mannes once wrote for The Times Magazine, in which she espoused child day-care centers, hardly a revolutionary idea. What impressed me about the flood of readers' letters was not their disapproval, but their rage. One woman called Miss Mannes a prostitute, and another wrote that she was dirty-minded and un-American and ought to go back to wherever she had come from, which happened to be New York.

"I do think we have to raise these questions," says Betty Friedan, with caution. "As an individual, not as a member of NOW, I can't help but raise them. Marriage, for example: It may be that we are asking too much of it, and that almost inevitably it will become a straitjacket for both sexes. The inefficacy of all this tinkering, the assumption of 'Can this marriage be saved?' makes you want to vomit.

"We work with the realities of American life, and in reality our job now is to make it possible for women to integrate their roles at home and in society. But as to whether we will finally have to challenge the institutions, the concepts of marriage and the nuclear family—I don't know. I just don't know.

"What I do know is this: If you agree that women are human beings who should be realizing their potential, then no girl child born today should responsibly be brought up to be a housewife. Too much has been made of defining human personality and destiny in terms of the sex organs. After all, we share the human brain."

Part 2

STUDENTS AND BOHEMIANS

IN THE LATE forties the public was concerned mainly with the collegiate experiences of ex-G.I.'s. In the fifties higher education suddenly boomed. During those years of rising enrollments the chief problems, apart from occasional flaps when a fraternity or sorority too obviously displayed its prejudices, were run-of-the-mill financial and pedagogical inadequacies. The students were no trouble. In fact, some critics worried that they were too docile, too much the "silent generation." Of course, most students in every generation are silent in this sense. The tone and flavor that inspire generational tags are produced by a small minority. What was surprising about college life in the fifties is that no minority of this type seemed to exist. The student culture lacked style. Students flamed not, neither did they agitate.

A group like this is hard to explain and harder to defend, as the effort of Professor Butz to do both in his article on the Class of '58 demonstrates. In particular his piece shows how difficult it is to find reasons for the behavior of trend-setting students at any given time. He thought his students were more moderate and realistic because they lived in a post-utopian atmosphere when everyone understood that the world could not be made better overnight. They were the products of America's new maturity. This seemed plausible at the time, but only six years later at Berkeley these same circumstances —affluence, maturity, the Cold War—produced a student elite with quite different views and modes of behavior. When A. H. Raskin, the *New York Times's* experienced labor reporter, went to Berkeley he took an opposite approach to the problem of explaining student behavior. Where Butz had viewed his students in the context of American life during the Eisenhower years, Raskin believed the Berkeley radicals were a consequence of the university itself. Yet most students at big universities like their institutions very much. This is especially true in California, where students have a great range of places to choose among. The University of California alone offers several distinct alternatives to students who want a good education. If they dislike the great size of Berkeley or U.C.L.A. they can go to branches of the system like Riverside, Davis, or Santa Barbara, where the level of instruction is nearly as high and student life more traditional than at the main campus. Thus, few Berkeley students resent the multiversity, for it is precisely because Cal is large and strong that they have come to it. In a general sense this is also true at other multiversities. Moreover, since 1964 similar eruptions have taken place not only at Wisconsin and Columbia but at small and medium-size institutions as well. It is clear now that whatever objections students have to the university as such, their rebellion is directed against more general conditions.

For this reason Thomas R. Brooks's article on Students for a Democratic Society is particularly helpful. SDS, as the largest and most visible organization of student radicals in the country, is even more important now than it was in 1965. It led the student battalions which put Columbia University out of business in 1968. Similar efforts may be expected from it in the future. As Brooks shows, radical students oppose the university not because it is uniquely defective but because it is the most accessible agency of the larger society that is their real target. SDS has changed somewhat since 1965 (indeed, it is always changing, as every issue of *Radical America,* SDS's historical journal, points out). It is less anarchistic and more conventionally socialistic than it was a few years ago. Escalation in Vietnam has forced it to concentrate on the war issue at the expense of its other projects, most of which had not worked out very well anyway. Its mood is harsher and its tone more strident than before. But Brooks's essay continues to be an excellent introduction to this contemporary student elite.

The two articles on bohemian life are important because they discuss what is rapidly becoming a central feature of American society. The Beat Generation was an early and abortive attempt to create a life-style contrary to dominant American values. The Beats rejected Western materialism in favor of Eastern spirituality—Zen Buddhism in particular. They attacked American rationalism and confronted the success ethic with a special failure ethic of their own. Properly speaking, the Beats were few in number, probably no more than four or five hundred people. But they foreshadowed a time when bohemian affectations would become much more common, and, as Clellon Holmes suggests, they acted out in a particularly vivid and public way the numerous vague discontents felt by millions of inarticulate, unrepresented young Americans. The Beats were also a literary clique. In works like Jack Kerouac's *On the Road,* and perhaps even Allen Ginsberg's *Howl,* they left worthy monuments of their confused encounter with modern life.

It seems unlikely that their hippie successors will produce anything of equal value. They may, however, be even more revealing as to the shape of our future. The Hashbury scene was a temporary thing. Most radical students did not drop out and turn on. Yet at its peak in the summer of 1967, when thousands of hippies converged on San Francisco, their numbers alone made the movement unique. All previous bohemian groups had been small and mostly obscure. Today, thanks to the mass media and a society so wealthy that middle-class youngsters can live indefinitely on handouts, free services, and money from home, it is possible for bohemianism to be a social force. Perhaps even, as Hunter S. Thompson believes, hippies are leading the way to a new bourgeois bohemianism that will compensate the middle class for its lost dream of political relevance.

Defense of the Class of '58

by Otto Butz

AS ANOTHER commencement season approaches, the American younger generation is in danger of being unfairly and tragically sold short. Unfairly, because its elders, in judging it by the forms of youthful expression current in the Nineteen Thirties, are misinterpreting its realism and prudence as ominous evidence of apathy and lack of idealism. Tragically, because, in so doing, these older Americans are depriving themselves of what should and could be their surest ground for confidence in the nation's future. What they fail to see is that the very qualities of realism and prudence, which they are inclined to find so disturbing in today's youth, may, in fact, mark these young men and women as the most mature and promising generation to emerge since the days of the American frontier.

After five years as a university teacher in this country, I fully agree that today's young Americans *are* a down-to-earth and matter-of-fact lot. What I would protest, however, is the conclusion, so frequently drawn from this fact, that contemporary young people are less adventurous than were earlier generations of Americans, that they lack positive political convictions, that they suffer from an impaired sense of individuality, and that, as one educator recently described them, they are little more than "gloriously contented . . . self-seekers on the American assembly-line."

That today's college-age Americans have become less ambitious and spectacular in the particular expressions of their beliefs is be-

From the *New York Times Magazine,* May 25, 1958.

yond dispute. The reasons for this development have been chiefly twofold. For one thing, the expectations from life of these young people, as compared with those earlier entertained by their fathers, have become more modest. Traditional America's admirable but unrealistic faith in the quick and easy liberal-democratic perfectability of man sooner or later had to be disappointed and revised. So did the radical and conservative utopias and conspiracy theories which at first replaced that faith. It was the fate of the young people of twenty-five years ago to have to experience these disappointments and to come to grips with themselves and the world in spite of them.

Today's young people, in contrast, have grown up as the heirs of this long and painful American coming-of-age. They have known from their very beginnings that economic security is important, that they would probably never become millionaires, that neither socialism nor communism is a panacea for the free-enterprise system's deficiencies, and that the world cannot be made safe for democracy in one war or one peace settlement. Would it not be remarkable if this fact were not reflected in a more realistic and moderate sense of the possible in the present younger generation?

It has, in addition, been the good fortune of these young people to be able to pursue their more modest goals in life under social and economic circumstances which, compared with those prevailing in the Nineteen Thirties, have been favorable indeed. On the one hand, job opportunities for the college graduate have, until this year, been almost unlimited. On the other, through such developments as broadened access to higher education, the reduction of various types of discrimination and the increased power of organized labor, many of at least the more crying injustices which stirred the hearts and minds of the young people of a generation ago have steadily been remedied.

The not unnatural predisposition in regard to what remains to be done has, therefore, been to avoid the more drastic and ideological type of argument and action in favor of sustained effort of a more piecemeal and administrative kind. And while the years since World War II have not been without their major international crises, even these have seemed amenable to being rationally understood and either accepted or matter-of-factly coped with.

The resulting, undeniable change in the expression of the present younger generation's beliefs need not, however, as is so often implied, be taken as evidence either of a dilution of the substances of the beliefs themselves or of a weakening of the intensity with which the beliefs are held. The truth of the matter, on the contrary, is that in a number of significant ways the present youth of America, at least as represented in the country's better colleges, gives promise of a good deal more inner direction and public dedication than their elders have demonstrated.

Consider, for example, the career plans of these contemporary college men and women. A Cornell University study, based upon 7,000 interviews at twelve colleges, shows today's students to be much less influenced by the promise of financial reward than by the prospect of what they may be able to contribute to the jobs of their choice. Asked what they wanted most from their work, 27 per cent said "an opportunity to use my special abilities," while only 10 per cent stressed "earning a good deal of money."

A similar inclination may very well be revealed in the rising percentages of today's college graduates who are heading for such service professions as governmental administration, medicine, teaching and scientific research. For example, a comparison of the career choices of the Princeton classes of 1935 and 1957 (as stated in the respective senior yearbooks) discloses the following notable differences:

The proportion of 1957 graduates planning to enter government service was more than 50 per cent greater than in 1935.

The proportion for medicine was 95 per cent greater.

The proportion for teaching was approximately 110 per cent greater, and for research in pure science more than 250 per cent greater.

Perhaps the most striking development in this regard has been the approximately 150 per cent rise, between 1935 and 1955, in the enrollment in the country's theological seminaries (as contrasted with a less than 30 per cent rise in the general population during the same period). Nor has this increase in the number of young Americans choosing the ministry as their lifework been purchased at the cost of intellectual quality. On the contrary, according to an editorial in Christianity and Crisis, the new theological students "represent a good cross-section of college graduates and include many top leaders of campus activities as well as members of Phi Beta Kappa. . . . Certainly the seminaries are getting abler men, on the whole, than in recent decades."

Nor is it correct to cite the present younger generation's lack of political militancy as proof that its members are any less deeply committed to the principles of their American heritage than were their parents. In a more conventional sense, it is true, they are unpolitical. The perennial "battle" between Republicans and Democrats and radicals and conservatives means very little to them; nor do they easily become agitated over the alleged moral superiority of the American position on this or that issue before the United Nations. But the important thing to notice is why they are thus inclined. The reason, largely, is that they believe these traditional polemics to be less and less meaningful and, as a result, find it more and more difficult to feel touched by them.

But if, on the other hand, the issue be one which they are convinced is truly of relevance, their response can be heartening indeed. There could be no more convincing illustration of this fact than the sense of involvement, outrage and agonized helplessness that swept the country's college campuses during the Hungarian revolt. "What can we do?" the cry rang out. In one of my classes, in a straw vote requested by several of the students, 70 per cent of those present declared their willingness to volunteer, if only it were possible without precipitating World War III.

I have found the same readiness to respond to what seems really to matter to them in intellectual life. In a recent undergraduate seminar which I conducted on "The United States and Sub-Sahara Africa," for example, not one of the score of participating students failed to develop a very real sense of personal concern. Without exception, their research papers gave evidence of the most serious-minded effort. And every one of our discussion sessions, scheduled for a maximum of three hours, continued heatedly from 7 in the evening until the early hours of the next morning. "What can we do about *apartheid* in South Africa? How secure is the cocoa economy of Ghana? What are the British doing about the grievances of the Kikuyu in Kenya? What are Nigeria's prospects for the successful development of representative democracy?"

"How earnest these American students are!" a young foreign student sleepily remarked to me at the conclusion of the seminar's final session. "You would never see this kind of thing in my country."

To the vast majority of these American citizens of tomorrow the goals to be implemented, both at home as well as throughout the world, appear in all essentials to be agreed upon. So do the conditions under which these goals must be implemented. The desirability of individual freedom and fulfillment, the importance of equality of social and economic opportunity, Government regulation of business, public spending, foreign aid, the permanent tensions and dilemmas of power politics, and the futility of resort to any of the world's competing "isms"—these have been facts of life for to-day's young people since they first learned to read. And in the few cases where they have not the "deficiency" has rapidly been made up in the first few years at college. Not so much, moreover, through the lectures of their professors as by the more persuasive impact of private bull sessions in the company of fellow-students.

"What is there to crusade about?" one bespectacled college junior half-complained to me the other day. As "corny" as it might sound, he added, with the inevitable touch of self-consciousness that seems to overcome today's youngsters when they speak of something that might be construed as "doing good," the thing to do was to get into the kind of work where you could bring your ideals and what-ever ability you had to bear on some practical problem. Unfor-tunately, he shrugged as he prepared to head back to the library, that wasn't very glamorous. But what could you do? That's the way it was!

Yet with all their soberness of purpose, at least a good many of these young Americans are by no means resigned to the morally hamstrung existence of the much-discussed organization man. I have seen no more encouraging evidence of this fact than in the symposium of autobiographical essays by Princeton seniors which I edited last year and which recently appeared in book form under the title of "The Unsilent Generation."

Nearly every one of the young contributors to this collection predicted that his most deep-felt personal problem in life would be the conflict between his desire for success and his determination to maintain his individual intellectual and moral independence against what he anticipated would be society's pressures for "con-formity." One boy defiantly announced his conviction that the secret of happiness is "to be true to one's self—and the rest of the world can go to hell." Another testified that "the most enduring and valuable idea" he had gained from his liberal education is "that each man must find his own truth after learning the realities and truths that exist for others; that each man, in other words, must decide for himself."

A third proclaimed his determination to make his life "a living testimonial that individual freedom is compatible with the welfare and progress of society." And another, expressing what I have found to be the most common and typical attempt to come to grips with the problem on today's college campuses, sought to comfort himself and his readers with the thought that, though the statistics pointing to his generation's tendency to "conformity" might be true, the fact that "we recognize them as true, and are becoming increasingly sensitive to their consequences in our lives, promises that many of us are going to escape the predictions set for our future."

Nor is this concern for responsible but free individual self-assertion merely a matter of apprehension and defensiveness in anticipating the future. It finds even more forceful expression in what these young people want to do in life. According to the Cornell University study already cited no less than 46 per cent of the sample of students interviewed stated that "ideally they would like to work in their own business or professional office." And the same individualistic inclination emerged as the most prominent feature of the abovementioned Princeton undergraduate essays. Most eloquently of all, perhaps, it was expressed by the young man who explained that the principal reason he wanted to be a leader in society was that "at the top and among the big boys, whether in business or in Government, the decisions to be made and the risks to be taken are as momentous and challenging as ever."

Reinforcing this deep-rooted, if politically unspectacular, individuality is a further most encouraging and rather general tribute to today's American student generation. That is its acute, analytical and uninhibited sense of complexities, including, above all, the sense of its own, its country's and mankind's limitations. The minds of these young Americans, and their sense of intellectual and moral honesty, are persistent almost to the point of irreverence. Mere stereotypes and clichés, no matter how hallowed by tradition or authority, will not appease them.

Above all, they want the truth—whether about God, democracy, communism, or what makes them and their parents tick. They are, to the limits of what they believe is realistically possible, determined to do their best but at the same time to live without false hopes, without unwarranted fears, and without apologizing, either to themselves or to anyone else, for being what they are.

As we know only too well, the members of the present younger generation of Americans are certainly not without a good many faults and shortcomings. Some of these are intrinsically human. Others are a reflection of the faults and shortcomings of the society that raised them. Yet in the respects in which these young people are unique, some of which have here been indicated, there are by no means grounds for pessimism about the American future. With them America may very well have come of age not only as the world power it is but, no less, as a nation of true adults.

Whether well-meaning but hasty parents recognize it or not, these American youths have *not* lost their fire. All that has happened is that they have become too mature merely to show it off, feel self-righteous about it or play with it. The future, indeed, may show that they are precisely the kind of realistic idealists which this country, in both its domestic and international life, has long been badly in need of.

The Berkeley Affair:
Mr. Kerr vs.
Mr. Savio & Co.

by A. H. Raskin

BERKELEY, CALIF.

WHAT TURNED the University of California's world-renowned campus into a snake pit of unrepressed animosities? As my helicopter rattled across the moon-dappled water of San Francisco Bay on its way toward this strangely riven academic center, it seemed to me two men were probably best equipped to supply the answer. In the process, they could go far toward explaining a simmering unrest on other campuses across the nation, and in every corner of our corporate society.

One man was Dr. Clark Kerr, 53, the quiet-spoken Quaker whose duties as president of the university make him Big Daddy to 72,000 students on nine California campuses. The other was Mario Savio, the charismatic 22-year-old undergraduate who has emerged as the archangel of student revolt at Berkeley.

My effort to get the answer from Savio got off to a rocky start. We had arranged to meet at the headquarters of the Graduate Coordinating Committee. This is a key unit in the Free Speech Movement (F.S.M.), the coalition of undergraduates, graduate students and teaching assistants that grew out of an ill-timed, worse-explained and now-rescinded administration order that barred all on-campus solicitation for political or civil-rights demonstrations mounted off the campus.

The committee office is a garret over the university's drama workshop, not far from the main gate to the huge, hillside campus. The visitor climbs a flight of wooden outside stairs and finds himself in a barren room that is dark despite the dazzling sunlight outside. The nearest thing to a real piece of furniture is a battered green sofa, with sags where the springs should be. A square table with a telephone fills one corner, and there are a half-dozen camp chairs. Under the table is a mound of picket signs. The mood is "Waiting for Lefty" done off-Broadway.

Savio, a slim six-footer with frizzy pale hair, peeled off the short, fleece-lined coat that has become a sort of personal trademark. His first words were a flat refusal to participate in any interview if I intended to focus on him as *the* communicator for the F.S.M. "Anything like that will just perpetuate a misrepresentation that the press has already done too much to build up," he said. "This is not a cult of one personality or of two personalities; it is a broadly based movement and I will not say anything unless it is made clear that the F.S.M. is not any single individual."

A way around that roadblock was ready at hand—a joint discussion with the six other members of the collective leadership who had accompanied Savio to the conference. It started with everybody sounding off against Sidney Hook's view in The Times Magazine (Jan. 3) that academic freedom was primarily for teachers and that the only imperative right for students was freedom to learn. Savio said they wanted equal space to reply; also they wanted to sue. I told them to go ahead if they thought they had a case. Finally, we got to what I wanted to talk about—namely, what they thought the issue at Berkeley had been and whether there was still any real issue left.

It was a somewhat formless encounter, a blend of a graduate seminar in political science and "Catch-22." People wandered out and others filled their chairs; getting in questions was harder than getting back answers. Yet, it was an engaging group—lucid in exposition, quick in rebuttal, manifesting no unease at differences of interpretation or emphasis within their own circle.

The Berkeley mutineers did not seem political in the sense of those student rebels in the turbulent Thirties; they are too suspicious of all adult institutions to embrace wholeheartedly even those ideologies with a stake in smashing the system. An anarchist or I.W.W. strain seems as pronounced as any Marxist doctrine. "Theirs is a sort of political existentialism," says Paul Jacobs, a research associate at the university's Center for the Study of Law and Society, who is one of the F.S.M.'s applauders. "All the old labels are out; if there were any orthodox Communists here, they would be a moderating influence."

The proudly immoderate zealots of the F.S.M. pursue an activist creed—that only commitment can strip life of its emptiness, its absence of meaning in a great "knowledge factory" like Berkeley. That is the explanation for their conviction that the methods of civil disobedience, in violation of law, are as appropriate in the civilized atmosphere of the campus as they are in the primordial jungle of Mississippi. It was an imaginative strategy that led to an unimaginable chain of events.

Trouble began on Sept. 14, a week before the opening of classes, when the dean of students suddenly shut off the only area on campus where students had been free to collect funds and enlist adherents for off-campus political or social action. This island for activists was a 26-by-60 foot patch of bricked-over ground, called the Bancroft Strip, just outside the principal pedestrian entrance.

The decision to embargo the Strip, made in the climactic days of an election campaign that would settle both the Presidency and the fate of California's controversial fair housing law, forged a united front of protest extending from campus Goldwaterites to Maoist members of the Progressive Labor party.

With the memory of the mutiny thick in the gloomy garret, the collective leadership of the F.S.M. spent the next three hours telling me what they thought the rebellion was *really* about.

They are convinced that the abrupt decision to close the Bancroft Strip represented a university capitulation to right-wing forces angered by the student picketing and sit-ins to compel the hiring of more Negroes in Bay area businesses. Specifically, they blame former Senator William F. Knowland, editor of The Oakland Tribune, whose paper was a special target. (Knowland says he didn't do it.)

The cutoff in political recruitment confirmed a conviction already held by some of the students that bankers, industrialists, publishers and other leaders of the Establishment in the Board of Regents were making a concentration camp out of the "multiversity"—a term coined by Kerr in a series of lectures at Harvard nearly two years ago to describe the transformation of a modern university, like Cal, into a vast techno-educational complex.

This conviction was not diminished by the extreme freedom the university has long allowed students to express their own political views, however unorthodox, at "Hyde Park" areas inside the campus. Even during the ban on the use of campus property for organizing off-campus political action, students retained their liberty to invite Communists, Nazis or Black Muslims to address meetings at the university. They also could—and often did—agitate for the right to smoke marijuana, to be able to buy contraceptives at the University Bookstore or for other far-out objectives.

All this has been going on for years in an atmosphere particularly congenial to the flowering of undergraduate rebellion. The whole Bay area has a long Left Bank tradition of hospitality to radical movements and off-beat behavior. Czeslav Milosz, a Polish poet and defector, who served on the faculty, left convinced that Berkeley and Greenwich Village were "the only two places in America you can be free." The mild year-round climate also helps. "There is no place in the world where uncomfortable people can feel so comfortable," said a visiting British professor.

Taken aback by the vehement student reaction to the recruitment taboo, the Regents in November restored the right to mount political action—not only in the Bancroft Strip but in several areas where it had never been allowed before. However, the F.S.M. is still unhappy because the new ruling specifies that only "lawful" off-campus activities can be planned on campus.

The rebels argue that students should have the same right as other citizens to participate in the political and social affairs of the outside community. What is "unlawful" ought to be determined solely by civil and criminal courts, not by a university administration or faculty. The university's only area of proper regulation over political activity should be the establishment of minimal time-place-manner rules to guarantee that anything the students do on campus does not interfere with classes or the orderly conduct of university business. Such is the current focus of what is left of the "free speech" issue.

Remembering centuries of "town vs. gown" controversies all over the world, in which universities had always fought to keep their campuses from coming under police rule, I asked the F.S.M. leaders whether their insistence on leaving disciplinary authority to the municipal law-enforcement agencies might not destroy the whole concept of academic sanctuary and expose them to much harsher treatment.

Savio, a philosophy major who graduated at the top of his class from New York City's Martin Van Buren High School, had a blunt answer: "That is a specious argument. The campus is already crawling with cops of the most insidious kind from the 'Red squad' and every other kind of undercover agency." Myra Jehlen, a comely, solemn Phi Beta Kappa from C.C.N.Y. and a Woodrow Wilson graduate scholar in English, added a postscript: "Immunity from police prosecution only applies to panty raids and fraternity guys. We're not interested in that."

She was the only coed in the group. Across the room was her husband, Carl Riskin, who had gone to Cambridge in England on a fellowship after graduating *magna cum laude* from Harvard and was now completing his Ph.D. thesis at Berkeley. He spoke seldom, but with force and precision.

Next to him sat Martin Roysher, a sophomore from Arcadia, Calif., whose casually correct clothes reflected the freshman year he spent at Princeton. He looked so young it was hard to believe he was out of high school, yet he, too, spoke crisply about everything from alienation to the importance of erasing any differentiation between the freedom of students and citizens to act upon their political beliefs.

Here, too, was Jack Weinberg, a former graduate student in math and now a civil-rights activist in CORE, who gained fame overnight as "the man in the police car" in the first of the mass upheavals last Oct. 1. Stephan Weissman, the red-bearded chairman of the Graduate Coordinating Committee, pulled a few picket signs from under the table and squatted on the floor. Robert Starobin, a Cornell B.A., who has been a teaching assistant in history at Berkeley for three years, is writing his Ph.D. dissertation on industrial slavery before the Civil War. Stocky and assertive, his talk bristled with complaints about the "power structure" and its determination to stifle civil-rights activity at Berkeley.

The one whose views evoked least challenge was the youth group's senior citizen, Hal Draper, a part-time librarian at the university who graduated from Brooklyn College in the Great Depression and is now fiftyish. A leader of the old American Student Union, he drifted through various wings of the Trotskyite movement and is currently an editor of New Politics, a journal intended to offer an outlet for all shades of Socialist thought. A Draper pamphlet called "The Mind of Clark Kerr" has become the F.S.M.'s bible in its fight against "the university factory." Dedicated to the students who immobilized the police car, the leaflet depicts Kerr as the preacher of docile submission to a technocratic juggernaut that will stamp out all individuality and all liberty.

The longer my conversation with the students went on, the clearer it became that the political battle was only a symptom of a larger revolt against the bigness and impersonality of the "multiversity" itself. If Clark Kerr is the high priest of the multiversity, social critic Paul Goodman is its Antichrist and thus beloved of the F.S.M. The opening theme of an F.S.M. pamphlet is a declaration by Goodman that in the United States today, "students—middle-class youth —are the major exploited class. . . . They have no choice but to go to college." Rejecting their role as factory workers on an academic assembly-line, the F.S.M. demands a humanized campus, a "loving community" based on comradeship and purpose.

"We must now begin the demand of the right to know; to know the realities of the present world-in-revolution, and to have an opportunity to think clearly in an extended manner about the world," says the F.S.M. credo. "It is ours to demand meaning; we must insist upon meaning!"

What is behind this manifestese? Does it betoken a desire to dismantle the University of California, or to establish a student soviet that would make all educational policy? The F.S.M. leaders disclaim such grandiose ideas.

"This is not a matter of rolling back the multiversity," says Myra Jehlen. "But it is our view that this university does neglect its students. We have no contact with the community of scholars, except to see a professor across 500 feet of lecture hall. Teaching assistants have to serve as parents for the students."

Savio deplores the extent to which the university's professors and facilities are involved in research for the Government and giant corporations. "It is a distortion, and too bad, that the university does not stand apart from the society as it is. It would be good to return to an almost totally autonomous body of scholars and students. But what we have now is that the Pentagon, the oil and aircraft companies, the farm interests and their representatives in the Regents consider the university as a public utility, one of the resources they can look on as part of their business."

And who should run things? Says Starobin: "Our idea is that the university is composed of faculty, students, books and ideas. In a literal sense, the administration is merely there to make sure the sidewalks are kept clean. It should be the servant of the faculty and the students. We want a redemocratizing of the university. Courses are clearly up to the faculty, but students should be able to convey their ideas. Dormitory regulations should be up to the students who live in the dorms. A bipartite or tripartite committee should have the final say in promulgating minimal rules on the time, place and manner of political activity."

There was much, much more before I asked whether they felt that the turmoil had accomplished anything. Myra Jehlen answered first: "Of course, you never win finally. New problems will always arise. But there has been a great strengthening of democratic institutions on the campus. The kind of actions we've taken, the important function of students in society—these have been vindicated. Yes, we have won, though how much is not clear."

Savio was more succinct: "We committed the unpardonable sin of being moral and being successful."

The setting was very different that evening when I visited Kerr at his home in El Cerrito, five miles from the campus. It is a glass-walled ranch house on a lofty bluff overlooking the Bay. Velvety lawns roll down to an old quarry in the canyon far below. There is a swimming pool, and flowers, shrubs and vines grow in jungle-like profusion in a great glass-roofed patio.

But Kerr is not a man for rich living, even though his salary of $45,000 a year puts him $900 ahead of Governor Edmund Brown as the state's highest-paid official. He is frugal even of time. If Kerr gets to an airport and discovers the plane will be 15 minutes late, he is furious at the lost time. But if it will be an hour late, he is contented; he will sit quietly in a corner of the airport, begin writing memos, speeches, articles or even a chapter for a book.

Kerr works with the same intensity at home. Each afternoon a squad of eight secretaries at his office in University Hall pack a great sheaf of papers into a cardboard box. A driver returns them before noon the next day. Each carries a notation in green ink written in an incredibly pinched, yet distinct, hand—the marching orders by which the biggest of big universities is run.

The commander's invariable uniform is a navy blue suit and white shirt. His mind has extraordinary range and a rare capacity for turning discord into consensus. Kerr ranks among the country's half-dozen most effective peacemakers in the volatile realm of labor-management warfare—a skill that has prompted every President since Harry S. Truman to enlist his help. In the middle of the disturbances at Berkeley, President Johnson asked him to accept appointment as Secretary of Health, Education and Welfare. All Kerr will say about that or any other post is that he still expects to be president of Cal on its centenary in 1968.

Among the many ironies of the Berkeley explosions is that Kerr now finds himself under savage attack from the left after more than a decade of demands for his ouster by right-wing critics. Leading the fight against a loyalty oath, he became so popular with the rest of the Berkeley faculty that in 1952, when the Regents decided to restore the goodwill they had lost in two bitter years, they named Kerr as chancellor. In 1959, a year after the Regents moved him up to president, Kerr again aroused right-wing ire by granting an honorary degree to Prof. Edward C. Tolman, who had been forced to resign for refusing to sign the oath. A year later he induced the Regents to name a new building in Tolman's honor.

When Berkeley students were arrested in 1960 for disrupting a hearing of the House Un-American Activities Committee in San Francisco, Kerr resisted demands to suspend or expel the demonstrators. He ignored similar conservative outcries last summer when undergraduates were arrested for a civil-rights sit-in at the Sheraton-Palace Hotel.

The liberalization of faculty and student rights during the Kerr administration earned for him and the Regents the American Association of University Professors' 1964 Alexander Meiklejohn award for conspicuous contributions to academic freedom. Less than six months later he was being denounced as an enemy of free expression by many on his own campus.

Kerr was not consulted on the fateful order shutting the Bancroft Strip. He was in Tokyo on his way home from a seven-week economic mission to the Iron Curtain countries on the day it was issued.

"It was perfectly apparent," Kerr says, "that the decision was a mistake, both in the action itself and in the way it was done. There was no advance consultation with the students, the over-all university administration or anyone else. When a privilege had been extended as long as that had been, there should have been consultation— and especially against the background of an impending national election and intense student involvement in civil rights."

(A Dostoevskian bit of background, still unknown to the students: Kerr foresaw in September, 1959, that the Strip would eventually be a source of trouble because there was no logical basis for exempting it from the no-politics rule that applied everywhere else on campus. He got the Regents to agree that it ought to be turned over to the city for use as a public plaza. But, for reasons still unexplained, the university's treasurer never carried out the instructions to deed over the Strip. If he had, the whole melancholy chain of events might never have begun.)

Kerr agrees with the F.S.M. thesis that students should have as much political freedom as anyone else in the community. The only difference is that he thinks they already have it. In his judgment, the rules governing political expression on campus, including the right to invite heretics of all political persuasions to speak at student meetings, give Berkeley undergraduates more freedom than bank clerks, factory workers or 99 per cent of the general citizenry.

He ridicules the notion that the university has been succumbing to the "power structure" in the dispute over civil-rights activity. "I had to fight some extremely tough battles against some very powerful legislators who felt we should kick out students who were arrested for sit-ins in the Bay area, but we never yielded an inch," Kerr says. "It just would not have been in character for us to say that the only place the students could fight for Negro rights was in Mississippi."

As for the Bancroft Strip, Kerr says that "whatever pressure preceded the order involved the loading of the galleries at the Republican convention with Berkeley students whooping it up for Scranton against Goldwater."

The F.S.M. indictment of the "multiversity" brings a special twinge to Kerr because every charge the insurgents now raise he foresaw with greater incisiveness as long ago as April, 1963, when he gave the Godkin lectures at Harvard.

Those talks described, with apparent fatalism but decided unenthusiasm, the evolution of a "mechanism held together by administrative rules and powered by money." Kerr predicted that undergraduates would feel so neglected and depersonalized that the revolt they once engaged in against the faculty *in loco parentis* would turn into an even more destructive uprising against the faculty *in absentia*. Everything Kerr warned of then is embodied now in the F.S.M. lament that the student is being downgraded to the status of an I.B.M. punch card in a computerized multiversity.

Kerr concedes that the multiversity is a disturbing place for many students, but he disputes that it is devoid of meaning. "One of the advantages of a big city or a big university—as against a smaller and more monolithic closed community—is that people find those things which may mean something to them," he says. "They are given a choice.

"It would be terribly stultifying to find yourself in a place which has a single meaning, and that meaning is the same for everyone. The only kind of society that has only a single meaning is an authoritarian one. It seems to me that is a place where you would really expect rebellion. Essentially, what the F.S.M. are saying is that they are rebelling against freedom of choice."

When I noted that the students objected not to too many meanings, but to the absence of any, Kerr replied:

"In fact, there is a lot of opportunity to participate, only it takes a little longer and requires more initiative to find it. Many tend to be overwhelmed by their opportunities; there are so many lectures to choose from, so many things to do, that they tend to become lost. They are torn too many ways and wind up condemning the whole structure."

The notion that the university, for all the magnitude of its Federal and industrial involvement (it is receiving $246 million this year for operating three giant atomic installations, plus $175 million in research grants and contracts), has become an arm of the Pentagon or big business also draws a rebuttal from Kerr. "The university," he says, "is intertwined with all society. And if it is overbalanced in any direction as compared with the surrounding society, it is in the fact that it is a source of dissent and social criticism. You could say it is a tool of the critics, and that is one of the things that make it so dynamic."

All this brought us back to the students' overriding complaint— the enormous size of Berkeley, with 27,500 students on a single campus, and the obliteration of the individual's relationship to faculty and administration. Kerr's answer dwelt more on society's inescapable needs than confidence that alienation could be overcome.

"Every day makes it clearer that the university's invisible product, knowledge, is likely to be the most powerful single element in our culture," he says. "With so many young people pounding at our gates, we're up against a tremendous assignment. To take the position that we won't grow would be a terribly irresponsible thing."

Kerr is a philosopher-pragmatist of the technocratic society, probably the ablest and most creative in the educational field. His guiding principle is individual disengagement. He preaches the idea that each person can best protect his own happiness in a society of bigness by developing pluralistic attachments. "If you invest all of yourself in an institution," he says, "you become a slave. It becomes a prison, not an agency of liberation." This road to the independent spirit is just the opposite of that traveled by the F.S.M. and its leaders. Their goal is commitment, but there is a good deal of confusion about precisely what it is they are committed to.

And who is listening, now that the clear-cut issue created by the closing of the Bancroft Strip and the blackout of political recruiting has been resolved? The signs are that the overwhelming support for F.S.M. aims among students of all political hues and of no hues has evaporated along with the issue.

Moreover, there are strong indications of strain inside the F.S.M. steering committee, now a much more ingrown group than in the initial days of across-the-board coalition. Many would like to disband the movement. Hal Draper said frankly that it might go into "an inactive phase." Ed Rosenfeld, the F.S.M.'s press officer, says that one thought under consideration is to establish a cooperative coffeehouse, on a nonprofit basis, near the campus. "It would be a civilized gathering place in the best European manner," he says, "a suitable forum for debates and discussion."

Back at the heliport for the return flight, I tried to evaluate the Berkeley uprising against the memories of my own days of rebellion as president of the C.C.N.Y. class of '31. It was a time when one worker in four was jobless and the misery of the Great Depression was beginning to grip the land. We had been ready to picket our own commencement in cap and gown, but we chickened out at the last minute for fear of losing our degrees.

These students, for all their talk of setting up an espresso joint as a monument to their mutiny, were a tougher, smarter breed, more ready to go for broke.

But what did they accomplish, besides effecting the cancellation of an order the university admits never should have been issued?

They have done one important thing that may prove of considerable help to Berkeley and all other big universities. They have cut through the multifarious concerns of an administration that must deal with every agency of government, including those in 50 countries abroad, and forced it to recognize that it is sitting on a volcano of neglected, seething students.

Kerr, who has always recognized the need for diversity in multiversity, already is hard at work on measures to improve the quality and the immediacy of instruction. He aims to break down the idea that research, not teaching, is the mission of the good professor. Both roles are vital, Kerr believes, and so does the man he has brought in as acting chancellor, Dean Martin Meyerson of the College of Environmental Design.

Last fall's earthquake also has shaken the administration and faculty into a heightened awareness of the need for teamwork to lessen the students' belief that no one cares whether they go or stay, that undergraduate needs are passed over in favor of lucrative research contracts, book-writing projects and traveling lectureships all over the world. Prof. Arthur M. Ross, the enterprising chairman of an emergency executive committee elected by the faculty in the blackest period last December, expresses confidence that a genuine educational overhaul is in prospect. Most of his colleagues agree.

What goes into the curriculum and who teaches what courses will be a matter for the faculty to determine, but both Kerr and Ross feel students can have a useful advisory role. A larger area of authority for students in disciplinary committees and in other forms of self-government also is in prospect. All these developments should help still the discord at Berkeley, but—much more important—they will help make it a better institution of learning.

One of the imponderables in trying to guess whether peace has really come to the campus is that some F.S.M. activists obviously have developed a vested interest in finding things to fight about. They seem to operate on the theory that, in a system they believe is basically corrupt, the worse things gets, the easier it will be to generate mass resistance.

This is not a novel theory in radical movements, but it is not one that makes for stability. When the police dragged Savio and the 800 others out of Sproul Hall, he exulted, "This is wonderful—wonderful. We'll bring the university to our terms." When Paul Jacobs told an F.S.M. leader that he had advised Kerr to enter Sproul on the night of the sit-in and talk to the students (advice Kerr did not take), the insurgent asked sourly, "What side are you on?"

The reckless prodigality with which the F.S.M. uses the weapon of civil disobedience raises problems no university can deal with adequately. Mass discipline carries the danger of martyrdom and a spread of sympathetic disorders to other campuses.

Garrisoning the grounds with police runs so counter to the essential concept of the university as a redoubt of tolerance and reason that it is perhaps the worst solution of all. At Berkeley it brought tration. Yet, the alternative of giving students total immunity could the faculty into open alliance with the students against the adminis- engender a situation akin to that in the University of Caracas, where student revolutionaries use the campus as a fortress from which to sally forth to attack the general society.

"We fumbled, we floundered, and the worst thing is I still don't know how we should have handled it," Kerr acknowledges. "At any other university the administrators wouldn't have known how to handle it any better."

Menacing as is this new disruptive device, one even graver danger sign outranks all others raised by the mess at Berkeley. That is the degree to which it evidences a sense of lost identity, a revulsion against bigness, that is affecting all of our society. On the campus it takes the form of antagonism against the multiversity. In the mass production unions this same feeling of impending obliteration recently spurred rank-and-file strikes against General Motors and Ford, and may erupt again in the basic steel industry this spring. The longshoremen, fearing the shiny face of automation, voted down contracts that gave them lifetime job security and a generous wage guarantee—principally because they felt the machine was grinding them and their jobs into nothingness.

A similar mood of irrationality, of vaporous but paralyzing apprehension, stalks all our institutions in a time of unmatched material prosperity and individual well-being. Young people, in particular, study the unemployment statistics and decide that society is in a conspiracy to provide security for the older generation at the expense of the youngsters outside waiting to get in. Education is the magic carpet over the hurdles that make the dropout the shutout in our society. But, even at this most distinguished of universities, bigness robs many students of individual dignity or purpose. This feeling helps explain the spread of drug addiction and senseless crime among many well-to-do youngsters. All are part of an alienation that turns even affluence and security into worthless prizes.

This may prove to be the nation's critical challenge, potentially more damaging than the international crises that monopolize so much of our concern and our budget. If Berkeley cannot imbue life with a sense of fulfillment and content, where will we find it? Kerr, the mediator-innovator, must become a gladiator—pioneering new paths in intergroup relations and giving new vitality to democratic standards that rest on knowledge.

Voice of the New Campus "Underclass"

by Thomas R. Brooks

THE ENTRANCE to the national office of the Students for a Democratic Society is between two vacant store fronts on East 63rd Street between Glenwood and University, not far from the University of Chicago but well within the slums of Woodlawn. Like everything else on the street, the leaflet-sized placards in the S.D.S. doorway are tattered and torn. One is the inevitable reproduction of a SNCC (Student Nonviolent Coordinating Committee) poster showing Negroes and whites clasping hands beneath the appeal: "Come Let Us Build a New World."

The others are photographic reproductions, too, including the cover of an S.D.S. Bulletin with a striking picture of a begrimed white boy standing in the backyard of a poverty-stricken neighborhood in Cleveland, and one of two demonstrators moving toward the camera ahead of a crowd of policemen, television cameramen and a train. Over this is a typed caption: "Cops chase S.D.S. pickets who are attempting to stop California train which is carrying troops to suppress the Revolutionary movement of the Vietnamese people."

At the head of the stairway, with its peeling green and white paint and chipped plaster walls, one finds what some students have come to view as the command center of student opposition to the war in Vietnam. Within this warren of badly scarred offices crowded with battered desks and wobbly chairs, telephones ringing and typewriters clacking, a group of some 15 young people, in their early twenties

From the *New York Times Magazine,* November 7, 1965.

and late 'teens and mostly male, worked around the clock one day recently to get out a referendum to the S.D.S. membership on the so-called "Draft Program," a proposal that S.D.S. agitate, educate and organize around a "legal" antidraft campaign. Posters of all sorts and conditions abound—"Stop Escalating Now," "Vote for Mad," and "Make Love, Not War" are just a few of the catchier slogans.

"They told me this job would take 15 minutes," a girl running an Addressograph machine said. "But I've been here three hours already."

In another office, several young men collated the 18-page mimeographed S.D.S. Bulletin carrying general news of S.D.S. as well as the referendum. Periodically, an elevated train rumbled past, rattling windows and drowning out the incessant conversation.

"This is alienating work," said Jeff Shero, Bulletin editor and S.D.S. vice president, as he stapled Bulletins, "so we can talk." Shero, a soft-spoken 23-year-old Texan who looks out at the world through troubled eyes, went on to say that he was taking a year off from his studies at the University of Texas "to help the organization out." Asked about his draft status, he answered that he was "C.O.'ing it," having applied for conscientious-objector status some time back. The referendum, he explained, was essential because the draft program had been "selected" for attack by the Government. "The June S.D.S. convention decided that any program that might involve legal or political recriminations against the organization should be submitted to the membership," he said.

One suspects that S.D.S. members—at least some—are flattered by the attacks on them from President Johnson as well as a number of other eminent public figures, including Senators Dodd, Dirksen and Jackson and Attorney General Katzenbach. In truth, the Attorney General did not attack so much as explain. Asked by newsmen about Communist influence in S.D.S., he said that in such groups "you are likely to find some Communists involved" (something not denied by S.D.S. people). Asked if Communists were leaders, he said, "By and large, no."

Katzenbach announced that the F.B.I. had started a national investigation of groups backing the antidraft movement. He also said that while he disagreed "strongly and violently" with the young antidraft demonstrators, they had the right to express their views and opinions. The S.D.S., however, viewed all this—and the stronger statements—as open attacks on S.D.S. and as Red-baiting.

Shero, however, also seemed disposed to view these attacks as a public-relations boon, a gift from the enemy opening up the opportunity to reach thousands of students.

"We figured," Shero told me, "if we'd mimeographed on our machines for 10 years we wouldn't have got as much attention as we got overnight because of the attacks on us." Then he added: "Whenever they attack us, you see, in our reply, we ignore the attack and talk about the war." As for the question of Communism: "That's irrelevant when bombing children in Vietnam." Besides, Shero insisted, "we have no line—the rationale is not all drawn out. We're a very beautiful group because so many different people are able to work together."

The S.D.S. people, these children of liberal, middle-class parents, are concerned about poverty, civil rights and the war in Vietnam. They spurn, however, parental solutions; they are scornful of the War on Poverty, skeptical about the voting-rights legislation, suspicious of President Johnson's willingness to negotiate in Vietnam. But their own war against poverty has not gone too well; Negroes are running the civil-rights struggle. So, the escalation of the war in Vietnam not only horrifies these youngsters, it also offers them a target that fulfills their need for commitment and demonstrations aplenty to absorb their energies.

S.D.S., of course, is not the only antiwar group on campus. The old pacifist organizations, such as the American Friends Service Committee, the Fellowship of Reconciliation and the War Resisters' League, and the peace-movement groups, such as the Committee for a Sane Nuclear Policy, Turn Toward Peace and many others, all have college contacts, members and chapters. The new Marxist-oriented groups, such as the May 2d Movement (named after an antiwar demonstration of a few years ago) and the Du Bois Society clubs, are also active in antiwar agitation.

In addition, a number of so-called *ad hoc* committees, such as the New York and Chicago Committees to End the War in Vietnam, have sprouted up. But these are united-front, or umbrella, committees —rather than membership organizations—embracing a wide range of campus and noncampus antiwar and peace groups.

There are about 100 of these around the country, loosely tied in with the National Coordinating Committee to End the War in Vietnam, whose headquarters are in Madison, Wis. Frank Emspak, a 22-year-old zoology graduate who is chairman, has announced plans for a national convention in Washington, D.C., over the Nov. 26-28 weekend, bracketing a SANE-initiated March on Washington for Peace in Vietnam scheduled for Nov. 27. Emspak says emphatically: "We're not in the business of writing programs. The local groups decide what to do. We're a communication and coordination organization with agreement on a minimal slogan."

S.D.S. is represented on the National Coordinating Committee along with representatives from various local groups and national organizations, including M2M, the Du Bois Society and others. Local S.D.S. chapters have been influential in the formation of a number of local End the War groups. In New York City, for example, S.D.S. and the New York Committee to End the War in Vietnam share the same office at 1165 Broadway. S.D.S., according to its president, Carl Oglesby, "plans to concentrate on the education program on the campus and in the community, not on mass demonstrations. We hope that the National Committee in Wisconsin will take over the organization of demonstrations." But Oglesby does want S.D.S. to explore the possibilities of a student strike along the lines of those in France over Algeria and in Japan over the Japanese-American treaty several years ago.

Relations between S.D.S. and the National Coordinating Committee are not always smooth. "Everyone and his brother is a member of the steering committee," S.D.S. National Secretary Paul Booth told me, "and I wouldn't want them making decisions for my membership." Who will do what where, I suspect, will be determined by the relative strength of the various members of this uneasy coalition. Roughly speaking, and with considerable overlap, the M2M is a big thing in the East, S.D.S. in the Middle West and the Du Bois Society on the West Coast.

Meanwhile, S.D.S. is the largest single radical student group on or around the nation's campuses. It claims a membership of 3,000 (spokesmen say that at least twice as many participate in its activities) with 90 chapters around the country, a national staff of 12 people and an annual budget of $80,000. Single staff members are paid $12.50 a week—when they get paid—plus rent. S.D.S. has rented two floors in a nearby house for use as a staff apartment. "We eat together a lot," one staff member said. Married staffers are paid $70 a week and are expected to pay their own rent.

S.D.S. is not entirely a traditional campus-based organization. It has some 50 volunteers, living on subsistence pay raised out of local chapter funds, working in some 10 poor neighborhoods in Northern cities. Many of these are in the slum neighborhoods that surround our major universities—such as those around Columbia University in New York. S.D.S. members seek to organize the residents into community unions, battle urban renewal, agitate for control of poverty programs by the poor, and work to form new political groupings of the poor.

The S.D.S. missions to the poor have been undergoing a change since a group of youngsters under the leadership of Tom Hayden, an S.D.S. "founder," moved into the Clinton Hill area of Newark and formed the Newark Community Union Project. N.C.U.P. is the prototype and most successful of such S.D.S. projects.

The youngsters who join N.C.U.P. as "community organizers" exist on a Spartan diet—mostly peanut-butter and jelly sandwiches and powdered milk. At first, these lay brothers of the poor roam the neighborhood getting acquainted, taking surveys—"Does your landlord provide heat?"—as a way of meeting residents and getting to know their grievances. Then come informal meetings and more formal protest organizations on a block basis. Rent strikes are encouraged, along with sit-ins in city offices aimed at securing housing inspection and enforcement of building codes. In Newark, such tactics have paid off in needed repairs, regularized garbage collection and the shelving of an urban-renewal project that would have displaced residents.

Despite this modest success, S.D.S. has had difficulty in keeping projects of this type going. Last summer, there was a shift in emphasis from the problems of the poor toward the building of opposition to the war in Vietnam. The S.D.S. Oakland Community Union Project, for example, apparently spent most of its time "combating Selective Service," according to a report in The S.D.S. Bulletin. On Manhattan's West Side, a similar group spent its time handing out antiwar leaflets to the crowds at New York's Shakespeare Festival. Literature tables were set up in the street as a means of distributing antiwar literature and engaging passers-by in "educational debate." Street-corner meetings were also held.

Susan Schwartz, an attractive Radcliffe graduate now a French instructor at New York State University in Stony Brook, L. I., who lives on the Upper West Side, told me: "We're trying to create a permanent radical constituency by linking up peace issues with domestic issues." It is an effort that has its hazards. Miss Schwartz, the daughter of a Hartford, Conn., eye specialist, recalled street-corner speakers being pelted with eggs, tomatoes and bottles. "The police," she said, "did nothing. All the neutrals were driven away and the situation got kind of ugly and frightening. We had to have the police escort us to the subway."

This West Side group plans door-to-door canvassing this fall "on questions of peace, housing, schools and other community issues." It has opened a store-front community meeting place, largely staffed by Columbia students, and "hopes to lay the basis for a Congressional campaign in 1966." Despite the groping for community support, the group seems to draw its strength from what might be termed the Columbia University "surround," where the S.D.S. constituency is to be found.

The S.D.S. constituency is that new intellectual underclass growing up around our universities—students, college dropouts, graduate students, graduates who have started on their careers but who have not left the university neighborhood (especially in the larger cities), teaching assistants and professors in the lower ranks. It is a mobile class, shifting with ease from Berkeley to Cambridge and all points between.

The traditional constituency of the left, the working class, is pretty much given up as lost, having fallen prey to the unions and the Democratic party, pillars of the Establishment in S.D.S. eyes. Informed estimates place at least a third, if not more, of S.D.S. membership among graduate students, dropouts, graduates and others who make up the new underclass.

The S.D.S. president, Carl Oglesby, may well be the representative man of this new underclass. "There is something very Emersonian about belonging to S.D.S.," he told me. Though a member of only several months' standing, he was elected—perhaps the better word would be "chosen"—at the last S.D.S. convention in June after a long debate over whether or not S.D.S. should elect officers at all.

Holding office or having officers seems to some in the movement "a form of oppression." Vice President Shero, for example, who is something of an anarchist, has proposed a referendum that would abolish the offices of president and vice president. He believes the organization is "over-structured." When he was asked about the office of national secretary, he said: "Don't worry, we'll get around to abolishing that, too." However, debate over this issue was temporarily resolved last June when Oglesby was elected to office.

The story of Oglesby's involvement in S.D.S. and his election tells a good deal about the style of the movement as well as about its uncertainties. Note, for example, that Oglesby at 30 is the same age as many of the teaching assistants, section men and younger professors who actually teach S.D.S. students in college. Also, though a new boy, he is of an age with the S.D.S. elder statesmen and founders.

When I interviewed Oglesby in the Greenwich Village apartment of a friend, he was dressed casually in a yellow pullover, white shirt, dark brown slacks, white socks and nondescript black shoes. As he talks, he uses his hands expressively and his eyes are sharp and quizzical behind black, thin-rimmed glasses. He is tall and thin and, with his beard and brown hair, he looks rather like the middle-period D. H. Lawrence.

One is not surprised at all to discover that Oglesby is a playwright and would-be novelist. He has had two plays, "The Peacemaker" and "The Hero," produced at the University of Michigan; another, "The Season of the Beast," was produced by the Margo Jones Theatre in Dallas, Tex., and closed, says Oglesby, "by fiat" of the Board of Directors for being "anti-fundamentalist." "The Peacemaker" also was given a reading by the Actors Studio here in New York. Oglesby told me that he would not now finish his first novel, finding it no longer "relevant," though he has hopes of writing another.

Oglesby is one of the few S.D.S.'ers who can claim a working-class background. He was born in 1935 in Akron, Ohio, the son of a rubber worker. His parents, now divorced, came from the South: his father from South Carolina—"He came North to get rich in a factory"—his mother from Alabama. Asked about family politics, Oglesby said, "My family is completely non-political, kind of pale Democrats. My father believes in the union and that's about it."

After graduating from the Akron public schools, Oglesby entered Kent State University. By his own account, he was not very happy there. "In 1953," he told me, "there wasn't any movement discernible from Kent." But, he adds, "I really wasn't entitled to complain. I had the option of leaving." Which he did, moving to New York, where he almost succeeded in getting a play produced on Broadway. After a year, he went back to Kent, where he met his wife-to-be and married her.

Then came a time of odd jobs, including a stint in the mill room of a rubber factory. "It was a tough place," he says. A job as a technical writer at Goodyear came as a welcome break. Later, "somewhat over-ecstatic" at the acceptance of his first play by the Dallas theater group, Oglesby packed up wife and daughter and took off for Maine where he spent "three really beautiful months."

But the money ran out and he became a technical writer again, this time with Bendix Systems Division at Ann Arbor, Mich., where he was soon promoted to supervisor of his department. Meanwhile, he reentered school, hoping to get his B.A. degree from the University of Michigan as well as perhaps win the university's Hopwood Literary Prize. "Bendix," he told me, "was very tolerant about employees going to school during working hours. It's part of corporate liberalism. They thought I was kind of eccentric, but despite myself I became the fair-haired boy of upper management."

Still, though Oglesby believed that "American society was so bad that there can't be anything between me and it" he felt ashamed about "drawing a moral blanket over the fact that for eight hours a day I was a hireling in the cold war." At about this time, he became involved in an S.D.S. project "to get a grass-roots theater going." The project didn't but Oglesby did within S.D.S.

He did some research on the war in Vietnam and published some lengthy communiqués on the subject in The S.D.S. Bulletin. Then came a series of soul-searching conversations with S.D.S. leaders Rennie Davis and Todd Gitlin over: "What to do with my life?" At the time of the teach-ins last year, S.D.S. offered Oglesby two jobs, one with a community project in Boston and the other as research director in Ann Arbor. He accepted the latter, despite possible financial hardship for his wife and three young children.

The election as S.D.S. president, Oglesby told me, "was an emotional experience for me and the organization, too." I asked him if he ascribed his election to the swing within S.D.S. toward organizational concentration on the anti-Vietnam war issue. He thought not. "I was the oldest of the lot [of five] running," he told me, "and consider that the people are perplexed over what happens when you leave school. Is it possible to stay with the movement when you take on a job and family responsibilities? My willingness to come to them from a $12,000-a-year job and to throw myself on their willingness to sustain us was moving to them." Oglesby added that he "wanted to push away" the nomination—"I felt that it was obtrusive of me"—but he also felt himself "becoming a moral center for people though I tried not to be."

This kind of mystique is as important to the S.D.S. youngsters as is morality and the need for consensus. "The movement" of which S.D.S. is a part depends on consensus just as much as—if not more than—President Johnson. "The Trotskyites," I was told by Paul Booth, S.D.S. national secretary, in the course of a discussion about the umbrella-type End the War in Vietnam Committees, "are so new to the coalition that they don't know how to act. So, the first thing they do when they come in is to form a faction immediately. And, no one knows how to handle them."

It seems that as a result of this "Trotskyist" factionalism at least one New Left united-front group actually has had to take votes on important decisions. "Within the New Left," Booth said, "you know, we work for consensus, but how can you get consensus if there is an already committed bloc?" He shook his head regretfully, saying, "The self-destructive forces within the coalition really shouldn't be underestimated. Outside of meetings, though, things work O.K."

Booth, a 22-year-old Swarthmore graduate, class of 1964, who majored in political science, told me, "I was brought back partly to repoliticalize the movement." Booth's parents were both active in Americans for Democratic Action and before his disillusionment with liberalism Paul worked—in 1960—for the Democratic National Committee. His father, a New Dealer, was chief of the Unemployment Security Bureau's Division of Program and Legislation before becoming a professor of social work and economics at the University of Michigan. Paul's mother worked as a psychiatric social worker in Washington, D. C., where Paul grew up.

He is an intense, lanky young man with curly, light brown hair, with hazel eyes bright in a triangular face. Walking to lunch, wearing a dark madras jacket, white shirt and stringy tie, dark slacks, he was oblivious of the pencil perched above his right ear. His words tumbled out in haste trying to catch up with his rapid strides along the sidewalk. "We contend that young people don't want to fight, so why don't they test it by allowing choice, offer something that builds? Work in Watts, with SNCC, in the Peace Corps—this should be seen as a duty as high as burning a village." We stepped into the best restaurant on the block—not very good but one step above cafeterias and drug-store counters—and Booth said, "This is where the local poverty warriors eat."

Booth worries over what he calls "our mumbling inarticulateness in the face of questions about our politics. We do have a sound critique of coalition politics [the alliance of liberal, labor and civil-rights forces advocated by people like Michael Harrington and Bayard Rustin] and we should articulate. We've got a lot to say to the world." S.D.S., Booth believes, "is filling the void left by the non-existence of an adult left."

Despite disclaimers, however, S.D.S. does owe something to an adult left. Seeking a "sustained community of educational and political concern . . . bringing together liberals and radicals, activists and scholars, students and faculty," S.D.S. originated in 1960 as the revived student department of the League for Industrial Democracy, a tax-exempt Socialist-oriented educational organization founded in 1905 by Upton Sinclair, Jack London, Clarence Darrow and others and dedicated "to increasing democracy in our economic, political and cultural life." The L.I.D., too, is experiencing a revival under its new executive secretary, 27-year-old Tom Kahn, and chairman, 38-year-old Michael Harrington.

Recently, however, the two organizations have parted company. The separation followed S.D.S.'s increasing participation in action programs that clearly transcended the limits imposed by law on tax-exempt organizations. S.D.S., in short, did not want to be inhibited by the L.I.D.'s tax exemption, nor did S.D.S. want to jeopardize the exemption. However, a joint statement, issued by Kahn and Booth, did say: "We do not conceal the fact that political differences between the two organizations have emerged in recent times."

The S.D.S. Port Huron Statement, drafted in 1962 and considered its founding document, contained denunciations of colonialism, Communism and anti-Communism. This summer, however, the S.D.S. convention struck from its constitution clauses barring "advocates and apologists" of totalitarianism and opposing "authoritarian movements both of Communism and the domestic right" because these sections were "negative and exclusionary" and "smacked of Red-baiting." "The New Left," The S.D.S. Bulletin said in reporting the deletions, "should not concern itself with this Old Left tactic."

The L.I.D. was no more pleased about this development than it was about a Viet Cong romanticism among some of the S.D.S. The Viet Cong are fighting "at bottom a legitimate war of liberation," says Oglesby. There is also a strong feeling that the S.D.S. antidraft program pushes demonstrations to the point of defeating their purpose—peace in Vietnam—by hardening the opposition, freezing out the middle ground, and bringing an end to debate. There have been some counter-demonstrations, angry verbal exchanges and occasional fisticuffs on campuses recently.

Recent weeks have been rather trying ones for the S.D.S. "We're in trouble all right," Paul Booth told me, "but such trouble I can live with. The organization is booming." S.D.S. leaders expect to double their membership shortly and hope to hit 10,000 before the year is out. But one suspects that they are now recruiting only the converted; for example, a "super late news" item in The S.D.S. Bulletin: "University of Chicago students have been piling into the office all morning to sign membership cards. One fellow said, 'If you are going to be Red-baited, I want to be on the list.'" Or, there is the girl who joined the University of Chicago meeting I witnessed. She said: "I've always *felt* this way; member or not, it made no difference. But now I have to tangibly show I'm committed." That day, the Chicago S.D.S. chapter picked up 20 new members, bringing total membership to about 50—and this, I am told, is a big chapter.

Until now, S.D.S. has been very lax about dues: "When we split —you know, left the bourgeoisie," Oglesby told me, "we left all those habits behind, like paying dues." But, worried lest its antidraft stand cause a drop-off in contributions from the "richies" and "friendly institutions," the S.D.S. leadership has intensified both recruitment and the collection of dues.

The S.D.S. draft referendum is couched in terms that emphasize its value as "a tool for expanding the antiwar movement." First, The S.D.S. Bulletin discusses its "relevance" as a "central factor in the lives of millions of people." Among the "possible approaches to the draftable kids" are tables outside physical-examination centers for distributing leaflets along the lines of "Why are they trying to draft you?" and urging that "kids file Form 150," a request for C.O. classification. Help should be offered in filling out such forms, "strictly legal, unlike 'draft refusal.'"

Speaking engagements at high schools should be sought along with debates with military recruiters. Organizing around an antidraft program, The Bulletin goes on, provides the opportunity to educate listeners about the "basic facts about the war in Vietnam, the undemocratic nature of the draft itself, and serves to illustrate the connections between the University and the military establishment."

The program opens up opportunities for protest, too. According to The S.D.S. Bulletin, "the act of filing for C.O. is, in itself, a gesture of personal protest."

On campus, the authorities should be stopped from turning over class-rank information to the military. (S.D.S. believes that the extension of the draft may hit students in the bottom quartile of their class this winter.) Recruiters "should be the focus of attention, challenged to debate, accused by picket signs of participation in war crimes." Ditto, the R.O.T.C. demonstrations may also be aimed at local draft boards.

The antidraft referendum, as is often the case with S.D.S. policy-making, embraces activities already under way in some individual chapters.

There is, incidentally, no hard cut-off date for the vote, return of ballots and the count. "S.D.S. chapters," Oglesby told me, "have the right to act autonomously and a lot have been moving independently on this [the antidraft program] already."

S.D.S. members, for example, were active in the International Days of Protest, Oct. 15 and 16, which brought out some 80,000 in protest marches and demonstrations across the country. In Ann Arbor, 38 people were arrested in an S.D.S.-sponsored draft-board sit-in. The North Carolina S.D.S. chapter marched against the biological weapons center at Fort Bragg—without discernible results, however.

In Oakland, S.D.S. members have handed out leaflets at recruiting centers urging young men of draft age to file C.O. forms. They also tried unsuccessfully to stop a troop train. "How did we know when the trains were coming? Answer—spotters up the line," reported Paul Booth in the summer S.D.S. Bulletin. (Booth spent the summer working in the S.D.S. Oakland Community Project.) But, he added: "All the dramatic troop train demonstrations and other demonstrations have still not added up to more than a handful of arrests."

"Like Berkeley last year," Booth told me, "the draft thing contributes to student class consciousness."

Todd Gitlin, a member of the S.D.S. National Administrative Committee, also believes that the antidraft program will rally broad student support. "Originally," he said, "I was more excited about rallying ordinary kids. Then they read me an interview with the head of the Michigan Selective Service. This worthy gentleman pointed out that there were 76,000 students in Michigan (presumably this includes part-timers, kids in junior and community colleges, etc.), and that 20,000 of the lousy brats would be drafted. If such is the case, the campus should be fertile soil for an antidraft movement."

Some S.D.S. members, however, do not agree. Lee Webb, another member of the S.D.S. National Administrative Committee, put his opposition in these terms: "The antidraft issue is not the best one around which to organize a mass opposition to the war . . . [It] raises just those emotional cold-war issues that make it a terrible choice. . . . S.D.S. should be concerned most with broadening the base of opposition to the war, not with escalating the antiwar movement to more militant tactics." To paraphrase Webb, if S.D.S. members are arrested, it should be because the Government can no longer tolerate "mass dissatisfaction" with its foreign policy, not because of an antidraft program. "We see the linkage between the war and that program," Webb said, but "most people will not—they will see us only as draft dodgers."

The S.D.S. youngsters, incidentally, while they admire those who protest by burning their draft cards, are not likely to emulate them. As one S.D.S. member put it: "Is going to jail for three years, say, going to help the peace movement?" Those who burn their draft cards in protest, like young David J. Miller, who burned his in New York City several weeks ago and was subsequently arrested, are members of avowedly pacifist organizations and not of S.D.S. in most cases. S.D.S. is not a pacifist group.

"We're not against violence, per se," Oglesby told me. "We don't like it. Who does? But we're not pretending to be pacifists. The aim of the antidraft program is to make it possible for people who feel as we do about the war to do something about it." S.D.S., I was told, is interested in expanding the definition of conscientious objector to include those who are not against all wars.

Another group opposed to the present antidraft program is the New York-At-Large chapter of S.D.S., most of whose members believe in the workability of a liberal-labor-civil-rights coalition in politics, a belief in Establishmentarianism frowned upon by most of the rest of S.D.S. Steve Max, an articulate former S.D.S. staff member, fears that S.D.S. faces "a progressive narrowing of options." The combined effect, he argues, "of the incautious attitude taken toward the Viet Cong, the removal of statements in our constitution differentiating our politics from Communist ideologies, and the antidraft proposal is to cut off S.D.S. from many individuals and groups who are not to its left. The total, uncalculated effect is to alienate present friends and prospective allies."

Even the supporters of the antidraft program, it seemed to me as I talked to them, approached it warily. They are a little nervous about what they consider the program's "legal ambiguities." The day the referendum was sent out, a page was added explaining possible legal consequences. A number of letters have come into the S.D.S. national office raising essentially the same question, "Are we engaged in a *draft-dodging* program?" (Italics mine.)

David Gilbert, a 21-year-old Columbia University senior, philosophy major and former Eagle Scout, spoke to a floor meeting of about 20 at Carman Hall recently on the S.D.S. antidraft program. "My mother called me up," he said, "all upset about me now doing something illegal." Gilbert paused, then added: "Well, no one laughed, so I guess we've all got mothers." To set all such troubled minds at ease, Booth and other S.D.S. leaders repeatedly insisted to me: "We are legal."

"We've become a bit too Vietnam-oriented," Steve Kindred, a husky Chicago University history major told me. Kindred's father is an Iowa Methodist minister and Steve himself has just returned to Chicago after a year of working with peace groups in England. Speaking of plans for the Chicago S.D.S. chapter, he said: "We don't want to get stuck on crisis issue stuff." The Chicago group is forming working committees on foreign policy, domestic social change and university reform. It also plans an "inquest" that will "get the facts out" on Vietnam. The French and Italian press are to be "researched" for material to present to the inquest. "We're trying to fit in a general framework and reach as wide a base as possible," Kindred told me. But, he added, draft program publicity "helped get people here."

Carl Davidson, president of the University of Nebraska S.D.S. chapter, insists on describing S.D.S. as being "extremely antitotalitarian, against both Fascism and Communism." (The quotation is from The Daily Nebraskan.) Although S.D.S. is only a few weeks old at Nebraska, Davidson reports a dozen members, the sponsorship of a teach-in on Vietnam, a proposed study of rules and regulations on campus, and a look into the possible unionization of university service employees. All this is traditional S.D.S. campus activity.

The antidraft program is a departure on a new course. It is rooted in aversion to the horrors of the Vietnam war. At the moment, S.D.S., I would say, is content to look no further. Some S.D.S. members may believe that the Viet Cong are fighting "a revolutionary war"; others agree with Oglesby that the war is fought by the United States "under the banner of cold-war colonialism." Most, I suspect, would agree with young David Gilbert, who told a group of Columbia students: "I wouldn't say North Vietnam is a democratic ideal but it is the only viable regime in the country"—meaning all of Vietnam.

Neither do the S.D.S. youngsters see Communist China as an aggressor; the U.S. seems to them to be playing that part. They simply are not concerned about the possibility of Chinese Communist domination over Asia; China is remote and perhaps revolutionary still. India, once a rallying point for idealists, is no longer, especially since her refusal to grant a plebiscite in Kashmir. Socialism and neutralism in the underdeveloped countries, say S.D.S. spokesmen, "in many places should be encouraged."

Beyond this, they do not go. In sharp contrast to radical movements of the past, even a short decade ago, there is no discussion or debate over the nature of the Soviet Union or of Communist China. At their age, Stalin, the Stalin-Hitler Pact, Hungary, even Khrushchev's revelations are already dim history. During most of their nonage, the Communist monolith has, in fact, been falling apart, or so they believe. Besides, the S.D.S. generation is a most ahistorical generation. Unlike earlier radicals, they do not relate themselves to any radical tradition. There is little or no citing of texts in the Marxist manner.

S.D.S. is planning a December membership conference "to look at ourselves intellectually and organizationally." Among the topics of discussion—the list is almost endless—is the question of "coalition." With whom? The Du Bois Clubs, M2M, etc., on the one hand, or the L.I.D., the A.F.L.-C.I.O., Socialist party and Reform Democrats on the other? Communism and the national liberation movements as well as "the structure of power" in the United States are due for scrutiny. The parental League for Industrial Democracy has been asked to participate.

Still, one suspects that it is the antidraft program that will shape the S.D.S.'s immediate future. As Oglesby told me: "It appears our resources are being allocated for us by the Administration." And, he might have added, television, the press and other mass media. In this context, what will happen may depend upon Government reaction. But it will also turn on the response of the new university-created underclass to a tighter draft and to the S.D.S.'s antidraft program. Campus polls, so far, show that students favor President Johnson's approach to the Vietnam war over that of the S.D.S. But no one has polled the new underclass. What they will do and how that will affect S.D.S. no one at present can say.

"This Is the Beat Generation"

by Clellon Holmes

SEVERAL MONTHS AGO, a national magazine ran a story under the heading "Youth" and the subhead "Mother Is Bugged at Me." It concerned an 18-year-old California girl who had been picked up for smoking marijuana and wanted to talk about it. While a reporter took down her ideas in the uptempo language of "tea," someone snapped a picture. In view of her contention that she was part of a whole new culture where one out of every five people you meet is a user, it was an arresting photograph. In the pale, attentive face, with its soft eyes and intelligent mouth, there was no hint of corruption. It was a face which could only be deemed criminal through an enormous effort of righteousness. Its only complaint seemed to be "Why don't people leave us alone?" It was the face of a Beat Generation.

That clean young face has been making the newspapers steadily since the war. Standing before a judge in a Bronx court house, being arraigned for stealing a car, it looked up into the camera with curious laughter and no guilt. The same face, with a more serious bent, stared from the pages of Life magazine, representing a graduating class of ex-G. I.'s, and said that as it believed small business to be dead, it intended to become a comfortable cog in the largest corporation it could find. A little younger, a little more bewildered, it was this same face that the photographers caught in Illinois when the first non-virgin club was uncovered. The young copywriter, lean-

From the *New York Times Magazine,* November 16, 1952. Reprinted by permission of The Sterling Lord Agency.

ing down the bar on Third Avenue, quietly drinking himself into relaxation, and the energetic hot-rod driver of Los Angeles, who plays Russian roulette with a jalopy, are separated only by a continent and a few years. They are the extremes. In between them fall the secretaries wondering whether to sleep with their boy friends now or wait; the mechanics, beering up with the guys and driving off to Detroit on a whim; the models studiously name-dropping at a cocktail party. But the face is the same. Bright, level, realistic, challenging.

Any attempt to label an entire generation is unrewarding, and yet the generation which went through the last war, or at least could get a drink easily once it was over, seems to possess a uniform, general quality which demands an adjective. It was John Kerouac, the author of a fine, neglected novel "The Town and the City," who finally came up with it. It was several years ago, when the face was harder to recognize, but he has a sharp, sympathetic eye, and one day he said, "You know, this is really a *beat* generation." The origins of the word "beat" are obscure, but the meaning is only too clear to most Americans. More than mere weariness, it implies the feeling of having been used, of being raw. It involves a sort of nakedness of mind, and, ultimately, of soul; a feeling of being reduced to the bedrock of consciousness. In short, it means being undramatically pushed up against the wall of oneself. A man is beat whenever he goes for broke and wagers the sum of his resources on a single number; and the young generation has done that continually from early youth.

Its members have an instinctive individuality, needing no bohemianism or imposed eccentricity to express it. Brought up during the collective bad circumstances of a dreary depression, weaned during the collective uprooting of a global war, they distrust collectivity. But they have never been able to keep the world out of their dreams. The fancies of their childhood inhabited the half-light of Munich, the Nazi-Soviet pact and the eventual blackout. Their adolescence was spent in a topsy-turvy world of war bonds, swing shifts and troop movements. They grew to independent mind on beachheads, in ginmills and U. S. O.'s, in past-midnight arrivals and pre-dawn departures. Their brothers, husbands, fathers or boy friends turned up dead one day at the other end of a telegram. At the four trembling corners of the world, or in the home town invaded by factories and lonely servicemen, they had intimate experience with the nadir and the zenith of human conduct, and little time for much that came between. The peace they inherited was only as secure as the next headline. It was a cold peace. Their own lust for freedom, and their ability to live at a pace that kills, to which war had adjusted them, led to black markets, bebop, narcotics, sexual promiscuity, hucksterism and Jean-Paul Sartre. The beatness set in later.

It is a post-war generation, and, in a world which seems to mark its cycles by its wars, it is already being compared to that other post-war generation, which dubbed itself "lost." The Roaring Twenties, and the generation that made them roar, are going through a sentimental revival, and the comparison is valuable. The Lost Generation was discovered in a roadster, laughing hysterically because nothing meant anything any more. It migrated to Europe, unsure whether it was looking for the "orgiastic future" or escaping from the "puritanical past." Its symbols were the flapper, the flask of bootleg whisky, and an attitude of desperate frivolity best expressed by Noel Coward's line: "Tennis, anyone?" It was caught up in the romance of disillusionment, until even that became an illusion. Every act in its drama of lostness was a tragic or an ironic third act, and T. S. Eliot's "The Wasteland" was more than the dead-end statement of a perceptive poet. The pervading atmosphere was an almost objectless sense of loss, through which the reader felt immediately that the cohesion of things had disappeared. It was, for an entire generation, an image which expressed, with dreadful accuracy, its own spiritual condition.

But the wild boys of today are not lost. Their flushed, often scoffing, always intent faces elude the word, and it would sound phony to them. For this generation conspicuously lacks that eloquent air of bereavement which made so many of the exploits of the Lost Generation symbolic actions. Furthermore, the repeated inventory of shattered ideals, and the laments about the mud in moral currents, which so obsessed the Lost Generation, does not concern young people today. They take it frighteningly for granted. They were brought up in these ruins and no longer notice them. They drink to "come down" or to "get high," not to illustrate anything. Their excursions into drugs or promiscuity come out of curiosity, not disillusionment.

Only the most bitter among them would call their reality a nightmare and protest that they have indeed lost something, the future.

But ever since they were old enough to imagine one, that has been in jeopardy anyway. The absence of personal and social values is to them, not a revelation shaking the ground beneath them, but a problem demanding a day-to-day solution. *How* to live seems to them much more crucial than *why*. And it is precisely at this point that the copywriter and the hot-rod driver meet, and their identical beatness becomes significant, for, unlike the Lost Generation, which was occupied with the loss of faith, the Beat Generation is becoming more and more occupied with the need for it. As such, it is a disturbing illustration of Voltaire's reliable old joke: "If there were no God, it would be necessary to invent Him." Not content to bemoan His absence, they are busily and haphazardly inventing totems for Him on all sides.

For the giggling nihilist, eating up the highway at ninety miles an hour, and steering with his feet, is no Harry Crosby, the poet of the Lost Generation who flew his plane into the sun one day because he could no longer accept the modern world. On the contrary, the hot-rod driver invites death only to outwit it. He is affirming the life within him in the only way he knows how, at the extreme. The eager-faced girl, picked up on a dope charge, is not one of those "women and girls carried screaming with drink or drugs from public places," of whom Fitzgerald wrote. Instead, with persuasive seriousness, she describes the sense of community she has found in marijuana, which society never gave her. The copywriter, just as drunk by midnight as his Lost Generation counterpart, probably reads "God and Man at Yale" during his Sunday afternoon hangover. The difference is this almost exaggerated will to believe in something, if only in themselves. It is a *will* to believe, even in the face of an inability to do so in conventional terms. And that is bound to lead to excesses in one direction or another.

The shock that older people feel at the sight of this Beat Generation is, at its deepest level, not so much repugnance at the facts, as it is distress at the attitudes which move it. Though worried by this distress, they most often argue or legislate in terms of the facts rather than the attitudes. The newspaper reader, studying the eyes of young dope addicts, can only find an outlet for his horror and bewilderment in demands that passers be given the electric chair. Sociologists, with a more academic concern, are just as troubled by the legions of young men whose topmost ambition seems to be to find a secure berth in a monolithic corporation. Contemporary historians express mild surprise at the lack of organized movements, political, religious or otherwise, among the young. The articles they write remind us that being one's own boss and being a natural joiner are two of our most cherished national traits. Everywhere, people with tidy moralities shake their heads and wonder what is happening to the younger generation.

Perhaps they have not noticed that, behind the excess on the one hand, and the conformity on the other, lies that wait-and-see detachment that results from having to fall back for support more on one's human endurance than on one's philosophy of life. Not that the Beat Generation is immune to ideas; they fascinate it. Its wars, both past and future, were and will be wars of ideas. It knows, however, that in the final, private moment of conflict a man is really fighting another man, and not an idea. And that the same goes for love. So it is a generation with a greater facility for entertaining ideas than for believing in them. But it is also the first generation in several centuries for which the act of faith has been an obsessive problem, quite aside from the reasons for having a particular faith or not having it. It exhibits on every side, and in a bewildering number of facets, a perfect craving to believe.

Though it is certainly a generation of extremes, including both the hipster and the "radical" young Republican in its ranks, it renders unto Caesar (i.e., society) what is Caesar's, and unto God what is God's. For in the wildest hipster, making a mystique of bop, drugs and the night life, there is no desire to shatter the "square" society in which he lives, only to elude it. To get on a soapbox or write a manifesto would seem to him absurd. Looking out at the normal world, where most everything is a "drag" for him, he nevertheless says: "Well, that's the Forest of Arden after all. And even it jumps if you look at it right." Equally, the young Republican, though often seeming to hold up Babbitt as his culture hero, is neither vulgar nor materialistic, as Babbitt was. He conforms because he believes it is socially practical, not necessarily virtuous. Both positions, however, are the result of more or less the same conviction—namely that the valueless abyss of modern life is unbearable.

A generation can sometimes be better understood by the books it reads, than by those it writes. The literary hero of the Lost Generation should have been Bazarov, the nihilist in Turgenev's "Fathers and Sons." Bazarov sat around, usually in the homes of the people he professed to loathe, smashing every icon within his reach. He was a man stunned into irony and rage by the collapse of the moral and intellectual structure of his world.

But he did nothing. The literary hero of the Beat Generation, on the other hand, might be Stavrogin, that most enigmatic character in "The Possessed" by Dostoevski. He is also a nihilist, or at least intimately associated with them.

But there is a difference, for Stavrogin, behind a facade very much like Bazarov's, is possessed by a passion for faith, almost any faith. His very atheism, at its extreme, is metaphysical. But he knows that disbelief is fatal, and when he has failed in every way to overcome it, he commits suicide because he does not have what he calls "greatness of soul." The ground yawned beneath Bazarov, revealing a pit into which he fell; while Stavrogin struggled at the bottom of that pit, trying feverishly to get out. In so far as it resembles Stavrogin, there have been few generations with as natural and profound a craving for convictions as this one, nor have there been many generations as ill-equipped to find them.

For beneath the excess and the conformity, there is something other than detachment. There are the stirrings of a quest. What the hipster is looking for in his "coolness" (withdrawal) or "flipness" (ecstasy) is, after all, a feeling of somewhereness, not just another diversion. The young Republican feels that there is a point beyond which change becomes chaos, and what he wants is not simply privilege or wealth, but a stable position from which to operate. Both have had enough of homelessness, valuelessness, faithlessness.

The variety and the extremity of their solutions is only a final indication that for today's young people there is not as yet a single external pivot around which they can, as a generation, group their observations and their aspirations. There is no single philosophy, no single party, no single attitude. The failure of most orthodox moral and social concepts to reflect fully the life they have known is probably the reason, but because of it each person becomes a walking, self-contained unit, compelled to meet the problem of being young in a seemingly helpless world in his own way, or least to endure.

More than anything else, this is what is responsible for this generation's reluctance to name itself, its reluctance to discuss itself as a group, sometimes its reluctance to be itself. For invented gods invariably disappoint those who worship them. Only the need for them goes on, and it is this need, exhausting one object after another, which projects the Beat Generation forward into the future and will one day deprive it of its beatness.

Dostoevski wrote in the early Eighteen Eighties that, "Young Russia is talking of nothing but the eternal questions now." With appropriate changes, something very like this is beginning to happen in America, in an American way; a re-evaluation of which the exploits and attitudes of this generation are only symptoms. No simple comparison of one generation against another can accurately measure effects, but it seems obvious that a Lost Generation, occupied with disillusionment and trying to keep busy among the broken stones, is poetically moving, not very dangerous. But a Beat Generation, driven by a desperate craving for belief and as yet unable to accept the moderations which are offered it, is quite another matter. Thirty years later, after all, the generation of which Dostoevski wrote was meeting in cellars and making bombs.

This generation may make no bombs; it will probably be asked to drop some, and have some dropped on it, however, and this fact is never far from its mind. It is one of the pressures which created it and will play a large part in what will happen to it. There are those who believe that in generations such as this there is always the constant possibility of a great new moral idea, conceived in desperation, coming to life. Others note the self-indulgence, the waste, the apparent social irresponsibility, and disagree.

But its ability to keep its eyes open, and yet avoid cynicism; its ever-increasing conviction that the problem of modern life is essentially a spiritual problem; and that capacity for sudden wisdom which people who live hard and go far possess are assets and bear watching. And, anyway, the clear, challenging faces are worth it.

The "Hashbury" Is the Capital of the Hippies

by Hunter S. Thompson

SAN FRANCISCO

IN 1965 BERKELEY was the axis of what was just beginning to be
called the "New Left." Its leaders were radical, but they were also
deeply committed to the society they wanted to change. A prestigious
faculty committee said the Berkeley activists were the vanguard of
"a moral revolution among the young," and many professors
approved.

Now, in 1967, there is not much doubt that Berkeley has gone
through a revolution of some kind, but the end result is not exactly
what the original leaders had in mind. Many one-time activists have
forsaken politics entirely and turned to drugs. Others have even forsaken Berkeley. During 1966, the hot center of revolutionary action
on the Coast began moving across the bay to San Francisco's Haight-
Ashbury district, a rundown Victorian neighborhood of about 40
square blocks between the Negro/Fillmore district and Golden Gate
Park.

The "Hashbury" is the new capital of what is rapidly becoming a
drug culture. Its denizens are not called radicals or beatniks, but
"hippies"—and perhaps as many as half are refugees from Berkeley
and the old North Beach scene, the cradle and the casket of the
so-called Beat Generation.

The other half of the hippy population is too young to identify

From the *New York Times Magazine*, May 14, 1967.

with Jack Kerouac, or even with Mario Savio. Their average age is about 20, and most are native Californians. The North Beach types of the late nineteen-fifties were not nearly as provincial as the Haight-Ashbury types are today. The majority of beatniks who flocked into San Francisco 10 years ago were transients from the East and Midwest. The literary-artistic nucleus—Kerouac, Ginsberg, et al.—was a package deal from New York. San Francisco was only a stop on the big circuit: Tangier, Paris, Greenwich Village, Tokyo and India. The senior beats had a pretty good idea what was going on in the world; they read newspapers, traveled constantly and had friends all over the globe.

The word "hip" translates roughly as "wise" or "tuned-in." A hippy is somebody who "knows" what's really happening, and who adjusts or grooves with it. Hippies despise phoniness; they want to be open, honest, loving and free. They reject the plastic pretense of 20th-century America, preferring to go back to the "natural life," like Adam and Eve. They reject any kinship with the Beat Generation on the ground that "those cats were negative, but our thing is positive." They also reject politics, which is "just another game." They don't like money, either, or any kind of aggressiveness.

A serious problem in writing about the Haight-Ashbury is that most of the people you have to talk to are involved, one way or another, in the drug traffic. They have good reason to be leery of strangers who ask questions. A 22-year-old student was recently sentenced to two years in prison for telling an undercover narcotics agent where to buy some marijuana. "Love" is the password in the Haight-Ashbury, but paranoia is the style. Nobody wants to go to jail.

At the same time, marijuana is everywhere. People smoke it on the sidewalks, in doughnut shops, sitting in parked cars or lounging on the grass in Golden Gate Park. Nearly everyone on the streets between 20 and 30 is a "head," a user, either of marijuana, LSD, or both. To refuse a proffered "joint" is to risk being labeled a "nark"—narcotics agent—a threat and a menace to almost everybody.

With a few loud exceptions, it is only the younger hippies who see themselves as a new breed. "A completely new thing in this world, man." The ex-beatniks among them, many of whom are now making money off the new scene, incline to the view that hippies are, in fact, second-generation beatniks and that everything genuine in the

Haight-Ashbury is about to be swallowed—like North Beach and the Village—in a wave of publicity and commercialism.

Haight Street, the Great White Way of what the local papers call "Hippieland," is already dotted with stores catering mainly to the tourist trade. Few hippies can afford a pair of $20 sandals or a "mod outfit" for $67.50. Nor can they afford the $3.50 door charge at the Fillmore Auditorium and the Avalon Ballroom, the twin wombs of the "psychedelic, San Francisco, acid-rock sound." Both the Fillmore and the Avalon are jammed every weekend with border-line hippies who don't mind paying for the music and the light shows. There is always a sprinkling of genuine, barefoot, freaked-out types on the dance floor, but few of them pay to get in. They arrive with the musicians or have other good connections.

Neither of the dance palaces is within walking distance of the Hashbury, especially if you're stoned, and since only a few of the hippies have contacts in the psychedelic power structure, most of them spend their weekend nights either drifting around on Haight Street or loading up on acid—LSD—in somebody's pad. Some of the rock bands play free concerts in Golden Gate Park for the benefit of those brethren who can't afford the dances. But beyond an occasional Happening in the park, the Haight-Ashbury scene is almost devoid of anything "to do"—at least by conventional stand-ards. An at-home entertainment is nude parties at which celebrants paint designs on each other.

There are no hippy bars, for instance, and only one restaurant above the level of a diner or a lunch counter. This is a reflection of the drug culture, which has no use for booze and regards food as a necessity to be acquired at the least possible expense. A "family" of hippies will work for hours over an exotic stew or curry in a communal kitchen, but the idea of paying $3 for a meal in a restau-rant is out of the question.

Some hippies work, others live on money from home and many are full-time beggars. The Post Office is a major source of hippy income. Jobs like sorting mail don't require much thought or effort. A hippy named Admiral Love of the Psychedelic Rangers delivers special-delivery letters at night. The admiral is in his mid-20's and makes enough money to support an apartmentful of younger hippies who depend on him for their daily bread.

There is also a hippy-run employment agency on Haight Street and anyone needing part-time labor or some kind of specialized work can call and order as many freaks as he needs; they might look a bit weird, but many are far more capable than most "temporary help," and vastly more interesting to have around.

Those hippies who don't work can easily pick up a few dollars a day panhandling along Haight Street. The fresh influx of curiosity-seekers has proved a great boon to the legion of psychedelic beggars. During several days of roaming around the area, I was touched so often that I began to keep a supply of quarters in my pocket so I wouldn't have to haggle over change. The panhandlers are usually barefoot, always young and never apologetic. They'll share what they collect anyway, so it seems entirely reasonable that strangers should share with them.

The best show on Haight Street is usually on the sidewalk in front of the Drog Store, a new coffee bar at the corner of Masonic Street. The Drog Store features an all-hippy revue that runs day and night. The acts change sporadically, but nobody cares. There will always be at least one man with long hair and sunglasses playing a wooden pipe of some kind. He will be wearing either a Dracula cape, a long Buddhist robe, or a Sioux Indian costume. There will also be a hairy blond fellow wearing a Black Bart cowboy hat and a spangled jacket that originally belonged to a drum major in the 1949 Rose Bowl parade. He will be playing the bongo drums. Next to the drummer will be a dazed-looking girl wearing a blouse (but no bra) and a plastic mini-skirt, slapping her thighs to the rhythm of it all.

These three will be the nucleus of the show. Backing them up will be an all-star cast of freaks, every one of them stoned. They will be stretched out on the sidewalk, twitching and babbling in time to the music. Now and then somebody will fall out of the audience and join the revue; perhaps a Hell's Angel or some grubby, chain-draped impostor who never owned a motorcycle in his life. Or maybe a girl wrapped in gauze or a thin man with wild eyes who took an overdose of acid nine days ago and changed himself into a raven. For those on a quick tour of the Hashbury, the Drog Store revue is a must.

Most of the local action is beyond the reach of anyone without access to drugs. There are four or five bars a nervous square might relax in, but one is a Lesbian place, another is a hangout for brutal-looking leather fetishists and the others are old neighborhood taverns full of brooding middle-aged drunks. Prior to the hippy era there were three good Negro-run jazz bars on Haight Street, but they soon went out of style. Who needs jazz, or even beer, when you can sit down on a public curbstone, drop a pill in your mouth, and hear fantastic music for hours at a time in your own head? A cap of good acid costs $5, and for that you can hear the Universal Symphony, with God singing solo and the Holy Ghost on drums.

Drugs have made formal entertainment obsolete in the Hashbury, but only until somebody comes up with something appropriate to the new style of the neighborhood. This summer will see the opening of the new Straight Theater, formerly the Haight Theater, featuring homosexual movies for the trade, meetings, concerts, dances. "It's going to be a kind of hippy community center," said Brent Dangerfield, a young radio engineer from Salt Lake City who stopped off in San Francisco on his way to a job in Hawaii and now is a partner in the Straight. When I asked Dangerfield how old he was he had to think for a minute. "I'm 22," he said finally, "but I used to be much older."

Another new divertissement, maybe, will be a hippy bus line running up and down Haight Street, housed in a 1930 Fagol bus—a huge, lumbering vehicle that might have been the world's first house trailer. I rode in it one afternoon with the driver, a young hippy named Tim Thibeau who proudly displayed a bathtub under one of the rear seats. The bus was a spectacle even on Haight Street: people stopped, stared and cheered as we rumbled by, going nowhere at all. Thibeau honked the horn and waved. He was from Chicago, he said, but when he got out of the Army he stopped in San Francisco and decided to stay. He was living, for the moment, on unemployment insurance, and his plans for the future were hazy. "I'm in no hurry," he said. "Right now I'm just taking it easy, just floating along." He smiled and reached for a beer can in the Fagol's icebox.

Dangerfield and Thibeau reflect the blind optimism of the younger hippy element. They see themselves as the vanguard of a new way of life in America—the psychedelic way—where love abounds and work is fun and people help each other. The young hippies are confident that things are going their way.

The older hippies are not so sure. They've been waiting a long time for the world to go their way, and those most involved in the hip scene are hedging their bets this time. "That back to nature scene is okay when you're 20," said one. "But when you're looking at 35 you want to know something's happening to you."

Ed Denson, at 27, is an ex-beatnik, ex-Goldwaterite, ex-Berkeley radical and currently the manager of a successful rock band called Country Joe and the Fish. His home and headquarters is a complex of rooms above a liquor store in Berkeley. One room is an art studio, another is an office; there is also a kitchen, a bedroom and several sparsely furnished areas without definition.

Denson is deeply involved in the hippy music scene, but insists he's not a hippy. "I'm very pessimistic about where this thing is going," he said. "Right now it's good for a lot of people. It's still very open. But I have to look back at the Berkeley scene. There was a tremendous optimism there, too, but look where all that went. The Beat Generation? Where are they now? What about hula-hoops? Maybe this hippy thing is more than a fad; maybe the whole world is turning on but I'm not optimistic. Most of the hippies I know don't really understand what kind of a world they're living in. I get tired of hearing about what beautiful people we all are. If the hippies were more realistic they'd stand a better chance of surviving."

Most hippies take the question of survival for granted, but it's becoming increasingly obvious, as the neighborhood fills with penniless heads, that there is simply not enough food and lodging to go around. A partial solution may come from a group called the "Diggers," who have been called the "worker-priests" of the hippy movement and the "invisible government" of the Hashbury. The Diggers are young and aggressively pragmatic; they have set up free lodging centers, free soup kitchens and free clothing distribution centers. They comb the neighborhood soliciting donations of everything from money to stale bread to camping equipment. Diggers' signs are posted in local stores, asking for donations of hammers, saws, shovels, shoes and anything else that vagrant hippies might use to make themselves at least partially self-supporting.

The name and spirit derive from small groups of 17th-century English rural revolutionaries, called both Diggers and True Levelers, who had a number of Socialist ideas. Money should be abolished, communal farms could support all those willing to work them, and individual ownership of land would be outlawed. The Diggers were severely harassed and the movement eventually caved in under the weight of public opprobrium.

The Hashbury Diggers have fared a bit better, but the demand for food and lodging is beginning to exceed the supply. For a while, the Diggers were able to serve three meals, however meager, each afternoon in Golden Gate Park. But as the word got around, more and more hippies showed up to eat, and the Diggers were forced to roam far afield to get food. Occasionally there were problems, as when Digger chieftain Emmett Grogan, 23, called a local butcher a "Fascist pig and a coward" when he refused to donate meat scraps. The butcher whacked Grogan with the flat side of his meat cleaver.

The Digger ethic of mass sharing goes along with the American Indian motif that is basic to the Hashbury scene. The cult of "tribalism" is regarded by many of the older hippies as the key to survival. Poet Gary Snyder, a hippy guru, sees a "back to the land" movement as the answer to the food and lodging problem. He urges hippies to move out of the cities, form tribes, purchase land and live communally in remote areas. He cites a hippy "clan" calling itself the Maha-Lila as a model (though the clan still dwells in the Hashbury):

"Well, now," Snyder says, "like, you are asking how it's going to work. Well, the Maha-Lila is a group of about three different families who have sort of pooled their resources, which are not very great. But they have decided to play together and to work together and to take care of each other and that means all of them have ways of getting a small amount of bread, which they share. And other people contribute a little money when it comes in. And then they work together on creative projects, like they're working together on a light-show right now for a poetry reading that we're going to give. And they consider themselves a kind of extended family or clan.

"That's the model. They relate it to a larger sense of the tribe, which is loose, but for the time being everybody has to be able— from time to time—to do some little job. The thing that makes it different is that you don't have a very tight monogamous family unit, but a slightly larger unit where the sharing is greater."

The tribal concept makes a lot better sense than simply depending on the Diggers. There are indications, however, that the youthful provincialism of the Haight-Ashbury is due for a forced consciousness-expansion. For the past few months, the scene has been filling up with would-be hippies from other parts of the country, primarily Los Angeles and New York. The real influx is expected this summer. The city is rife with rumors, reliable and otherwise, that anywhere from 50,000 to 200,000 "indigent young people" will descend on San Francisco as soon as the school year ends.

The Diggers are appalled at the prospect. "Where are they going to stay?" says one. "What are they going to do?" A girl who works in one of the Digger kitchens shrugs and says: "The Diggers will continue to receive the casualties of the love generation." Local officials, from the Mayor down, are beginning to panic. Civic leaders in the Haight-Ashbury have suggested that sleeping facilities be provided in Golden Gate Park or in nearby Kezar Stadium but Police Chief Tom Cahill said no.

"Law and order will prevail," he insisted. "There will be no sleeping in the park. There are no sanitation facilities and if we let them camp there we would have a tremendous health problem. Hippies are no asset to the community. These people do not have the courage to face the reality of life. They are trying to escape. Nobody should let their young children take part in this hippy thing."

In March, the city's Health Director, Dr. Ellis Sox, sent a task force of inspectors on a door-to-door sweep of the Haight-Ashbury. Reports of as many as 200 people living in one house or 50 in one apartment had stirred rumors of impending epidemics in the neighborhood. In a two-day blitz, eight teams of inspectors checked roughly 1,400 buildings and issued a total of 65 deadline notices to repair sanitation faults. But only 16 of the 65 notices, according to The San Francisco Chronicle, were issued to occupants "whose bizarre dress and communal living habits could class them as hippies."

Dr. Sox had no choice but to back off. "The situation is not as bad as we thought," he said. "There has been a deterioration [of sanitation] in the Haight-Ashbury, but the hippies did not contribute much more to it than other members of the neighborhood." Dr. Sox went on to deny that his mass inspection was part of a general campaign against weirdos, but nobody seemed to believe him.

The Haight-Ashbury Neighborhood Council, a nonhippy group of permanent residents, denounced Dr. Sox for his "gratuitous criticism of our community." The council accused city officials of "creating an artificial problem" and harassing the hippies out of "personal and official" prejudice.

As recently as 1962, the Haight-Ashbury was a drab, working-class district, slowly filling with Negroes and so plagued by crime and violence that residents formed vigilante patrols. Housewives were mugged on the way to the grocery store, teen-agers were slashed and stomped in gang rumbles, and every drunk on Haight Street was fair game for local jack-rollers.

Now, with the coming of the drug culture, even the squarest of the neighborhood old-timers say the streets are safer than they have been for years. Burglaries are still a problem but violence is increasingly rare. It is hard to find anyone outside the hippy community who will say that psychedelic drugs have made the neighborhood a better place to live. But it's even harder to find a person who wouldn't rather step over a giggling freak on the sidewalk than worry about hoodlums with switch-blades. The fact that the hippies and the squares have worked out such a peaceful coexistence seems to baffle the powers at City Hall.

A lot of cheap labels describe what is happening in the Hashbury, but none of them make much sense: the Love Generation, the Happening Generation, the Combine Generation and even the LSD Generation. The last is the best of the lot, but in the interest of accuracy it should probably be amended to the Head Generation.

A "head," in the language of hip, is a user of psychedelic drugs: LSD, marijuana ("grass"), mescaline, peyote, methedrine, benzedrine, and a half-dozen others that are classified in the trade as mind-stimulating, consciousness-expanding, or "head" drugs. At the other end of the spectrum are "body" drugs: opium, heroin, barbiturates and even alcohol. These are basically depressants, while head drugs are stimulants. But neither type comes with a manufacturer's guarantee, and the Hashbury is full of people whose minds have been jerked around savagely by drugs that were supposed to induce peaceful euphoria.

Another hazard is the widespread tendency to mix two or three drugs at one time. Acid and alcohol can be a lethal combination, causing fits of violence, suicidal depression and a general freak-out that ends in jail or a hospital.

There is widespread concern, at least in San Francisco, about the dangers of so many people using so much LSD. A doctor at San Francisco General Hospital says there are at least 10,000 hippies in the Haight-Ashbury, and that about four of them a day wind up in a psychiatric ward on bad trips. He estimates that acid-heads make up only 1½ per cent of the city's population, but that the figure for the Haight-Ashbury is more like 100 per cent.

The estimate is absurd; if every hippy in the Hashbury took acid every day, the number of users in the neighborhood would still be less than 50 per cent. Many of the local squares try grass from time to time, but few have worked up an appetite for LSD; the difference in potency is roughly the same as the difference between beer and grain alcohol. Even among hippies, anything more than one dose of acid a week is considered excessive.

Most heads are relatively careful about their drug diets, but in recent months the area has attracted so many young, inexperienced hippies that public freak-outs are a fairly routine thing. Neighborhood cops complain that acid-heads throw themselves in front of moving cars, strip naked in grocery stores and run through plate-glass windows. On weekdays, the action is about on a par with Macdougal Street in Greenwich Village, but weekend hippies and nervous *voyeurs* from the suburbs make Saturdays and Sundays a nightmarish traffic jam. The sidewalks are so crowded that even a mild freak-out is likely to cause a riot.

Municipal buses no longer use Haight Street on weekends; they were rerouted after mobs of hippies staged sit-down strikes in the street, called mill-ins, which brought all traffic to a standstill. The only buses still running regularly along Haight Street are those from the Gray Line, which recently added "Hippieland" to its daytime sightseeing tour of San Francisco. It was billed as "the only foreign tour within the continental limits of the United States" and was an immediate hit with tourists who thought the Haight-Ashbury was a human zoo. The only sour note on the tour was struck by the occasional hippy who would run alongside the bus, holding up a mirror.

Last year in Berkeley, hard-core political radicals who had always viewed hippies as spiritual allies began to worry about the long-range implications of the Haight-Ashbury scene. Students who once were angry activists were content to lie back in their pads and smile at the world through a fog of marijuana smoke—or, worse, to dress like clowns or American Indians and stay zonked for days at a time on LSD.

Even in Berkeley, political rallies during 1966 had overtones of music, madness and absurdity. Instead of picket signs and revolutionary slogans, more and more demonstrators carried flowers, balloons and colorful posters featuring slogans from Dr. Timothy Leary, the high priest of acid. The drug culture was spreading faster than political activists realized. Unlike the dedicated radicals who emerged from the Free Speech Movement, the hippies were more interested in dropping out of society than they were in changing it. They were generally younger than the political types, and the press dismissed them as the "pot left," a frivolous gang of druggies and sex kooks who were only along for the ride.

Then Ronald Reagan was elected Governor by almost a million-vote plurality. Shortly afterward, Clark Kerr was fired as president of the University of California—a direct result of Reagan's victory. In that same November, the G.O.P. gained 50 seats in Congress and served a clear warning on the Johnson Administration that despite all the headlines about Berkeley and the New Left, most of the electorate was a lot more hawkish, hard-nosed and conservative than the White House antennae had indicated.

The lesson was not lost on the hippies, many of whom still considered themselves at least part-time political activists. One of the most obvious casualties of the 1966 elections was the New Left's illusion of its own leverage. The radical-hippy alliance had been counting on the voters to repudiate the "right-wing, warmonger" elements in Congress, but instead it was the "liberal" Democrats who got stomped.

So it is no coincidence that the Haight-Ashbury scene developed very suddenly in the winter of 1966-1967 from the quiet, neo-bohemian enclave that it had been for four or five years to the crowded, defiant dope fortress that it is today. The hippies, who had never really believed they were the wave of the future anyway, saw the election returns as brutal confirmation of the futility of fighting the establishment on its own terms.

There had to be a whole new scene, they said, and the only way to do it was to make the big move—either figuratively or literally—from Berkeley to the Haight-Ashbury, from pragmatism to mysticism, from politics to dope, from the hang-ups of protest to the peaceful disengagement of love, nature and spontaneity.

The credo of the Haight-Ashbury was expressed, about as well as it can be, by Joyce Francisco, 23-year-old advertising manager of the new hippy newspaper, The San Francisco Oracle. She was talking a few months ago to a columnist from the establishment press, trying to explain what the hippy phenomenon meant: "I love the whole world," she said. "I am the divine mother, part of Buddha, part of God, part of everything."

"How do you live?" the columnist asked.

"From meal to meal. I have no money, no possessions. Money is beautiful only when it's flowing; when it piles up it's a hang-up.

We take care of each other. There's always something to buy beans and rice for the group, and someone always sees that I get grass or acid. I was in a mental hospital once because I tried to conform and play the game. But now I'm free and happy."

Next question: "Do you use drugs often?"

"Fairly. When I find myself becoming confused I drop out and take a dose of acid. It's a short cut to reality; it throws you right into it. Everyone should take it, even children. Why shouldn't they be enlightened early, instead of waiting till they're old? Human beings need total freedom. That's where God is at. We need to shed hypocrisy, dishonesty, phoniness and go back to the purity of our childhood values."

The columnist then asked if Miss Francisco ever prayed.

"Oh, yes," she said. "I pray in the morning sun. It nourishes me with its energy so I can spread my love and beauty and nourish others. I never pray *for* anything; I don't need anything. Whatever turns me on is a sacrament: LSD, sex, my bells, my colors . . . that is the holy communion, you dig?"

The columnist wasn't sure if she did or not, but she passed on the interview for the benefit of those readers who might. Many did. Anyone who thinks all the hippies in the Bay Area are living in the Hashbury might just as well leave his head in the sand.

In normal circumstances, the mushrooming popularity of psychedelics would be a main factor in any article on hippies. But the vicious excesses of our drug laws make it impossible, or at least inhuman, to document the larger story. A journalist dealing with heads is caught in a strange dilemma. The only way to write honestly about the scene is to be part of it. If there is one quick truism about psychedelic drugs, it is that anyone who tries to write about them without firsthand experience is a fool and a fraud.

Yet to write from experience is an admission of felonious guilt; it is also a potential betrayal of people whose only "crime" is the smoking of a weed that grows wild all over the world but the possession of which, in California, carries a minimum sentence of two years in prison for a second offense and a minimum of five years for a third. So, despite the fact that the whole journalism industry is full of unregenerate heads—just as many journalists were hard drinkers during Prohibition—it is not very likely that the frank, documented truth about the psychedelic underworld, for good or ill, will be illuminated at any time soon in the public prints.

If I were to write, for instance, that I recently spent 10 days in San Francisco and was stoned almost constantly . . . that in fact I was stoned for nine nights out of 10 and that nearly everyone I dealt with smoked marijuana as casually as they drank beer . . . and if I said many of the people I talked to were not freaks and dropouts, but competent professionals with bank accounts and spotless reputations . . . and that I was amazed to find psychedelic drugs in homes where I would never have mentioned them two years ago—if all this were true, I could write an ominous screed to the effect that the hippy phenomenon in the Haight-Ashbury is little more than a freak show and soft-sell advertisement for what is happening all around them . . . that drugs, orgies and freak-outs are almost as common to a much larger and more discreet cross section of the Bay Area's respectable, upward-mobile society as they are to the colorful drop-outs of San Francisco's new bohemia.

There is no shortage of documentation for the thesis that the current Haight-Ashbury scene is only the orgiastic tip of a great psychedelic iceberg that is already drifting in the sea lanes of the Great Society. Submerged and uncountable is the mass of intelligent, capable heads who want nothing so much as peaceful anonymity. In a nervous society where a man's image is frequently more important than his reality, the only people who can afford to advertise their drug menus are those with nothing to lose.

And these—for the moment, at least—are the young lotus-eaters, the barefoot mystics and hairy freaks of the Haight-Ashbury—all those primitive Christians, peaceful nay-sayers and half-deluded "flower children" who refuse to participate in a society which looks to them like a mean, calculated and soul-destroying hoax.

As recently as two years ago, many of the best and brightest of them were passionately involved in the realities of political, social and economic life in America. But the scene has changed since then and political activism is going out of style. The thrust is no longer for "change" or "progress" or "revolution," but merely to escape, to live on the far perimeter of a world that might have been—perhaps should have been—and strike a bargain for survival on purely personal terms.

The flourishing hippy scene is a matter of desperate concern to the political activists. They see a whole generation of rebels drifting off to a drugged limbo, ready to accept almost anything as long as it comes with enough "soma."

Steve Decanio, an ex-Berkeley activist now doing graduate work at M.I.T., is a good example of a legion of young radicals who know they have lost their influence but have no clear idea how to get it back again. "This alliance between hippies and political radicals is bound to break up," he said in a recent letter. "There's just too big a jump from the slogan of 'Flower Power' to the deadly realm of politics. Something has to give, and drugs are too ready-made as opiates of the people for the bastards (the police) to fail to take advantage of it."

Decanio spent three months in various Bay Area jails as a result of his civil rights activities and now he is lying low for a while, waiting for an opening. "I'm spending an amazing amount of time studying," he wrote. "It's mainly because I'm scared; three months on the bottom of humanity's trash heap got to me worse than it's healthy to admit. The country is going to hell, the left is going to pot, but not me. I still want to figure out a way to win."

Meanwhile, like most other disappointed radicals, he is grimly amused at the impact the hippies are having on the establishment. The panic among San Francisco officialdom at the prospect of 200,000 hippies flocking into the Hashbury this summer is one of the few things that ex-Berkeley radicals can still laugh at. Decanio's vision of the crisis was not written as prophecy, but considering the hidden reality of the situation, it may turn out that way: "I can see Mayor Shelley standing on the steps of the Civic Center and shouting into TV microphones, 'The people cry bread! Bread! Let them turn on!'"

Part 3

RIGHT AND LEFT

THE POLITICAL FRINGE groups discussed in the articles that follow are interesting because they are not concerned so much with electoral politics as with the kind of society America is and should be. Of the two, there is no question that the right wing is by far the most important. Millions of votes have been cast for extremists like George Wallace and Strom Thurmond. The right enjoys extensive support in small towns all over America. It is well financed. Not only multimillionaires like H. L. Hunt contribute to rightist causes, but a great many ordinary people as well. It is just this grass roots character that makes the right dangerous.

Two of the articles in this section describe indigenous movements typical of the extreme right. A great amount of energy is expended in fights, like that over book-branding in San Antonio, which have only ideological meaning. Whether books were marked red or not surely meant nothing to the quality of life in San Antonio, but the attempt to stamp them was a ritual act of great significance all the same. The censoring of textbooks and the struggles against fluoridated water, while slightly more consequential, are also of this type. To individuals anxious about the future, demoralized by the passing of traditional values and customs, deluged with Cold War propaganda of the vilest sort, and powerless to influence events, there is some comfort to be gained from enterprises which ease the mind even if they have few practical effects.

The Parents and Taxpayers, however, represents a much more

troublesome and complex set of problems. Unlike the remote, abstract questions which arouse doctrinaire rightists, school busing is an issue of real concern to parents. Peggy Streit's article shows that the members of PAT were no more prejudiced than the average American. Probably few objected to integration in principle. But the transportation of their children to distant schools, and the importation of Negro children into their own neighborhoods, threatened, as they saw it, their whole way of life. Education is thought crucial to advancement in American society, and if integrated schools were poorer schools, as many believed, then their children's future was being compromised. And if, as they feared, integrated schools led to integrated neighborhoods, then their houses too—the only asset most possessed—were also in the balance. These may not be morally impressive arguments, but they were nonetheless urgent and compelling, even when false. While this particular issue will probably recede as Negroes lose interest in school integration, it is the kind of problem certain to become more common. As Negroes press harder they rub up against the same upper working-class and lower middle-class whites described here.

Although the John Birch Society is a well-financed subversive conspiracy, its trouble-making capacities are modest by comparison with white backlash groups like the PAT. When it first surfaced many thought the Birch Society so grotesque that laughter would dispose of it. But Robert Welch and his minions plugged doggedly along, and after a while people stopped laughing. In truth, the Birch Society is not very funny. At the same time, it now seems that the society's capacity for mischief is less than was once believed. Like most rightist conspiracies, its main impact is in local areas where particular conditions render the citizenry vulnerable to paranoid visions. It is possible, however, that such organizations as the Birchers (but not psychotic groups like the Nazis and the Minutemen) also have a therapeutic function of sorts. It seems desirable, in a way, for people whose minds have been unbalanced by changing times to have a social outlet for their fears and hostilities. Instead of festering at home, they can join the Birch Society, go to cell meetings, distribute literature, create innocuous front groups, and plan elaborate coups against the PTA. This creates an illusion of effectiveness among people who would otherwise be confronted with their real impotence. Who knows, in its twisted way the Birch Society may be a kind of safety valve bleeding off poisonous emotions in a relatively safe fashion?

The left-wing group with which the Birch Society is most often compared, and on which, by his own admission, Robert Welch modeled it, is the Communist party. We can get some notion of what the CPUSA had been from A. H. Raskin's article written just before it was destroyed. Already by 1947 the CPUSA was past the years of its greatest influence. The Depression and the Russo-American alliance during World War II had enabled the party to recruit some distinguished supporters and to build a solid organizational base. The Cold War changed all this. The turnover of members, always high, grew higher. Organized labor conducted a successful purge of Communists which in a few years left the party with no union influence at all. Communist affiliations became fatal to the careers of professional men and women. The government jailed, fined, and harassed in a variety of ways the party's leadership. Even before Senator Joseph McCarthy rose to power on the communist issue in the early fifties, the CPUSA had been reduced to insignificance. Fortunately, Raskin visited party headquarters when it was still very much in business under the direction of some of its most legendary figures. William Z. Foster, onetime Wobbly, leader of the great steel strike of 1919, was national chairman. Robert Minor, a superb editorial cartoonist who had given up a brilliant career to become a party functionary, was alive and well, and so was Elizabeth Gurley Flynn, who had been the IWW's "Rebel Girl" in its glory days before World War I. Still, as Raskin's quotations demonstrate, the party by this time was far removed from its revolutionary origins. The bureaucratic rigor which, together with its Soviet connections, was so destructive to the party's prestige could not be disguised.

When the left began to revive in the 1960's, its initial tendency was to stay as far from the doctrinaire, highly organized old-line leftists as possible. This produced a variety of impulses ranging from SDS to Joan Baez's school for nonviolence, easily the most charming of all radical groups. Joan Didion's gently incisive essay on the school points up the striking difference between left and right, despite the current cliché which holds that extremists are all alike: the Birch Society is the right counterpart of the CPUSA, black nationalism resembles the white nationalism of Klansmen and Minutemen, and so forth. Some radical tendencies defy this neat formula altogether. The nonviolent, revolutionary, flower-power ethic has deep roots in the rich American utopian and perfectionist tradition. Whatever its failings, this strain obviously has nothing in common with the paranoid suspiciousness and strident hatreds so characteristic of the extreme right. It is easy to make fun of this benevolent mystique, but at least it harms no one, and at best it offsets a trifle the general bloodymindedness of our times.

"Book Branding" – A Case History

by Stanley Walker

SAN ANTONIO

THIS FINE OLD cosmopolitan city of almost 500,000 persons, famous for its devotion to liberty and its tolerance of non-conformists, is in the midst of a book burning, or, more accurately, a book-branding controversy which has aroused much local bitterness and at the same time attracted nation-wide attention. The showdown will come in the next month when the board of trustees of the library system and the newly elected city council meet and resume their arguments. The main question is: Should books on the public library shelves whose authors are either identified as Communists or suspected of Communist sympathies be branded with a red stamp?

How could this happen? And in San Antonio, of all places? A study of the situation leads to the conclusion that, given the right climate and a handful of persistent and plausible agitators, it could happen almost anywhere. All that the situation requires is a few hard-working zealots and a more or less supine population which likes to be told that a certain course of action will help national security and make society better and cleaner.

San Antonio, notwithstanding its conglomerate population, is full of what might be called typical Texans, well-meaning persons who sometimes are easy prey for patrioteers, roaring nationalists and

From the *New York Times Magazine,* July 12, 1953.

reformers with apparently simple devices for making the world better and safer. The typical citizen shapes up roughly something like this: He loves his country. He would not, willingly and with his eyes open, do anything to injure it. He really wants to be "fair." He is suspicious of labor unions, and especially of what have come to be called "labor bosses." He is conservative, definitely anti-Communist, and he wants his children to grow up to be God-fearing, respectable persons—and, if possible, well educated and well heeled. Often he has a constitutional inability to size up a new proposal for what it is and to visualize its inevitable secondary effects.

Ask this fellow: "Don't you believe in free discussion?" "Don't you believe it necessary to know what communism is all about before you can fight it effectively?" "Don't you think workers have a right to band together to improve their working conditions and to bargain collectively?" To these questions, and to others like them, you will get a grudging "Yes." Or, perhaps more often, a "Yes—but." In other words, he is slightly confused, and even his best friends would not describe him as a profound or far-seeing thinker.

Prohibition was fastened on Texas by the so-called good people, the better people, who had been convinced that booze was bad and that the proposition, "It is bad; therefore let's abolish it," made perfectly good sense. After a long period it dawned on the Texans, along with most other persons, that the proposition had holes in it.

Similarly, for a time in the early Nineteen Twenties, it looked as though Texas was going to be controlled by the Ku-Klux Klan. At the beginning the Klan professed to be the organization of "the better people," and many decent men were sucked into it because the proposition, "Law and order are getting out of hand, and society seems to be in danger; therefore let us, as good citizens, organize and clean it up," seemed to be sensible enough. Many of the members did not realize the fundamental hollowness of the argument nor could they at the beginning see the things which were bound to follow. A Dallas dentist, Dr. Hiram Wesley Evans, started the ball rolling for the Klan, and before he and his cohorts were un-horsed the whole state was thrown into a disgusting turmoil.

It was true then, and it is true now, that all such strange and repressive movements seem to carry, in a sense, their own antidote. Strong voices almost at once begin to be heard; powerful citizens, often of widely different types, come forward to mock the alleged reformers. In Texas, the main enemies of the Klan were such leaders as Dan Moody and James E. Ferguson—men who were bitter personal and political opponents.

Something of the sort has happened in San Antonio. At first it appeared that the book branders might have a walkover. But it was not so easy. Calmer citizens—among them, as usual, men and women of widely varying tastes and backgrounds—came forward to oppose the move and to caution, "Now wait a minute; let's see if you realize what you are about to do." When the showdown comes it is probable, though by no means a cinch, that the voices of caution will prevail.

Eleven members of the fifteen-member library board are newly appointed and many of them have no great familiarity with library work—or, indeed, with books. However, a private poll indicates that at least eight members of the board, including the four hold-overs, will stand firmly against the book-branding scheme. The city council is another matter. It holds the purse strings. Some of its members looked with great favor at first on book branding when it seemed the popular and patriotic thing, but they are cooling off. And they, like most politicians, are sensitive to the breezes of public opinion.

Many observers think it odd that this could happen in San Antonio. The Alamo stands here. This is the home town, the long-time seat, of the Maverick family, who by tradition and definition and practice wear no man's brand. This is the charming though sometimes turbulent city where several civilizations have met and more or less blended. The leading crusader for book branding in San Antonio is Mrs. Myrtle Glasscock Hance. Her parents for many years conducted a school for acrobatic dancing. She describes herself as a housewife. She has never made any pretense to literary attainments or wide acquaintance with books.

Mrs. Hance's position, she says, is simply this: She does not seek the removal from the library shelves of any books by authors suspected of Red bias, nor would she burn them. She professes to recognize "constitutional rights." What she does request is that books by a long list of suspected authors be stamped, or branded, on the inside front cover with a red stamp, "large enough to be seen immediately," showing that the author has Communist affiliations or sympathies, and the number of "citations." "The reader," she says, "will then realize that in many instances he is reading Communist propaganda."

And how did Mrs. Hance, who admits she is "not a learned Ph.D.," get started on her crusade? Her own story is that she went to work checking the library books after reading two magazine articles: "Why You Buy Books That Sell Communism," by Irene Corbally Kuhn, in the American Legion Magazine of January, 1951, and "A Slanted Guide to Library Selections," by Oliver Carlson, in the Freeman of Jan. 14, 1952. After reading these articles, she says, she enlisted the aid of six other women as a committee. Several of these women, including Mrs. Hance, are members of a national organization, patriotic by profession, called the Minute Women.

After much labor, Mrs. Hance had her report ready. It listed more than 500 books which she felt should be branded. Her report in many respects is a curious document. The authors listed include not only some known Communists but many persons who at one time or another have been mentioned as having had some sort of affiliation with Communist-front organizations. The report recommends the branding of books by these authors without regard to the actual subject-matter of the books.

Thus, an edition of "The Canterbury Tales," by a whimsical old Englishman named Geoffrey Chaucer, would be branded with a red stamp because it is illustrated by Rockwell Kent. The scientific works of Dr. Harlow Shapley and Albert Einstein would be branded. Everything by Dorothy Parker, including the short stories, would get the red stamp. Thomas Mann would get the full treatment.

The new city council, along with the Mayor, Jack White, granted Mrs. Hance and her group a hearing. She presented her long list of allegedly dangerous literature, along with her suggested remedies. Mayor White and most of the councilmen seemed at first to think that her proposals were reasonable enough. Mayor White's wife, by the way, is a member of the Minute Women. But the opposition to book branding was also present at the hearing.

The council adjourned to think, and, presumably, is still thinking. As for Mayor Jack White, he is brooding, apparently hooked by one of those dilemmas that try men's souls. There is his wife, the Minute Woman, to be considered. He doesn't want to be accused of showing sympathy to Communists and their works. On the other hand, he knows something of politics, and he hesitates to antagonize the powerful and respectable citizens who are calling the book-branding idea preposterous. Mr. White does not desire that his city get an illiberal reputation throughout the country. Privately, he has sent word to some of the opponents of the branding idea to "sit tight," that "everything will be all right."

Probably everything will turn out "all right," at that. But Mrs. Hance's crusade, starting so quietly, has impressed many ordinary citizens and quite naturally has brought out many crackpots and red-hot patriots. The curious suggestion was made from one quarter that watchers be set to spy upon persons who consulted the branded books and their names be turned over to the Federal Bureau of Investigation. One prominent San Antonio capitalist, a leading supporter of something called the Constitution Party, told an acquaintance in a telephone conversation that branding was not enough. He favored burning, and he was eager to start the fire himself.

Meanwhile the friends of the library and all who oppose book branding on general principles have been busy. Impetuous, freedom-loving Maury Maverick, former member of Congress, former Mayor of San Antonio, and coiner of the word "gobbledygook," jumped into the fight against the branders, though he is pretty much out of political affairs these days. Maverick's son, Maury, Jr., is a chip off the old block and as a member of the last Legislature carried on an eloquent battle against a state book-branding bill which had been introduced by another member from San Antonio, Marshall O. Bell. Largely because of the younger Maverick's efforts, the bill which finally passed was so watered down that it means next to nothing. It is permissive, giving municipal bodies the right to label books if they so desire; it is quite probable that they already had this legal right.

It is probably fair to say that, as of the moment, the sentiment in San Antonio has turned definitely against Mrs. Hance's scheme. She did her cause harm by going into the libraries at Brackenridge and Thomas Jefferson High Schools and demanding that she be allowed to go through all their books for Red bias. To many, this seemed a little too much.

The San Antonio papers, no lovers of Vox Pop, usually pay little or no attention to letters to the editor, but when The San Antonio News opened its editorial page to letters on the book-branding issue, the tide was about ten to one against. Moreover, President Eisenhower carries tremendous prestige in San Antonio. His Dartmouth remarks on book burning and the right of the individual to read what he pleases, along with his later message to the meeting of librarians in Los Angeles, have had considerable influence in San Antonio.

The old gray champion of books in San Antonio is M. M. (Mike) Harris, for many years editor of The San Antonio Express. More than any other person, though he has able help, he must get the credit for building up the excellent city-county library system in San Antonio and Bexar County. He is the inventor and popularizer of the bookmobile, the traveling library which takes books to people's homes. He is now head of the library trustees and is in the middle of the fight.

He is powerful in San Antonio. He and Maury Maverick are friends and allies, though when Maverick was Mayor the two had a misunderstanding which estranged them for a time. Maverick is a roaring liberal, an ex-New Dealer from way back; Harris is a steadfast conservative in politics and economics. But, as so often happens in controversies such as the book-branding fight, they stand side by side when the right issue comes along.

The other day, Mr. Harris, sitting in his breezy tower room on the sixth floor of The Express Building, where he can look out over the enormous and motley expanse to the southeast, Mr. Harris said he believed he and the friends of the library would win. The margin, however, might be narrow. Soon he will call the board of trustees of the library into session (as soon as some of the members get back from cooling themselves in the Rocky Mountains) and have a showdown. If he loses, he says, he will quit the board.

"I do not propose," said old Mike Harris, "to preside over the degradation of the San Antonio library system."

Close-Up of the Birchers' "Founder"

by George Barrett

THE VISITOR . . . a pallid, 61-year-old retired business man from the Boston suburb of Belmont, who a little earlier had slipped quietly into town, linked hands piously with his hosts around the dinner table to offer family grace. The sound of crickets, relayed across Louisiana bayous and neat, clipped lawns, broke the night's stillness outside.

Robert Henry Winborne Welch, Jr., head of the Right-Wing super-patriotic John Birch Society, engaged in pleasant chit-chat that night, not long ago, with his Southern hosts in their home in a well-to-do section of Shreveport.

His hosts, however, were nervous. Though followers of Mr. Welch, they felt the strain of entertaining the man who has suddenly and dramatically emerged as one of the country's most controversial figures, a former fudge-and-candy manufacturer who a little more than two years ago organized the John Birch Society. This was to be—and is—a semi-secret network of "Americanists" dedicated to fighting Communists by deliberately adopting some of communism's own clandestine and ruthless tactics and, simultaneously, intent on working—again deliberately—to destroy government by democracy, which Mr. Welch describes contemptuously as government by "mobocracy."

One of those at the dinner table addressed Mr. Welch by the wrong name. But he was in good spirits, laughed over the mistake,

From the *New York Times Magazine*, May 14, 1961.

and launched into a detailed discourse on the etymology of his name. He concluded by explaining quietly, that the root word for Welch means "stranger."

The "Stranger" from Massachusetts is even now something of a shadowy figure, although he has been generating some intense reactions throughout the country with his wild-swinging blows against the "Communist conspiracy" and has inspired, in some communities, the deadly game of look-again-and-more-closely at your neighbor.

Within recent weeks, North Dakota's Republican Senator Milton R. Young expressed fears that a reprisal campaign conducted by Welch's society might cost him his Senate seat because he opposes the society's demand that the Government abandon the Federal Reserve System, the Commodity Credit Corporation, and veterans' hospitals; a two-star general has been relieved of his command pending studies of charges that he fostered some of Welch's extremist teachings among his troops; the United States Attorney General has called the John Birch Society "ridiculous," and President Kennedy has taken occasion at a press conference to rebuke the society for being too fast on the draw in search for Communists.

The "Stranger" has just completed a number of quick visits to towns around the country. He travels alone, and is so close-mouthed about his schedule that even his chapter chiefs are not sure of his precise arrival time until shortly before he comes to town. When he alights from his plane (usually a commercial liner but occasionally a private plane placed at his disposal by one of his wealthy sponsors) Mr. Welch, carrying his briefcase and suggesting in his appearance a worn Southern preacher, gets into a waiting car and takes off for a private home that is seldom identified. And somewhere in town—again an unidentified place—he meets with his chapter leaders and members, talking softly through puffs of cigar smoke.

Each chapter numbers between ten and twenty members. At these sessions, there is talk about policy, which has been already laid down in the regular monthly bulletin each member gets from headquarters in Belmont. There is also a routine that Mr. Welch checks: each month after the bulletin arrives the chapter "Leader" (appointed, not elected) gathers his group, calls on each member in turn to report point by point what he has done to carry out the society's program for the previous month, and then spells out the specific local action each member must next take to put through Mr. Welch's newest campaign.

The major target for the Birchers right now is Chief Justice Earl Warren, whom Mr. Welch wants to have impeached in order, as he puts it, to give a dramatic setback to the Communist conspiracy.

The plan of action calls for all members to send letters to Senators, Representatives and state legislators, as well as local newspapers, urging the impeachment action, to paste "Impeach Warren" stickers on their car bumpers, to persuade other organizations of which they are members to pass impeachment resolutions and finally, if practicable, to form "Impeach Warren Committees" in their home towns.

There are times when the chapters get a little rough. Those in Wichita are said to have trained their members to inform their Leaders of "Communist" influences in the classrooms, and parents then get on the telephone to direct a concentrated attack against teachers and principals. A "new type" of secret student organization, described as a unit of the John Birch Society, has apparently encouraged students at the University of California at Santa Barbara to become informers on constant lookout for Communists.

Mr. Welch has been following up his chapter sessions with "public" rallies, convened by the local groups for those in the community they believe might be wooed into the society. Attempts are usually made to keep the tickets—generally $1 each—controlled enough to bar dissidents; in some places each purchaser must give his name, and the policing is so efficient that in one community a college professor—an anti-Bircher—tried several ways quietly to wangle a ticket to a large rally and failed.

At these rallies, Mr. Welch seems to be unaware of his audience, talking to his lecture cards and keeping almost word-for-word to the same ninety-minute speech in each town. He is touchy, however; if there is a shuffle in the audience he hesitates, and looks up suspiciously. At one meeting an attendant paced about, searching for a physician who was in the audience. Mr. Welch stopped his talk and wanted to know why the man was "walking around like that." He did not wait for a reply but told his audience that that kind of distraction was a typical "dirty Communist trick."

His speech centers on the theme that Communists can be anywhere (in Harvard and in pulpits, as well as in Moscow), and that they must be understood in terms of what he calls the principle of reversal," which holds that everything the Communists seem to be they are not, and practically everything they seem not to be they probably are.

He likes to give this example: The Russians make a great show in the United Nations of trying to oust Dag Hammarskjöld from his job as Secretary General and replace him with a three-member panel, but this is only a ruse, because the Russians—according to this logic—know that the United States will vigorously defend Mr. Hammarskjöld and he will, therefore, remain in the United Nations, which is what the Russians really count on because, Mr. Welch says, Mr. Hammarskjöld "is one of the most contemptible agents of the Kremlin ever to be supported by the American taxpayers."

Actually, Mr. Welch contends, Russia will not leave the United Nations, despite its boycott of Mr. Hammarskjöld, because the Soviets see the world organization as paving the way for the "intended Communist Internationale."

Mr. Welch discourages question-and-answer periods to let listeners try to unscramble all this. And, colorless as he is, when he rides away from town after delivering his set speech, the divisions of the community usually are even more sharply, and angrily, drawn.

For one part of the community, for the ultra-conservatives who look on Senator Goldwater as at least a couple of shades too liberal and for those Birchers who have made the late Senator Joseph R. McCarthy the lamented prophet of their movement, the "Stranger" from Massachusetts is a kind of deliverer, a strong man who has sounded the tocsin just in time and is summoning his patriotic bands for the decisive battle against the Communist conspirators, who have already, he tells his followers, maneuvered such stunning fifth-column victories as the foreign-aid programs.

Most of the domestic programs, in the Welch view, are socialistic "welfareism" and part of the major evils of a central Federal collectivism. The foreign-aid program dangerously depletes the nation's strength. The billion-dollar defense programs (they likewise involve heavy taxes and Mr. Welch wants to abolish the Federal income tax) also dangerously deplete the nation's strength and are part of the Communist plot because the Soviet Union obviously never intends to go to war with the United States since it could not conquer even tiny Finland.

Finally, Mr. Welch seeks to overturn the Supreme Court decision outlawing public-school segregation, which he regards as the product of that kind of radical thinking (the "whole Supreme Court is a nest of Socialists and worse") which is subverting the nation and making it ripe for a merging, without struggle, with Russia.

These are examples, and Mr. Welch has many more, and although certain of his admirers who are not society members cannot go for the whole program, he has endeared himself to some reactionaries because his position in general concerning government and economic systems falls somewhere to the Right of King Louis XIV.

For another part of the community, however, the "Stranger" is an ominous figure, and they see all the horrors of the witch hunt in his passionate crusade to track down parents (in the Parent-Teacher Associations) and military officers, ministers and others he considers to be Communists or dupes or what he calls "Comsymps," which, he told one group, is a "beautiful word, because you don't have to say how much the person is a Communist and how much he is a sympathizer."

There are many who call him a "little Hitler" and, while some say that it is bordering on the absurd to take very seriously the balding, fusty figure who drones out his message, they are quick to note that extremists are notoriously ready to rally to a banner, and they recall that Hitler himself was generally considered a clown —at first.

They not only find elements of the authoritarian state in Mr. Welch's program, but see specific resemblances to the Nazi framework of *Gauleiters* and Fuehrer, of tight control and no questions, of shock tactics and emotional rantings. For them there are scary echoes of the past in the John Birch Society's system of small, anonymous groups and in the command hierarchy of "Leader," "Voluntary Coordinator," "Coordinator," "Major Coordinator" (a future rank when the society expands) and, on the summit, "Your Founder," as Mr. Welch calls himself, or "The Founder," as his followers often refer to him.

He boasts of his "fanaticism," and describes himself as the "hard-boiled, dictatorial and dynamic boss" of the semi-secret society. He insists that the society operates as a monolithic force, and that the members generally either accept assignments without question, through a chain of command in which all decisions are made at the top, or get out (they do not, incidentally, receive an accounting of their dues and contributions). The "Founder" favors the polemic approach, including his most infamous accusation, repeated in various circulars, that President Eisenhower was "a dedicated, conscious agent of the Communist conspiracy."

It is easy in some communities to scoff at the John Birch Society, but it is a little harder to poke fun in communities where a number of business men, management executives, physicians, lawyers and other "solid" people have joined chapters. It is then, sometimes, that the scoffer becomes cautious. And caution can give way to quiet fright, the kind of fright that stirred this comment that recent night when Mr. Welch arrived in Shreveport: "Even the crickets sound sinister tonight."

The Birchers themselves are bitter about remarks like this. They contend that they have been maligned, and falsely convicted, in much of the public mind.

While the Birchers usually protest vehemently that they do not go in for secrecy they admit that the number of society members is a secret. (It is believed that there are chapters now in thirty-four states and the District of Columbia, with a total membership expected to reach 100,000 by the end of this year and with an ultimate national goal calling for 1,000,000 members.)

The Birchers further acknowledge that the names of the members are not revealed, although they point out that any member who wants to say publicly that he belongs to the society is free to do so.

It is true that many of them speak up promptly. Dallas Wales, the 38-year-old father of three teen-age daughters, was a radio personality in Shreveport, La., who gave up his job with a popular interview program to become the paid, full-time Coordinator of the John Birch Society for all of Louisiana and the southern half of Mississippi.

Mr. Wales is forthright, contemptuous of anything conspiratorial, and completely convinced that the society is his best way of combating the Communist menace he sees closing in steadily on the free world.

He was a Marine Corps sergeant at Guadalcanal and Tarawa, and he says he can never forget one May Day in New York, when he was taking his master's degree in speech at Columbia University and saw men in Marine Corps uniforms walking up Eighth Avenue with May Day paraders who carried this sign: "Communist Party, Brooklyn, U.S.A."

Mr. Wales, like many of his fellow Birchers, sees things simply, and while there may be some indecipherable jargon in Mr. Welch's philosophy (Mr. Wales does not admit this) he is eager to follow him as the leader in an anti-Communist crusade. He readily explains that he is a "hero man," and makes it clear that he has no intention of questioning the head of the John Birch Society on any of the aims contained in Mr. Welch's anti-Communist program.

The non-salaried Voluntary Coordinator for Florida is David Murphey 3d, a partner in the brokerage firm of The Pierce, Carrison, Wulbern Corporation, and for him, too, the issue comes in stark, uncomplicated images. "The Communists are after us, you and me, all of us, and particularly us, the stock brokers, and"—he points to the door—"I want to stop that Communist before he comes through there, with a machine gun in his hands."

In some towns a rally of Birchers could well be taken for a typical, quiet group of Sunday-night worshipers. But it seems clear that the anti-Communist tactics of the John Birch Society take their coloration from the customs of the particular community, and there can be little doubt that "The Blue Book"—the outline of basic aims and general philosophy which Mr. Welch has supplied as a kind of manual—gives a wide enough range for individual Birchers to operate tactically pretty much as their individual consciences dictate.

This writer, for example, was refused entry to a Welch rally in Houston by angry and suspicious officials of the local patriotic group, the Sons of the American Revolution, which on that occasion served as the kind of "front" favored by Mr. Welch, who frankly admits borrowing this ploy from the Communists. It took a bit of careful smuggling with the help of some well-placed anti-Birchers to get into a safe recess of the chamber. But in Tampa and in Shreveport the writer was courteously received by Coordinators who were willing and eager to answer most questions.

Not so Mr. Welch. Only rarely has he agreed to talk with reporters, and he is now so convinced that there is a Communist conspiracy at work within the press that he refuses to grant interviews.

The man who sits at the society's summit and masterminds the operation from his headquarters in a two-story brick office building in Belmont decided four years ago to give up his job as a vice president of the family candy company to devote all his time to anti-Communist activities.

Mr. Welch had first become interested in the problem of Communist infiltration in the early Nineteen Fifties. As time went on his brother, the president of the company, felt that he was away too often. Mr. Welch faced a choice: communism or candy. He gave up the candy, and closed a twenty-year career that had included service as a bank director and seven years as a board member of the National Association of Manufacturers.

One of his first forays into the field of Communist thought, before he established the John Birch Society, fizzled completely. He sent out a prediction that the Russians were planning an imminent invasion of the United States, but the deadline he gave has long since come and gone.

Something of an intellectual dabbler who likes to flit quickly from Emerson to Santayana to Voltaire to Spengler to Spencer to Tennyson, Mr. Welch also dabbled a bit when it came to deciding on a career. After graduating from the University of North Carolina at the age of 17, he entered Annapolis, in 1917, but left after one academic year (he was near the top of his class) because the war was over and, as he told the Naval Academy, he wanted to be a writer.

However, he went instead to Harvard Law School, where he completed two years and again withdrew, again after getting good grades. He wound up in the family's candy business, and it is interesting that Mr. Welch, who now urges less government, served during World War II on the O.P.A. advisory committee for the candy industry.

It was on a wintry morning a little over two years ago that he summoned eleven of his friends to a meeting in Indianapolis to start the John Birch Society. For two days he talked, with breaks for coffee and snacks and brief discussions by the others present.

He covered quite a bit of territory in that talk. He told the men in the room that he was really a North Carolina boy, born in Chowan County, and that he came from a long line of farmers and Baptist preachers but that, forty years before, he had broken through the intellectually restricting bonds of Southern Baptist fundamentalism. He recited a poem that he had written about apes inheriting the earth, a poem he always recites on his tours of society chapters. If by chance the eleven men were nodding, he must have pulled them up with this:

"And democracy, of course, in government or organization, as the Greeks and the Romans both found out, and as I believe every man in this room clearly recognizes—democracy is merely a deceptive phrase, a weapon of demagoguery and a perennial fraud."

The men in the room approved his program, created a national council, whose members include Spruille Braden, former Assistant Secretary of State, and decided to name the society for John Morrison Birch, a missionary turned captain in the Office of Strategic Services, who was killed by Chinese Communist guerrillas in 1945, shortly after V-J Day. Mr. Birch was the first victim of World War III, according to Mr. Welch.

The system of chapters was also set up, including a home chapter for members who could not be enlisted in a local chapter, and dues were placed at $24 a year for men and $12 for women (more if any member wanted to pay it) with a life membership costing $1,000.

Granting that the Birchers demonstrate anew that every society, in every time, produces well-meaning and honest citizens who, like crackpots, are willing to follow extremist leadership, and without minimizing the potential danger that this constitutes for the country, it seems certain that the John Birch Society, in itself, is not nearly the potent force it has been represented to be.

Moderates and liberals in some of the communities where Birchers are fairly active say that the telephone campaigns and other pressure tactics are no greater now than they have ever been. It is a fact that in many cases the Bircher who issues an angry protest these days is the same person who protested before in the name of a local patriotic group.

The signs are that the society has not only been overrated in terms of applied power, but that it has been increasingly subjected to counterattacks and scorn since its program became public. Mr. Welch admits that the recruiting of new members has slowed down "materially" in some areas of the country and to some degree in all areas.

But worst of all, for the Birchers, the laughs are beginning to rise. In Houston a Gridiron Club skit entitled "Jane Smirch" mocked the John Birch Society, and two disk jockeys have been making cracks about starting a John Burp Society with Robert Belch as the boss. In Tampa, a Catholic manager of a finance company proclaiming a blow for "freedom from fear," deliberately disrupted a Welch meeting, and a young girl in the balcony shouted sarcastically to the Birchers: "Call the Gestapo!"

One Coordinator of the society tells ruefully about trying to hire a hall for Mr. Welch, and explaining to the girl at the desk that the John Birch Society was a group whose slogan was "less government and more responsibility." She looked at the Coordinator, her face dark, and said: "What are you guys, anyway, Communists?"

Why They Fight for the P.A.T.

by Peggy Streit

In its campaign to end segregation in New York City's schools the Board of Education last spring decided to begin a program of school "pairing." Under this plan, a predominantly white school is linked with a predominantly Negro–Puerto Rican school—some grades attending one school and the remaining grades attending the other, thus achieving a racial mixture in both. This integration, proponents of the plan maintain, would end the "ghetto complex" that has held Negro children back. In some cases, a pairing scheme requires the busing of some children from their neighborhoods. A militant organization called Parents and Taxpayers has sprung up to fight the plan, however. This article records the views of members of one chapter, South Richmond Hill–South Ozone Park, Queens.

"THE WAY I see it, it's like this," said the taxi driver. "If I had kids of school age I'd join P.A.T. And I'd keep the kids out of school just as long as we white people didn't get our rights. Now don't get me wrong. I ain't got nothing against colored people. If they want good schools, they ought to have good schools. But they ought to go to schools in *their* neighborhood—just like white kids ought to go to school in *their* neighborhood."

The taxi stopped at a red light. The traffic on Van Wyck Boulevard rumbled by the drab, squat commercial buildings—a bar, a

From the *New York Times Magazine*, September 20, 1964.

hardware store, a beauty parlor, a real-estate office advertising a six-room two-story, one-family house for $15,000.

"You know Queens?" he asked. "South Richmond Hill? South Ozone Park? No? I was born and raised here," he said proudly. "Just like my folks. There's a lot of second- and third-generation families out here. It's a real neighborly place—not like New York City where nobody cares who lives next door and nobody owns their own home."

Leaving behind the pounding commercial traffic, the taxi turned off abruptly into a more tranquil world of narrow residential streets lined by modest homes—house after identical house, like rows of ditto marks. But they shared the sedate dignity of a clean, orderly neighborhood, their aging ungracious architecture softened by the sycamore trees.

"Like I was saying," continued the taxi driver, "you buy a house because you want your kid to go to a school nearby and the church is just around the corner. And then, here comes the government or school board and what do they say? They say, 'Mister, you can't send your kid to school near you. You got to bus him to school in a Negro neighborhood, 20 blocks away, that's been—what do they call it—*paired* with a white school because of racial imbalance.' Now I ask you, is that right? And I say to you, no—that ain't right. We're losing our freedoms in this country. Next thing you know, they'll be telling you where to go to church."

The taxi slowed to a halt outside the home of P.A.T. official June Reynolds. "I'm sure glad I'm not that school-board guy, Gross," he chuckled, with wry satisfaction. "You know how women's voices go up when they get mad? Tell the ladies: 'God bless them.' "

"Now," said Mrs. Reynolds, "what would you like to know about our group?" Her cluttered desk was the only disorder in a living room like countless others in the neighborhood—wall-to-wall carpets, meticulously vacuumed; modern furniture gleaming with polish; earthenware lamps, their orange shades still protected by plastic wrappers; a large-screen television set; reproductions of oriental art on the walls . . . a picture of modest but proud possession.

Size? "There are about 2,700 of us," she replied, "with 300 hard-core members doing most of the work—the executive board, the telephone girls who call about P.A.T. meetings and poll members, and the block captains who ring doorbells for new members."

Membership? "Mostly parents with elementary-school kids, of

course, but some people without children. This is a moral issue, too, not just an educational one."

Purpose? "To protect our children, preserve our neighborhood-school system, and keep our children from being bused into strange districts."

Activities? "Well, we organize protests against pairing and busing, and we've been urging members to write to their newspapers and councilmen. Things like that."

The racial issue? She paused irresolutely. "The racial issue doesn't have anything to do with what we want," she said. "We believe in open enrollment. If Negroes want to go to white schools where there's room, they should be allowed to. And we believe in the improvement of Negro schools. It's not true what people say—that we don't like Negroes and we don't want them in our schools. If they live in our neighborhood they have a right here. But nobody has a right to send our children *away* from our neighborhood."

The telephone jangled again and she turned her young, earnest face back to business. "Membership meeting this evening," she said to the caller with urgency. "Try to make it. This is a battle we're fighting, and without your support we'll lose it. Yes, everybody will be there."

That night, everybody included a trim, distinguished-looking man graying at the temples, who stated the central position of the group, again claiming that the P.A.T. stand has nothing to do with race.

"I'm sick of hearing us all called bigots," he said with exasperation. "What we want is the best possible deal for our children. My wife and I bought a house where we did because we like the neighborhood and the schools close by. Now we think our kids may be offered second best and we'd be rotten parents if we didn't oppose that. Why do people think that all opposition to pairing has to be equated with bigotry? Please believe me when I tell you that there isn't a person out here who would willingly hurt anyone."

Stanley Smigiel, president of the South Richmond Hill–South Ozone Park P.A.T. and a grease monkey by trade, was also there. A man of hefty body and voice, he was faintly nervous in his new role as civic leader, mopping his steaming brow with a handkerchief.

"When they told me, 'You got to do this and you got to do that,' that's when my dandruff went up," he said. "I lived in South Jamaica in a Negro area for 30 years. I don't have nothing against Negroes, but the only thing I care about is this: I don't want my child traveling no further than he has to to school. What if the bus breaks down? What about snowy days? What if he gets sick and it's an emergency and my wife can't get to him? And furthermore, I don't like him going into classes with a lot of slow readers who will pull down his I.Q. I was a dropout in school and I learned my lesson. I don't want nothing going wrong with my son's education."

June Reynolds, a young, fresh-faced, bright-eyed, dedicated dynamo, doesn't have anything against Negroes either. "I went to school with Negroes when I was a girl," she said. "If I were a Negro, how would I see to it that my kids got a better education and a chance in the world?" She answered herself without hesitation. "I'd move into an interracial neighborhood. I wouldn't live in Harlem for anything in the world. I'd scrub floors. I'd take in laundry. I'd get any kind of job to get out of Harlem—and I know I'd succeed because I believe that in the United States anybody can do anything if he tries hard enough.

"Look at my father. Negroes can at least speak English, but when my father came here from Italy he had to learn the language, so he went to night school. Then he got a job as a wrapper in a bakery. He worked there 47 years and was a supervisor when he retired. The way I see it," she added with finality, "if a Negro lives in Harlem, it's because he likes it there and because he doesn't want to work hard enough to get out of that environment."

Hannah Edell, a round, small, blond woman with soft pink cheeks and a troubled voice, was a little less dogmatic.

"Yes, I think the Negro has been discriminated against," she said, "and I think they should be helped along. But I don't think their problem is educational. It's social. I know that some Negroes think, 'Why should I bother to get an education if I can't get a job afterwards?'—and that's what I mean by a social problem. It's up to large corporations to give them jobs."

She acknowledged the obvious question with a long, hard sigh. "Yes, I know," she said. "Why *shouldn't* large corporations give their jobs to the best-educated—and they are usually white."

She paused then reflected sadly: "It's a vicious circle, isn't it? One hardly knows where to begin. But one thing I *do* know," she went on, gaining assurance. "They shouldn't begin with our children. Integration isn't a problem for children to solve—or their parents. It's up to the politicians, big corporations—other people. And the Board of Education. This problem has existed for a long time. Why didn't the board do something to improve Negro education a long time ago, so things wouldn't have got to this state?"

Joe Lamanna, project manager for a contractor, saw the problem differently. A large young man, dark-eyed, handsome, well-turned-out and the possessor of a college degree earned after five and a half years of night school, he is proud of his Italian ancestry, of his home in one of Ozone Park's more affluent districts and of a gigantic new car, which he won in a church raffle.

"This is most of all a moral issue," he said. "What right does anybody—*anybody*—have to tell me what to do? Where does it all end? I worked with Negroes on a construction job for seven years. They don't work hard or help their children in school or care about their families or keep their homes clean. But that's not the issue. I just won't tolerate anybody telling me I've got to send my son into another neighborhood to school."

His small, chic wife agreed. "I don't think I have a moral obligation to anyone—to my family, my husband and child maybe, but no one else. If Negroes have been deprived of some rights it's because they haven't worked for them. They don't deserve them. And the only way they're finally going to get them is through hard work—not by having our children bused into their schools." Her voice rose in distress.

"People just aren't psychologically ready for all this—this mixing," she complained. "We're not bad people out here in Ozone Park. We don't want to hurt anybody. We are decent, hard-working, church-going, law-abiding people—but we're bewildered. Bewildered by this bombshell of racial integration. Why do things have to change overnight? Why can't it be gradual?"

Though differently expressed, the views of P.A.T. members coincide on most questions.

Slavery? Sure Negroes were slaves once and that was terrible. But they haven't been slaves for 100 years. How could they use that anymore as an excuse for not getting ahead?

Color? It wasn't their color that was holding them back. It was the kind of people they were and the things they did and things they didn't do.

Discriminated against? Not really. In the South, maybe, but there was no segregation in New York City. They could go into any restaurant. Look at the Jews. They lived in ghettos once. They couldn't get certain kinds of jobs once. They had been discriminated against much longer than the Negroes, and look how well they had done.

Substandard schools? But why hadn't they *done* something about their schools before now? White mothers would have. Why had they been so apathetic all these years?

"If I were God, what would I do to improve the lot of the Negro?" echoed a P.A.T. supporter. "If I were God, I'd make everybody white."

*   *   *

Liberty Avenue is a crawling, congested business artery of Richmond Hill flanked by two-story buildings and dotted with the red and purple patterns of tomatoes and eggplants on the fruit stands. It has the vibrant air of a not-too-distant Italy or Germany or Ireland or Israel. The elevated trains roar and rattle overhead, quaking the buildings that border the tracks.

In a two-flight walk up, John and Felicia Petosa live in six cramped but immaculate rooms. There was a miniature organ against one wall of the living room and a television set, to which a small boy was glued, against another. A narrow hall led to small bedrooms miraculously clean despite the gray elevated, an arm's reach beyond the windows.

Felicia Petosa, married to a cook, is a warm, ardent woman. Her breathless commentary on the world and its problems was stalled only occasionally by the need for a fresh breath. She has two children, the eldest of whom spent his first years in a school in East Brooklyn—an area 70 per cent Negro and Puerto Rican.

"Pathetic," began Mrs. Petosa, taking a deep breath. "The school had no hallway. You got to the second classroom by walking through the first, and the third by walking through the first two. P.T.A. meetings were held next to the boiler room. I could never get interested. Fights all day. When the kids finished fighting at school they fought at home. Just on our block there were over 75 kids. The Puerto Rican lady who lived next door had five and 15 people lived in four rooms. We paid our own exterminator bills, but finally the man said he wouldn't do our place no more because it wouldn't do no good unless the whole block got done. We lived upstairs and the landlord lived down and every day he'd complain about the noise my kids made and I'd say to him, 'Excuse me, I'll go put them in a freezer and take them out for supper.'

"Finally, my husband was getting along better in his business and we moved, and the first day my little boy went to school here his conduct improved so much I took his temperature. I don't have anything against Negroes," added Mrs. Petosa, "but I believe in the neighborhood-school system. Why do our children have to be inconvenienced, just to satisfy the Negroes' whims?"

She picked up her bag, turned the fire off under the kettle, cautioned her young son to behave himself and said: "I'm going out into the neighborhood to distribute P.A.T. literature. I do it whenever I have a free minute. Come along."

The narrow, elderly streets seemed comfortable and secure in their monotonous uniformity, with cement driveways squeezed between identical houses, small patches of neat green yard, stone stoops.

A statue of the Virgin Mary stood in one yard, an empty, dry birdbath in another. A Good Humor man with his tinkle bells trailed children behind him.

"I don't want to buy anything today," called an irritated housewife from her kitchen.

"No, my mommy isn't home. She's at the hospital having another baby."

"Yes, I know about Parents and Taxpayers." This was the indignant voice of a grandmotherly woman, baby-sitting for two youngsters securely attached to her skirts. "It's terrible, I think, just terrible what people are trying to do to our neighborhood. There was a girl where we used to live—she must have been Polish or something—who married a colored man and had one of those chocolate-colored babies. Terrible. When you start mixing people up, that's when the trouble begins."

A woman paused on the street, a large, brown-paper shopping bag in her arms, and said: "What do they think they're going to accomplish with this pairing? They say they want to bring Negro and white kids together so they can get to know each other. And the Board of Education thinks Negroes will get a better education in schools with white children. But what's really going to happen? Just sitting next to each other isn't going to change things.

"There's a little boy on our street," she went on, "who uses bad language and doesn't do his school work and won't behave. *He* goes to school with our kids, but *he* doesn't change just because he sits next to a well-behaved child. He stays the way he is because that's the way his parents are. And as for raising the educational standards, give me one example—just one example—where mixing Negroes and whites hasn't pulled standards down to the Negro level rather than raising them to the white level. I don't know why the Negroes are behind. But they are, and I don't want them hurting my child's chances in school."

Farther down the street, now quiet with the heavy calm of a late-summer afternoon, an elderly lady sat on a camp chair in her front yard, her plump arms stretching the short sleeves of her house-dress.

"If the Negroes come into our neighborhood schools, does that mean they will be *moving* in?" she asked with a worried frown. "Eight years ago we paid $12,000 for this house. We scraped together every penny we had and borrowed more. Now it's worth at least $16,000. My husband and me we worked so hard to get it and it's all we have. And now, if the Negroes start coming into the neighborhood it won't be worth a cent."

A yapping dog subsided into friendliness behind a screen door and his mistress said: "I'm worried. I've got a 10-year-old boy and I don't want him going to school in no Negro neighborhood. Maybe nothing would happen. Then again, maybe it would. What if there's a riot, like there was in Harlem? And what if he goes into a drugstore and some of the older kids give him a jelly apple with dope in it? You never know, do you?"

"People keep saying that we members of Parents and Taxpayers just don't like Negroes," said a neat, brushed young man, seated amidst his bowling trophies. "But that isn't the issue. The fact is, I want my children to go to school where *I* went to school, and that's just two blocks away. My sister—she lives two doors up the street —*she* went there. My two cousins who live just around the corner *they* went there. We know the principal—a fine woman. This is our neighborhood."

A cluster of children on tricycles moved politely out of the way. In the street, two more youngsters chalked in the outlines for a game of hopscotch. On a porch, a woman, her hands in a pail of water, paused from her window washing.

"Yes, I'm one of P.A.T.'s telephone girls," she said. "Recently I've been polling people on their feelings towards the boycott. Oh, *everybody* was for it. People kept saying, 'Well, it's about time.

We've been conducting ourselves like ladies and gentlemen and where has it got us?' And then you know what they said—without my even asking? They said, 'I'm going to vote for Goldwater.' If other communities are like ours," she said, with satisfaction, "Goldwater's going to be our next President."

"I don't know what to think," said an elderly woman plaintively. "Please come in and sit down." She settled onto an ancient divan covered with a green tasseled throw.

"My son comes home a couple of weeks ago and when I say I think it's shocking, the thought of busing our neighborhood children into Negro schools and Negro children into our schools, my son gets furious and he says, 'You're a bigot!' Then he says to me, 'Don't you know Negroes were slaves once and they have been discriminated against for 150 years? That people haven't given them decent jobs and have forced them to live in Negro ghettos? Can you imagine what that does to people psychologically?' he says to me. And I say, 'But look how dirty they are and how bad their morals are and would you want your children going to school with Negroes?' And he gets mad again and he says I ought to be ashamed. 'Don't you understand that if you don't give people a decent education, or home, or chance, they lose hope and don't bother to work or study or keep their homes clean? If you treat them inferior, they *act* inferior,' he says. And then he says, 'If a Negro and white person asked you for a job and both were equally qualified, which would you choose?' I didn't know what to say, but finally I said I guessed the white person. And then"—and the old lady shook her head in distress and disbelief—"then he said, 'You're a bigot!' and he walked out."

The shadows and sounds of the afternoon grew longer and mellower. Someone was having a piano lesson. A car door slammed and a child cried, "Mommy, daddy's home." Homeowners came out on the stoops to take the air, and in the distance, a church bell chimed.

Standing before his church, a rector talked about his parishioners. "I've worked here much of my life," he said, "and I know that by most of the world's standards, these are good people, endowed with many of the great American virtues. They are hard-working and thrifty. They're honest and devoted to their families. But many of them have worked their way out of real poverty and in the process they haven't had much time or inclination to worry about other people's problems or think about the Negro and why he is the way he is; why they made out and the Negro hasn't. And they're not yet secure enough socially or economically to add to their American virtues the great human virtues of understanding, tolerance and compassion.

"Now," he continued, "they're scared. For years, Van Wyck Boulevard has been a psychological Berlin Wall. The Negroes tended to live on one side, the whites on the other, and the whites fear the wall will be breached if busing goes through. Many people here feel that their most precious possessions are in jeopardy, that their children may be endangered educationally and socially and their property devalued. These fears may be unfounded but that doesn't make them any less real. And then, you know, mothers do genuinely find comfort in having their little ones as close to home as possible. And I can't blame them.

"People come to me and ask, 'Why does integration have to begin with *our* children?'" he said sadly, "and I tell them it has to begin somewhere. But they're not very satisfied with my answers . . ."

Report on the Communist Party (U.S.A.)

by A. H. Raskin

THE NINE-STORY loft building at 35 East Twelfth Street looks exactly like a thousand other musty old buildings in downtown Manhattan. Still visible on its aging walls are the faded signs of clothing and knitgoods manufacturers who moved their sewing machines and cutting tables out of the building nearly twenty years ago.

Today it houses the national headquarters of the Communist party. It is the American Kremlin to those who regard the party as part of the world-wide fifth column fostered by Soviet Russia, but the party's 70,000 members indignantly reject this appellation. To them the Twelfth Street headquarters is a fountainhead of inspiration from which pours a flood of literature and counsel designed to protect the masses from the onslaught of "Wall Street reaction" and to point the way to eventual establishment of a Socialist America.

A wheezing elevator carries visitors past floors that contain the offices of The Daily Worker and The Freiheit, the party's Jewish-language newspaper; retail and wholesale book departments, and the headquarters of the Communist state and county organizations. On the top floor are the offices of the national leaders. So pervasive is their authority that "the ninth floor" is as familiar an address to Communists as No. 10 Downing Street is to Britons.

The elevator landing opens into a sparsely furnished reception room. On its walls are pictures of Franklin D. Roosevelt, Washing-

From the *New York Times Magazine,* March 30, 1947.

ton, Jefferson, Lincoln, Lenin, Stalin, Marx and a half-dozen pioneers in the American Communist movement. Conspicuously absent are such "renegades" as Earl Browder, Jay Lovestone and Ben Gitlow, once all-powerful in the party's councils but now branded as "enemies of the working class," with whom no Communist may associate on pain of expulsion from the party.

On a small table is a bust of Ella Reeve Bloor, 84-year-old crusader whom the Communists compare with "La Pasionara," flame of the Spanish Loyalist forces in the war against Franco and his Axis allies. A couch and three chairs in a leatherette covering complete the room's appointments. A railing fences off the locked metal door leading to the party offices. Behind a desk in the enclosure sits a youth wearing in his lapel the emblem of the Silver Star, third highest Army combat decoration. He controls a ticker that opens the locked door.

Alongside a dimly lit corridor beyond the reception room are the offices of the Communist high command. Most of them are tiny, with battered desks and chairs. Even the slightly larger offices occupied by William Z. Foster, the party's national chairman, and Eugene Dennis, its general secretary, are furnished in Spartan style. A map of the world hangs behind Mr. Foster's desk and a few Marxist tomes straggle across the shelves of his bookcase. Mr. Dennis's bookshelf is bare. A framed copy of the Declaration of Independence adorns his wall.

In the period when Mr. Browder was general secretary and the party was soft-pedaling its Socialist aims the most striking item on the ninth floor was a huge mural bearing the slogan "Communism Is Twentieth Century Americanism." Today the mural is gone and the slogan has been dropped along with other trappings of Browder's "right opportunism."

By way of reminder that the Communists hold no patent on the idea of governmental change, portraits of Washington and Jefferson alternate with those of Lenin and Stalin in almost every office.

The library is a shock to persons accustomed to hushed reading rooms in which the studious find sanctuary from the noises of the world. The Communist bibliophile must pick his way through a maze of mimeograph machines, packing cases and other obstructions to reach the magazines, books and pamphlets that crowd the racks. In the center of the room a giant roll of corrugated paper is suspended from the ceiling. The atmosphere is as conducive to repose and contemplation as the Times Square subway station in rush hour. For those who feel the need of more cloistered surroundings there is a conventional reading room in the State headquarters four floors below.

In the party's legislative office this correspondent found Robert Minor, who abandoned a well-paid job as a newspaper cartoonist thirty years ago to promote radical causes. Mr. Minor has had his ups and downs since joining the Communist movement. Son of a Texas judge, he has known the inside of many jails. He has clashed with police and vigilante bands from one end of the country to the other.

During the years of Browder's leadership, Minor rose to the pinnacle of party authority. He was recognized as Browder's second in command and during the year Browder spent in Federal prison for passport fraud, Minor was the party's national head. When Browder was cast into outer darkness a year and a half ago, Minor's star plummeted even though he was quick to renounce adherence to Browder's policies of friendly collaboration between capital and labor. He was dropped from the national board, the party's inner circle of policy makers, and was sent to the South, where he spent a year in organizing activity for the party. A few months ago, having redeemed himself sufficiently, he was recalled to New York to serve in the national legislative department.

None of these vicissitudes has shaken Minor's faith in the cause he serves. The greatest compliment ever paid him, he believes, was the statement of his successor as cartoonist on The St. Louis Post-Dispatch, Daniel R. Fitzpatrick, that from the day Minor embarked on his mission of economic liberation for the masses he never carried out an employer's wish.

"You do not consider the party an employer?" I asked.

A benign smile spread across his face.

"The party," he said softly, "is father, mother, brother and sister. It is not an employer."

What is this party that is able to command such complete devotion from its members? Many say it is not one but two parties. One functions openly. It is organized in community and industrial clubs and in county, State and national committees. It advertises its adherence to the principles and practices of democracy in every page of its constitution. It sponsors shop-gate and street-corner meetings to trumpet its views. It thrives on mass demonstrations. It distributes upward of 10,000,000 leaflets a year. It uses every avenue of communication to din into the consciousness of all who will listen its admiration for the Soviet system and its hostility to "fascist" trends in American life.

The other party shuns the limelight. It is a shadowy underground organization whose outlines emerge dimly in testimony before Congressional committees and in "confessions" by ex-Communists. It is a party whose members travel under bogus names and flout all the commandments of "bourgeois morality" to advance the party's fortunes. This party is organized under a discipline as absolute as that of an army. It has its own spies and secret police. It is responsive to the dictates of "C. I. reps" sent by Moscow to direct the activities of native Communists. It is charged with laboring tirelessly to betray democratic institutions to the greater glory of Moscow and the Soviet brand of totalitarianism.

It is hard for an outsider to know where to draw the dividing line between fact and fiction in this story of clandestine chicanery. The official leaders of the party are not much help in this direction. They dismiss all talk of ties between the party and the U.S.S.R. as the malicious invention of "turncoats, stool pigeons and Benedict Arnolds."

Some, like Elizabeth Gurley Flynn, only woman member of the national board, say there is nothing secret about the party—that it is as open and aboveboard as the Statue of Liberty, all lit up out in the harbor. Others, like Mr. Dennis, are somewhat more candid. The party's No. 2 man admits that some Communists do not parade their party affiliation. But he says this is because they fear loss of jobs or other forms of persecution and not because they wish to mislead those who might otherwise refuse to associate with them. All Communists, Mr. Dennis maintains, would be proud to proclaim themselves as party members if their civil and personal rights were adequately protected.

In its literature the party depicts the United States as "the entrenched citadel of capitalism" where fascist-minded elements are working to foment a war with Russia as a necessary step along their road to world domination. Samsonlike, the party intends to thwart this design by transforming itself into a "mass party of mass action."

How far it is from fulfilling this ambition is indicated by its own membership reports. Its total enrollment at the beginning of this year was only a little above 70,000, and one-quarter of these members had forfeited their good standing by failing to register.

These figures do not do full justice to the Communist strength in State and national elections. In New York State, where the party claims 30,000 members, it rolled up 96,000 votes for its candidate for Attorney General last November. If the same proportion of three voters for every enrolled member holds in the rest of the country, the party's probable strength in a national election would be between 200,000 and 250,000.

Despite the regularity with which it is accused of dominating unions, the party has made relatively little headway in winning workers to the class struggle. There are some 30,000 workers who hold cards in unions and also in the Communist party, or a ratio of one Communist for every 500 organized workers. Concededly, this membership is unevenly distributed, with about twice as many Communists in the CIO as in the AFL. But even in the CIO, where they control a dozen strategic unions, party members represent only one-half of 1 per cent of the rank and file.

The party professes confidence that it will raise its over-all membership to 100,000 by the time it reaches its twenty-eighth birthday next September. It had originally promised itself this total as a 1946 birthday present, but the results were disappointing.

In fact, when the national committee held its last "plenum" in December, it received such gloomy reports on the state of the party that some members favored shelving any organized drive this year and taking a "breathing spell" during which local clubs could be consolidated and their internal situation stabilized. This suggestion was rejected as leading to stagnation and retrogression.

"It would have the effect," said Henry Winston, the party's 35-year-old organization secretary, "of narrowing down the party to a small core of activities concerned only with administrative problems, at a moment when history compels us to assume greater responsibility and to multiply manyfold our mass work and our numerical strength."

Four-fifths of the party members are now organized in community clubs and the rest in shop or industrial clubs. The community clubs, which are the backbone of the party's structure, are supposed to translate the fight against monopoly and for Soviet-American friendship into terms the average housewife and shopkeeper can understand. They give out handbills and organize meetings and picket lines on such issues as higher prices, higher rents and the 5-cent fare. Their instructions are to turn their members into "good neighbors" who will be able to lead their communities toward the rosy-Red dawn of the new Communist day.

To strengthen its trade union base, the party is concentrating most of its current organizing activity on the development of more shop and industrial clubs. These clubs serve as spearheads for spreading the Communist program in industry and for bringing more workers into the party. Most of the shop clubs function secretly. Some are so covert that outside Communists are not allowed to attend their meetings without special invitation. In such "factions" one member will act as link between the shop workers and the party. By virtue of this association he often becomes endowed with all the authority of a "commissar" in his relations with the other Communists in the shop.

At the December plenum the trade union representatives were sternly reminded that it was not enough for Communist shop clubs to campaign for higher wages and other issues of immediate economic concern to the workers. Communists had the larger mission, the plenum was told, of using these issues to develop class consciousness among the workers and prepare them for "struggles on a higher level."

"Especially is it necessary," Mr. Winston admonished, "for the shop and industrial clubs to master the tactic of the united front, which remains a phrase until it is specifically applied to each shop, each department, each industry and section of industry."

The united front is the device through which a comparative handful of Communists exert their influence over a broad area of American affairs. J. Edgar Hoover, chief of the Federal Bureau of Investigation, calls it the "Trojan horse" policy and says it has become a "Trojan snake" on which the party relies to impose "a godless, tyrannical, communistic dictatorship on the United States."

The Communists put it quite differently. They herald the party as the vanguard element in forging a powerful democratic coalition to fight for jobs, security and equality, for progress, democracy and peace. To this end, they appeal to workers, to Negroes, to veterans, to young people and to "progressives" of every persuasion to rally beside them in a common struggle against "monopoly reaction."

Inside the mass organizations Communists shape their basic policy to conform to the dictates of the party line, but enjoy a considerable measure of latitude on tactics. They get their day-to-day guidance on what the party expects them to do from The Daily Worker, and regular readership of this and other party publications is prescribed in the constitution as a *sine qua non* of good standing in the party.

Specialized instructions and reprimands for "incorrect" conduct are passed down the chain of command by word of mouth.

It would be absurd, however, to conceive of the average Communist as an unwilling prisoner in a dictatorial political machine. In the minds of most Communists there is no conflict between the party's blind defense of every facet of Soviet domestic and foreign policy and nominal allegiance to the United States. They ignore all evidence of Soviet autocracy and aggression and identify themselves with the great social crusaders of history.

Every shortcoming in our democracy provides bricks for building the Communist united front. Lynchings, evictions, high living costs, inadequate housing, unemployment, laws to shackle labor— all these are grist for the party's mill. The more people it can involve in mass demonstrations, mass picket lines and general strikes, the more successful it counts its contribution to the never-ending "war" between the "people" and the "trusts."

Maintaining a united front policy requires considerable ability, particularly for a group that is as sensitive to each shift of the Moscow winds as the Communist party is.

Problem No. 1 is to convince its partners in the united front that each abrupt reversal in the party's attitude toward world affairs is based on American considerations. The embarrassments the party has suffered on this score are too familiar to need repetition.

Problem No. 2 is to prevent the party from being swallowed up in the united front. This was the essence of the case against Browder, who was accused by his comrades of having betrayed the principles of Marxism-Leninism by his advocacy of class collaboration after the war.

Problem No. 3 is to restrain the tendency of the more militant Communists to go all-out for third-party action and a swift démarche toward socialism. When Browder was booted out, many Communists advocated severing the party's ties with those who refused to share its Socialist goal. They were slapped down.

Today the party is attempting to steer a middle course between the Scylla of "right revisionism" and the Charybdis of "left sectarianism." The new line is a hard one to follow and the editorial writers of The Daily Worker, chained to the exigencies of a daily deadline, constantly find themselves in hot water for veering too far to the right or the left.

The current bible of party policy is the program adopted at the

December plenum. It puts principal emphasis on mobilizing a united front of all labor against the passage of repressive legislation. The party also calls for outlawing the Ku Klux Klan, the Columbians, American Action, Inc., and "all other Fascist organizations and activities."

It wants the House Committee on Un-American Activities abolished. It is for higher taxes on high incomes and lower taxes on low incomes; more housing; bigger social security and veterans' benefits; Federal subsidies to farmers; legislation to protect Negroes; nationalization of railways, mines, public utilities, communications and "the meat and dairy trusts," and prosecution of "the wealthy, the big monopoly war profiteers, especially in the steel, munitions, chemical, fuel, food, automotive and transport industries."

On the international front, the party wants us to stop making atomic bombs, to cut our military and naval expenditures and to promote universal and immediate world-wide disarmament. It calls on the United States to withdraw all troops from China and the Philippines and to withhold all support from the Chiang Government. It is against the proposed Inter-American Military Defense Act and it demands that this country sever all military ties with Britain. It pleads for Big Three unity, with the accent on American-Soviet amity and cooperation.

Hostility toward American Communists is based less on their stated program than on the belief that they are agents of the Soviet Union, that they are working toward violent overthrow of our form of government and that the system they would put in its place is essentially totalitarian.

What follows are the opposing points of view on these theses—comments on five charges that are frequently made against the party.

The Communist view is stated by Eugene Dennis, general secretary of the party. The opposite point of view is expressed by Matthew Woll, vice president of the American Federation of Labor. Both comments on the charges were made in longer form and have been condensed with the approval of the authors.

The Charge

> "The first loyalty of the Communist party is to the Soviet Union and it is only secondarily concerned with the American welfare."

Mr. Dennis Says:

The first and second loyalty of American Communists is to our working class, our people and our country, of which we are an integral part. As I stated in Madison Square Garden on Sept. 19, 1946: "We American Communists give allegiance to only one power: to the sovereign power that resides in the American people. We are American workers, Marxists and patriots. Today and on the morrow, as in the past, in war or in peace, we will loyally defend the genuine national interests of our people, of our country."

Some 15,000 Communists sealed this sacred pledge with loyal and exemplary service in the war against Hitlerism and Japanese militarism; and, years before that, some 4,000 American Communists likewise honored this principle by fighting and dying in freedom's cause and our country's interests against Franco fascism.

What is really at the bottom of the unfounded charge that we are "disloyal" is the fact that we have worked tirelessly for American-Soviet cooperation. Because of our resolute position in favor of American-Soviet friendship the anti-Sovieteers, the warmongers, who are intensely anti-American, try to brand us as "foreign agents." But this slanderous charge will not deter us from continuing to advocate and consistently fight for Franklin D. Roosevelt's program for U.S.A.-U.S.S.R. amity and collaboration which is so vital to our country's national security and the cause of world peace.

It is not the Communists but the trusts—the duPonts, Westinghouses, U.S. Steel, General Electric, etc.—who have a loyalty other than to the United States and the American people. They—the trusts—are the ones who put their monopoly and cartel interests above the interests of the nation. They are the ones who are ready at all times to betray the nation.

Mr. Woll Says:

The Communist party and its subdivisions in the United States have only one loyalty. This loyalty is to the Russian Communist party machine which dominates the Soviet Government. The Communists in our country are not really interested in improving the conditions of the American workers. When Communists do fight for such improvements it is only a means to an end—to enable them to win influence over workers so as to snare them into the Communist party or its myriad of satellite organizations.

Let me illustrate: Before June 22, 1941, the Communists were for strikes in American industry in order to cripple its war potential, as shown by the North American aviation strike. Then they were against the Selective Service Law and against all measures for adequate national defense. The heads of various CIO unions who follow the Communist party line organized a telegram drive on Congress against the enactment of the Selective Service Law.

However, the moment Hitler attacked Russia, the Communists—without any explanation as to any change of conditions in the United States—suddenly switched tactics completely. Overnight, in response to the changed conditions in which Russia found itself, they became super-patriots. They were now for clamping down on every effort of the labor movement to better the conditions of the workers. Higher wages and shorter hours no longer concerned them in the least.

These Communist party line followers forgot about the needs and interests of their members—in order to insure continued production for Russia. It was not American but Russian patriotism that explained the Communist party anti-strike policy after June 22, 1941, and during the rest of the war period. It was solely in the interest of their Russian masters and not out of concern for the safety of America that the Communists then resisted and denounced every attempt by American labor to preserve their rights and promote their basic interests.

The trade unions have always been considered by the Communists as their central and most vital field of operations. By capturing trade unions, the Communist minority hopes to be able to control or paralyze the economic life of whole nations. Domination of the trade unions is particularly important for the Communists at this critical international moment, since the world is grappling with the central problem of post-war reconstruction. This is especially true for war-ravaged countries in Europe and Asia. It is through their control of the French trade union movement that the French Communists have been able to score huge successes in elections and to have a paralyzing hold and veto power on the economic life of France.

The Charge

> *"The party is part of a 'world-wide fifth column' serving the interests of the U.S.S.R."*

Mr. Dennis Says:

The Communist party is an American working-class party. It bases itself on the needs and aspirations of the American people and utilizes the universally applicable principles of the social science of the working class, Marxism. The C.P.U.S.A. unmasks and combats all native and imported fifth columnists—the reactionary and Fascist elements, the agents of monopoly capital. That is why, over the years, we have waged political warfare against the Gerald L. K. Smiths, the Father Coughlins, the K. K. K., the Silver Shirts, the Hearsts and McCormicks, and now also against American Action, Inc.

Far from being a "world-wide fifth column," Communist parties throughout the world, as in France, Yugoslavia, China, Brazil, etc., have already won the respect of their people as being the best patriots, the best defenders of the national interests of their countries. That is the role to which the Communists in the United States are equally and ardently committed.

What is true of the allegation that we Communists are part of a "world-wide movement" is the fact that we are not only American patriots but also working-class internationalists. This, in fact, makes us better Americans devoted to the genuine interests of our country. In this—in our solidarity with all freedom-loving peoples—we are true to the tradition of Paine, Jefferson and Lincoln. We subscribe fully to Lincoln's declaration that ". . . the strongest bond of human sympathy, outside of the family relation, should be one uniting all working people, of all nations and tongues, and kindreds. . . ."

Mr. Woll Says:

No one can show a single instance where a Communist party organization in any country took a position on any question differing from the stand taken by the Russian Government. No Communist anywhere can show a single line of criticism of any Russian policy or difference with any Russian pronouncement. No matter how important a leader or group of leaders in any Communist party may be, if he or they should show the slightest sign of independence of opinion or intention to differ with the line handed down from Moscow, he or they are quickly removed, dropped, exiled or liquidated.

This is what makes a Communist party monolithic—one loyalty, one inspiration, one source of instructions, one aim—to serve the interests of their Russian Communist masters. Hence the Communist parties of all countries, at all times, carry out all orders as part of an international machine for a common purpose—to weaken all governments that are not in accord with, that do not lend support to, and that do not yield to Russian pressure and purpose.

For instance, the Communists denounced Roosevelt as a Fascist when he was for the NRA and against the Stalin-Hitler pact. But the same Roosevelt was perfect at Teheran and Yalta.

When Russia was against Perón the Communists in the United States were against Perón. But when Perón and Russia signed a commercial pact and established close diplomatic relations, the Communists in the United States, the Argentine and throughout the world stopped their attacks on Perón and began to seek increasing collaboration with him. Prior to Russia's getting together with Perón the WFTU publications denounced the Argentine Government. But the moment Russia changed its line toward Perón the WFTU publications stopped questioning, criticizing and denouncing Perón.

This is fifth-column work and performing the work of an agency of an alien Government. There is no doubt that these operations are directed from an international center. The moves, maneuvers and shifts of all Communist parties in all parts of the world are made simultaneously upon a central signal and for a common objective.

Of course, formally the Communist International may be dissolved. Actually it is working on all eight cylinders and using a high-octane gas.

Today Paris is formally the central headquarters of the actively functioning, but officially nonexistent, Comintern. The American Communist party leader Foster and all Communist leaders and agents visit Paris as correspondents and authors to our State Department, but really for getting instructions and new lines from Moscow. Often there may even be a Pravda correspondent on hand to serve simultaneously in three capacities—Comintern agent, NKVD or MVD listening post, and correspondent for his Moscow paper.

Whenever possible, such "3 in 1" agents in Paris are individuals with experience particularly in Anglo-Saxon countries—like the United States. Of course, these Russian fifth-columnists operate under different names at different times. Shingle or no shingle, new name or old name, it's the same nefarious conspiracy of totalitarian communism against human dignity, democracy and free trade unionism.

The Charge

> "The party receives instructions and financial support from Russia."

Mr. Dennis Says:

The Communist party has never received "instructions and financial support from Russia." If by "Russia" is meant, repeating a deliberate confusion, the former Communist International whose headquarters were at Moscow, then the statement is in place that before 1940 we were affiliated with the Communist International and occasionally exchanged fraternal opinions with Communist parties of other countries.

In 1940, however, upon passage of the Voorhis Act—which we then denounced as destructive of the democratic rights of the people and designed to destroy the Communist party as an open, legal political party—we severed all ties with the Communist International. In 1943 the Communist International itself was dissolved.

Any identity of views reflected then or now in the positions taken by our party and other Communist parties did not nor does not result from "international ties" or "instructions" from the Soviet Union. The identity of views which does exist on one question or another results solely from an independent interpretation of our universal science of Marxism, of problems common to the working class of the world, and in promoting world peace and democracy.

This does not mean that the views of all Communist parties are identical on all matters. In the independent development of views it often happens that differences of opinion develop on specific questions. Such differences develop because each party works out its policy independently, in accord with national needs. They are ultimately resolved because Communists everywhere work on the basis of a science whose principles are internationally valid.

It is notorious that British and American imperialism have given and are giving instructions and financial support to every backward and reactionary force throughout the world, as in Kuomintang China, Spain and Greece, to stem the advancing tide of the world's democratic forces. However, our party's only financial support comes from the advanced sections of the American working class and people. Our only "instructions" come from the dictates of the historic and immediate needs of the American working class and people.

Mr. Woll Says:

When Communist officials in the United States deny that they receive instructions or financial support from Russia they are torturing the truth and over-working their imagination. A perusal of the Communist press in the United States or in any other non-Russian country will prove beyond a shadow of doubt that these sheets regularly and religiously reflect Russian state policy. Among Communists, Moscow is often spoken of as "Mecca."

Being conspiratorial organizations, the Communist parties do not operate according to the rules of normal democratic procedure, which we commonly associate with American political life. In fact, communism today is nothing else but a conspiracy operating in the sole interest of Russia. Hence, it would indeed be very hard to find receipts in the United States to prove financial support from some banks, Kolhoz in Russia, or the Soviet publishing house. Underground business is never conducted with overground methods. Funds need not be transmitted openly or directly.

The Communist conspirators are not that careless these days. Funds might be transmitted through business institutions which make a profit in commercial relations with friendly trusts in friendly countries. Sometimes, when collections are made at public meetings, big sums might be announced as donations by American "angels" but they might well have come on the wings of Moscow.

The Charge

> "The party's aim is the violent overthrow of the American system."

Mr. Dennis Says:

The position of the Communist party on this question is definitively embodied in the constitution of the Communist party, which states:

". . . Adherence to or participation in the activities of any clique, group or circle, faction or party which conspires or acts to subvert, undermine, weaken or overthrow any or all institutions of American democracy, whereby the majority of the American people can maintain their right to determine their destinies in any degree, shall be punished by immediate expulsion. . . ."

Force and violence—resistance to the process of basic social change—have always been initiated and exercised by reactionary classes bent on maintaining their power and privileges against the will of the overwhelming majority. The counter-revolution of the Southern slavocracy in our own Civil War—1861-65—is proof of this historic truth.

And at this very moment, throughout the world, Communist parties, as in Poland, Czechoslovakia, Yugoslavia, Bulgaria, etc., are contributing all their energies to helping insure a peaceful course of social development for their countries. At the same time, American and British imperialists are giving aid and comfort to the pro-Fascists in these countries, as well as in France, who seek to foment disorder and bloodshed calculated to bring the reactionaries into power.

However, in the interests of democracy and peace, we American Communists place as the central task of the coming period the need of rallying the broadest labor and democratic coalition for the defeat of the forces of pro-Fascist reaction at home and abroad. And this is the only way to orderly social advancement.

We have made abundantly clear the character of our immediate and long-range aims. Our immediate objective is to protect the living standards and democratic rights of the American people and to prevent fascism from coming to power. We work to defeat the anti-labor legislation of the G. O. P. and the Southern Bourbons; to promote the economic security of the people; to help win equal rights for the Negro people and full civil liberties for all; and to safeguard and implement the cause of peace and Big Three unity, particularly through the fulfillment of the Potsdam, Moscow and Teheran agreements.

Our ultimate objective is socialism, that is, the common ownership and operation of the national economy under a government of the people, led by the working class.

Mr. Woll Says:

When Communist party officials deny that they are for the violent overthrow of the American democratic system, they know they are telling anything but the truth. The lie is an old and oft-used weapon of the Lenin-Stalin arsenal. The "A B C of Communism" preaches it. Lenin's manual of Communist strategy and tactics—"The Infantile Sickness of Left Communism"—proudly proclaims the lie as a keystone of Communist action, especially in the trade unions.

The program of the Communist International, which has never been revised or replaced, categorically states that the struggle for power is not a peaceful one and that the revolutionary overthrow of the capitalist system will be and must be a violent one. Oh, yes! When Communists in any country talk patriotic at any time, they are only maneuvering and camouflaging their basic aim. These tactical maneuvers are not changes in purpose or principle. The Communists will use any means to justify and attain their ends. To Communists, the end justifies all means. What's a little lie as a means to achieve their big end? Flexibility of tactics and rigidity of purpose are the inseparable twins of world communism. It is this dual feature which explains the ease with which Communist parties adapt themselves to sudden shifts of line ordered from Moscow.

The Charge

> "There is no difference between communism and fascism in so far as totalitarian disregard for personal rights and freedom is concerned."

Mr. Dennis Says:

Communism and fascism are as different as day is from night. As I stated on Sept. 19 at the Madison Square Garden:

". . . We say to American labor: the criminal falsehood that communism and fascism are Siamese twins, this pro-Fascist attempt to identify opposites is an old trick. . . . Not only the Communists but also millions of non-party anti-Fascists know fascism is the open, ruthless dictatorship of the most reactionary monopolies, of the Sixty Families; socialism is the rule of the workers in alliance with the working farmers and all common people. Fascism is race hatred, pogroms and lynching; socialism is the equality and friendship of peoples and nations. Fascism is the debasement and destruction of all cultural values, of human decency; socialism means the flourishing of culture, the achievement of the dignity of man. Fascism organizes war; socialism champions peace. These are facts, proved by life, by history. . . ."

This is not just a question of theory. In the great anti-Fascist war which was for our country as well as for others, as President Roosevelt said, a war of survival, the Socialist Soviet Union was our stanchest ally and bore the brunt of the war; and in every country the Communists were among the best and most self-sacrificing fighters for the preservation of the democratic achievements of their peoples and for liberation of their countries.

This was not an accident. It followed from the position of the Communists of all lands as great patriots, as the most resolute fighters for democracy and social progress, and the most uncompromising foes of fascism, which is the mortal enemy of all democracy. One does not have to be a Communist to recognize that the greatest issue of our time is the conflict between democracy and fascism, and that communism and fascism are diametrically opposite and the struggle between them is to the death. The history of the anti-Axis war, including the role of the Communists in all national resistance movements, makes this crystal clear.

As to personal rights, under capitalism, the personal freedom and "dignity" of the individual is determined, in the last analysis, by how much money one has. It is only under socialism that the masses of the people can come into their own, and that the full flowering of the individual will be possible. The truth of this is attested from time to time even by some of the correspondents of The New York Times when reporting objectively on the U.S.S.R.

Mr. Woll Says:

Of course there are differences between communism and fascism. Yet, though there is no total *identity*, there is enormous *affinity* between them. They are totalitarian in theory and practice. Communism, fascism, nazism, falangism are based on the one-party system

—on a monopoly of power in the hands of a single party—without any other organization having the right to have an office, publish a leaflet or paper or get any radio time.

Communism, nazism, fascism and falangism rely on terror as the last court of justice and decision. This system of terror is used against dissidents within the Communist party as well as against the people in Communist Russia at least as much as it was in Nazi Germany.

These four "isms" strive not only to have complete political power in the hands of their ruling bureaucracy, but to gather up in the hands of their chiefs all other instruments of social, economic and even moral power. In this respect, communism as practiced in Russia represents the most totalitarian of all totalitarian systems. In Russia there are no capitalist corporations or church institutions to share power, in the least, with the monolithic party dictator. Here poets and politicians are purged alike.

In Russia, even the church is now an organic part of the state apparatus. Thus the Russian Greek Orthodox patriarchs have recently been given clean and new uniforms to replace the old soiled ones described by Willkie. Today, the Russian patriarchs are harnessed as agents of Russian foreign policy in the Middle East and in the struggle to extirpate Catholic influence in the Balkans. Stalin has learned more than a lesson from the Czars of old, from the imperial Kremlin of yesterday.

In the last three weeks the party has been engaged in a fight for its life. The fight began with President Truman's message on foreign policy, the Communist party and President Truman's order that no Communist could enter or remain in the Federal Government. It continued last week in hearings before the House Labor Committee.

Many anti-Communists have voiced opposition to outlawing the party. Such suppression, they contend, would be a denial of democratic rights and would have the effect of driving the party underground, rather than destroying it.

The party is not tearing up its long-range plans. Looking beyond its current difficulties, it is already thinking about the next depression, which it expects to arrive late this year or early next year. If millions are thrown out of work, it believes the nation will turn toward Communist solutions.

Just Folks at a School for Nonviolence

by Joan Didion

OUTSIDE THE Monterey County Courthouse in Salinas the Downtown Merchants' Christmas decorations glittered in the thin sunlight that makes the winter lettuce grow. Inside, the crowd blinked uneasily in the blinding television lights. The occasion was a meeting of the Monterey County Board of Supervisors, and the issue, on this warm afternoon before Christmas, was whether a small school in the Carmel Valley owned by Miss Joan Baez, the Institute for the Study of Nonviolence, was in violation of Section 32-C of the Monterey County Zoning Code, which prohibits land use "detrimental to the peace, morals, or general welfare of Monterey County." Mrs. Gerald Petkuss, who lives across the road from the school, had put the issue another way. "We wonder what kind of people would go to a school like this," she asked quite early in the controversy, "why they aren't out working and making money."

Mrs. Petkuss is a plump young matron with an air of bewildered determination, and she came to the rostrum in a strawberry-pink knit dress to say that she had been plagued "by people associated with Miss Baez's school coming up to ask where it was, although they knew perfectly well where it was—one gentleman I remember had a beard."

"Well, I don't *care*," Mrs. Petkuss cried when someone in the

From the *New York Times Magazine,* February 27, 1966. Reprinted by permission of Farrar, Straus & Giroux, Inc., from *Slouching Towards Bethlehem* by Joan Didion. Copyright © 1966, 1968 by Joan Didion.

front row giggled. "I have three small children, that's a big responsibility, and I don't like to have to worry about . . ."—Mrs. Petkuss paused delicately—"about who's around."

The hearing lasted from 2 until 7:15 P.M., five hours and 15 minutes of participatory democracy during which it was suggested, on the one hand, that the Monterey County Board of Supervisors was turning our country into Nazi Germany and, on the other, that the presence of Miss Baez and her 15 students in the Carmel Valley would lead to "Berkeley-type" demonstrations, demoralize trainees at Fort Ord, paralyze Army convoys using the Carmel Valley road, and send property values plummeting throughout the county.

"Frankly, I can't conceive of anyone buying property near such an operation," declared Mrs. Petkuss's husband, a veterinarian.

"We don't start until 1," someone from the school objected. "Even if we did make noise, which we don't, the Petkusses could sleep until 1. I don't see what the problem is."

The Petkusses' lawyer jumped up. "The problem is that the Petkusses happen to have a very beautiful swimming pool; they'd like to have guests out on weekends, like to use the pool."

"They'd have to stand up on a table to see the school."

"They will, too," shouted a young woman who had already indicated her approval of Miss Baez by reading aloud to the supervisors a passage from John Stuart Mill's "On Liberty." "They'll be out with spyglasses."

"That is *not* true," Mrs. Petkuss wailed, injured now. "We see the school out of three bedroom windows, out of one living-room window. It's the only direction we can *look*."

Miss Baez sat very still in the front row. She was wearing a long-sleeved navy blue dress with an Irish lace collar and cuffs, and she kept her hands folded in her lap. She is extraordinary-looking, far more so than her photographs suggest, since the camera seems to emphasize an Indian cast to her features and fails to show either the startling fineness and clarity of her bones and eyes or, her most striking characteristic, her absolute directness, her absence of guile. She has a great natural style, and she is what used to be called a lady.

"Scum," hissed an old man with a snap-on bow tie who had identified himself as "a veteran of two wars" and who is a regular at such meetings. *"Spaniel."* He seemed to be referring to the length of Miss Baez's hair, and was trying to get her attention by tapping with his walking stick, but her eyes did not flicker from the rostrum.

After a while she got up and stood until the room was completely quiet. Her opponents sat tensed, ready to spring up and counter whatever defense she was planning to make of her politics, of her school, of beards, of her association with "Berkeley-type" demonstrations and income-tax rebellions and disorder in general.

"Everybody's talking about their forty- and fifty-thousand-dollar houses and their property values going down," she drawled finally, keeping her clear voice low and gazing levelly at the supervisors. "I'd just like to say one thing. I have more than one *hundred* thousand dollars invested in the Carmel Valley, and I'm interested in protecting my property, too." The property-owner smiled dazzlingly at Dr. and Mrs. Petkuss then, and took her seat amid complete silence.

Although all Baez activities tend to take on certain ominous overtones in the collective consciousness of Monterey County, what actually goes on at Miss Baez's Institute for the Study of Nonviolence, which was allowed to continue operating in the Carmel Valley by a 3-2 vote of the supervisors, is so apparently ingenuous as to disarm even veterans of two wars who wear snap-on bow ties.

Four days a week, Miss Baez and her little band of 15 meet at the school for lunch: potato salad, Kool-Aid, and hot dogs broiled on a portable barbecue. After lunch they do ballet exercises to Beatle records, and after that they sit around on the bare floor beneath a photo-mural of Cypress Point and discuss their reading: Gandhi, Thoreau, McLuhan, etc.

On the fifth day they meet as usual, but spend the afternoon in total silence, which not only involves not talking but also not reading, not writing and not smoking. Even on discussion days, this silence is invoked for regular 20-minute or hour intervals, a regimen described by one student as "invaluable for clearing your mind of personal hangups" and by Miss Baez as "just about the most important thing about the school."

There are no admission requirements, except that applicants must be at least 18 years old; entrance to any session is granted to the first 15 who write and say they want to come. They come from all over, and they are on the average very young, very earnest and not very much in touch with the larger scene—less refugees from it than children who do not quite apprehend it. They worry a great deal about "responding to one another with beauty and tenderness," and their response to one another is in fact so tender that an afternoon at the school tends to drift perilously through the looking glass. They debate whether or not it was a wise tactic for the Vietnam Day Committee at Berkeley to send an emissary to try to reason with the Hell's Angels "on the hip level."

"O.K.," someone argues. "So the Angels just shrug and say, 'Our bit's violence.' How can the V.D.C. guy answer that?"

They discuss a proposal from Berkeley for an International Nonviolent Army: "The idea is we go to Vietnam and we go into these villages, and then if they burn them, we burn, too."

"It has a beautiful simplicity," someone says.

They talk about Allen Ginsberg, "the only one, the only beautiful voice, the only one talking." Ginsberg had suggested that the V.D.C. send women carrying babies and flowers to the Oakland Army Terminal.

"Babies and flowers," a pretty little girl breathes. "But that's so beautiful, that's the whole *point*."

A dreamy boy with curly golden hair is holding a clear violet-colored marble up to the window, turning it in the sunlight. "Joan gave it to me," he says. "One night at her house when we all had a party and gave each other presents. It was so beautiful. It was like Christmas, but it wasn't."

Joan Baez (pronounced By-*ez*) grew up in the more evangelistic thickets of the middle class, the daughter of a Quaker physics teacher, the granddaughter of two Protestant ministers, an English-Scottish Episcopalian on her mother's side, a Mexican Methodist on her father's. She was born on Staten Island, but raised on the edges of the academic community all over the country; until she found Carmel, she did not really come from anywhere.

When it was time to go to high school her father was teaching at Stanford, and so she went to Palo Alto High School, where she taught herself "House of the Rising Sun" on a Sears Roebuck guitar, tried to achieve a vibrato by tapping her throat with her finger, and made headlines by refusing to leave the school during a bomb drill. When it was time to go to college, her father was at M.I.T. and Harvard, and so she went a month to Boston University, dropped out, and for a long while sang in coffee bars around Harvard Square. She did not much like the Harvard Square life ("They just lie in their pads, smoke pot, and do stupid things like that," complained the ministers' granddaughter about her acquaintances there), but she did not yet know another.

In the summer of 1959, a friend took her to the first Newport Folk Festival. She arrived in Newport in a Cadillac hearse with "JOAN BAEZ" painted on the side, sang a few songs to 13,000 people, and left with her future in her pocket. Her first album, released by Vanguard toward the end of 1960, sold more copies than the work of any other female folk singer in record history.

By the end of 1961 Vanguard had released her second album, and her total sales were behind only those of Harry Belafonte, the Kingston Trio and the Weavers. She had finished her first long tour (12 concerts, most of them at colleges, which made her about $15,000), had given a concert at Carnegie Hall which was sold out two months in advance, and had turned down $100,000 worth of concert dates because she would work only a few months a year.

She was the right girl at the right time. She had only a small repertory of standards from Child's "The English and Scottish Popular Ballads" ("What's Joanie still doing with this Mary Hamilton?" Bob Dylan would fret later), never trained her pure soprano and annoyed some purists because she sang everything "sad" and was indifferent to the origins of her material. But she rode in with the folk wave just as it was cresting. She could reach an audience in a way that neither the purists nor the more commercial folk singers seemed to be able to. If her interest was never in the money, neither was it really in the music: she was interested in something that went on between her and the audience. "The easiest kind of relationship for me is with 10,000 people," she says. "The hardest is with one."

She did not want, then or ever, to entertain; she wanted to move people, to establish with them some communion of emotion. By the end of 1963 she had found, in the protest movement, something upon which she could focus her emotion. She went into the South. She gave concerts at Negro colleges, and she was always where the barricade was—Selma, Montgomery, Birmingham.

She sang at the Lincoln Memorial after the March on Washington. She told the Internal Revenue Service that she did not intend to pay the 60 per cent of her tax which she estimated went to the defense establishment. (The Government then placed a $50,000 lien on her income; she has now agreed to pay the tax.) She became the voice that meant protest, though she always maintained a curious distance from the movement's more ambiguous moments. ("I got pretty sick of those Southern marches after a while," she could say later. "All these big entertainers renting planes and flying down.") She had made only a handful of albums (she has still made only six), but she had seen her face on the cover of Time. She was only 22.

Joan Baez was a personality before she was entirely a person, and, like anyone to whom that happens, she is in a sense the hapless victim of what others have seen in her, written about her, wanted her to be and wanted her not to be. The roles assigned her are various, but they are variations upon a single theme. She is the Madonna of the disaffected. She is the pawn of the protest movement. She is the unhappy analysand. She is the singer who would not train her voice, the rebel who drives the Jaguar too fast, the Rima who hides with the birds and the deer.

Above all, she is the girl who "feels" things, the girl who has hung on to the freshness and pain of adolescence, the girl ever wounded, ever young. But she is 25 now, an age when the wounds begin to heal whether one wants them to or not.

The school owned by Miss Baez is an old whitewashed adobe house quite far out among the rolling yellow hills and dusty scrub oaks of the upper Carmel Valley. Oleanders support a torn wire fence around the school, and there is no sign, no identification at all. The house was a one-room county school until 1950; after that it was occupied in turn by the So Help Me Hannah Poison Oak Remedy Laboratory and by a small shotgun-shell manufacturing business, two enterprises which apparently did not present the threat to property values that Miss Baez does.

She bought the place last fall, after the County Planning Commission told her that zoning prohibited her from running the school in her own house, which is on 10 acres a few miles away. Miss Baez is the vice president of the institute, and its sponsor; the $120 fee paid by each student for each six-week session includes lodging, at an apartment house in Pacific Grove, and does not meet the school's expenses. Miss Baez not only has a $40,000 investment in the school property but is responsible as well for the salary of Ira Sandperl, who is the president of the Institute, the leader of the discussions, and in fact the *eminence grise* of the entire project.

In a way, it is impossible to talk about Joan Baez without talking about Ira Sandperl. "One of the men on the Planning Commission said I was being led down the primrose path by the lunatic fringe," Miss Baez giggles. "Ira said maybe he's the lunatic and his beard's the fringe."

Ira Sandperl is a 42-year-old native of St. Louis who has, besides the beard, a shaved head, a large nuclear disarmament emblem on his corduroy jacket, glittering and slightly messianic eyes, a high cracked laugh and the general appearance of a man who has, all his life, followed some imperceptibly but fatally askew rainbow. He has spent a good deal of time in pacifist movements around San Francisco, Berkeley and Palo Alto, and was, at the time he and Miss Baez hit upon the idea of the institute, working in a Palo Alto bookstore.

Sandperl first met Joan Baez when she was 16 and was brought by her father to a Quaker meeting in Palo Alto. "There was something magic, something different about her even then," Sandperl recalls. "I remember once she was singing at a meeting where I was speaking. The audience was so responsive that night that I said: 'Honey, when you grow up we'll have to be an evangelical team.'" He smiles, and spreads his hands.

The two became close, according to Sandperl, after Miss Baez's father went to live in Paris as a UNESCO adviser. "I was the oldest friend around, so naturally she turned to me." He was with her when she appeared at Sproul Hall during the Berkeley demonstrations in the fall of 1964. "We were actually the 'outside agitators' you heard so much about," he says. "Basically, we wanted to turn an unviolent movement into a nonviolent one. Joan was enormously instrumental in pulling the movement out of its slump, although the boys may not admit it now." ("Have love as you do this thing," she had told the students, "and it will succeed.")

A month or so after her appearance at Berkeley, Joan Baez talked to Sandperl about the possibility of tutoring her for a year. "She found herself among politically knowledgeable people," he says, "and while she had strong *feelings,* she didn't know any of the socio-economic-political-historical terms of nonviolence."

"It was all vague," she interrupts, nervously brushing her hair back. "I want it to be less vague."

They decided to make it not a year's private tutorial but a school to go on indefinitely, and enrolled the first students late last summer. The institute aligns itself with no movements ("Some of the kids are just leading us into another long, big, violent mess," Miss Baez says), and there is, in fact, a marked distrust of most activist organizations.

Sandperl, for example, has little use for the V.D.C. because the V.D.C. believes in nonviolence only as a limited tactic, accepts conventional power blocs and, in fact, has considered running one of its leaders for Congress, which is anathema to Sandperl.

"Darling, let me put it this way. In civil rights, now, the President signs a bill; who does he call to witness it? Adam Powell? No. He calls Rustin, Farmer, King, *none* of them in the conventional power structure." He pauses, as if envisioning a day when he and Miss Baez will be called to witness the signing of a bill against violence. "I'm not optimistic, darling, but I'm hopeful. There's a difference. I'm hopeful."

The gas heater sputters on and off, and Miss Baez watches it, her duffel coat drawn up around her shoulders. "Everybody says I'm politically naive, and I am," she says after a while. It is something she often says. "So are the people running politics, or we wouldn't be in wars, would we?"

The door opens and a short, middle-aged man wearing handmade sandals walks in. He is Manuel Greenhill, Miss Baez's manager, and although he has been her manager for five years and accompanied her on a tour of Britain in the fall, he has never before visited the school, and he has never before met Ira Sandperl.

"At last!" Ira Sandperl cries, jumping up. "The disembodied voice on the telephone is here at last! There is a Manny Greenhill! There is an Ira Sandperl! Here I am! Here's the villain!"

Miss Baez believes that her quiet life in Carmel and her days at the institute talking and listening to Ira Sandperl are bringing her closer to contentment than anything she has done so far. "Certainly closer than the singing. I used to stand up there and think I'm getting so many thousand dollars, and for what?"

She is defensive about her income ("Oh, I have some money from somewhere"), vague about her plans. "There are some things I want to do. I want to try some rock 'n' roll and some classical music. But I'm not going to start worrying about the charts and the sales, because then where are you?"

Exactly where it is she wants to be seems an open question, bewildering to her and even more so to Manny Greenhill. If he is asked what his most celebrated client plans to do in the future, Greenhill talks about "lots of plans," "other areas" and "her own choice." But he is hoping to get Miss Baez to write a book, to be in a movie and to get around to recording rock 'n' roll. She has let him schedule only one concert for this year (down from an average of 30 a year), has accepted only one regular club booking in her entire career, and is virtually never on television. "What's she going to do on Andy Williams?" Greenhill shrugs. She did participate in a couple of folk specials before she was well-known, and has since appeared twice on "Night Life," once with Shelley Berman and once with Pat Boone.

Greenhill keeps an eye on her political appearances (she appeared at a demonstration against the Vietnam war in Washington last summer, and when the pickets failed to elicit a response from the White House, commented: "I don't think the President gives a damn"), and tries to prevent the use of her name. "We say, if they use her name, it's a concert. The point is, if they haven't used her name, then if she doesn't like the looks of it she can get out." Greenhill is resigned to the school's cutting into her schedule. "Listen, I've always encouraged her to be political," he says. "I may not be active, but let's say I'm concerned." He squints into the sun. "Let's say maybe I'm just too old."

To encourage Joan Baez to be "political" is really only to encourage Joan Baez to continue "feeling" things, for her politics are still, as she herself said, "all vague." Her approach is instinctive, pragmatic, not too far from that of any League of Women Voters member. "Frankly, I'm down on communism" is her latest word on that subject. On recent events in the pacifist movement she has this to say: "Burning draft cards doesn't make sense, and burning themselves makes even less."

She makes occasional appearances for Democratic Administrations and is frequently quoted as saying, "There's never been a good Republican folk singer." It is scarcely the diction of the new radicalism. Her concert program includes some of her thoughts about "waiting on the eve of destruction":

"My life is a crystal teardrop. There are snowflakes falling in the teardrop and little figures trudging around in slow motion. If I were to look into the teardrop for the next million years, I might never find out who the people are, and what they are doing."

Although Miss Baez does not actually talk this way when she is kept away from the typewriter, she does try, perhaps unconsciously, to hang on to the innocence and turbulence and capacity for wonder, however ersatz or shallow, of her own or of anyone's adolescence. This openness, this vulnerability, is, of course, precisely the reason that she is so able to "come through" to all the young and lonely and inarticulate, to all those who suspect that no one else in the world understands about beauty and hurt and love and brotherhood. Perhaps because she is 25 now, Miss Baez is sometimes troubled that she means, to a great many of her admirers, everything that is beautiful and truthful.

"I'm not very happy with my thinking about it," she says. "Sometimes I tell myself, 'Come on, Baez, you're just like everybody else,' but then I'm not happy with that, either."

"Not everybody else has the voice," Ira Sandperl interrupts dotingly.

"Oh, it's all right to have the voice, the *voice* is all right . . ."

She breaks off, and concentrates for a long while on the buckle of her shoe.

So now the girl whose life is a crystal teardrop has her own place, a place where the sun shines and the ambiguities can be set aside a little while longer, a place where everyone can be warm and loving and share confidences. "One day we went around the room and told a little about ourselves," she confides, "and I discovered that, *boy,* I'd had it pretty easy."

The late afternoon sun streaks the clean wooden floor and the birds sing in the scrub oaks and the beautiful children sit in their coats on the floor and listen to Ira Sandperl.

"Are you a vegetarian, Ira?" someone asks idly.

"Yes. Yes, I am."

"Tell them, Ira," Joan Baez says. "It's nice."

He leans back and looks toward the ceiling. "I was in the Sierra once." He pauses, and Joan Baez smiles approvingly. "I saw this magnificent tree *growing* out of bare rock, *thrusting* itself . . . and I thought *all right, tree,* if you want to live that much, *all right!* O.K.! I won't chop you! I won't eat you! The one thing we all have in common is that we all want to *live!*"

"But what about vegetables?" a girl murmurs.

"Well, I realized, of course, that as long as I was in *this* flesh and *this* blood I couldn't be perfectly nonviolent."

It is getting late. Fifty cents apiece is collected for the next day's lunch, and someone reads a request from the Monterey County Board of Supervisors asking citizens to fly American flags to show that "Kooks, Commies and Cowards do not represent our County," and someone else brings up the V.D.C. and a dissident member who had visited Carmel:

"Marv's an honest-to-God nonviolenter," Sandperl declares. "A man of honesty and love."

"He said he's an anarchist," someone interjects doubtfully.

"Right," Sandperl agrees. "Absolutely."

"Would the V.D.C. call Gandhi bourgeois?"

"Oh, they must know better, but they live such bourgeois lives themselves . . ."

"That's so true," says the dreamy blond boy with the violet-colored marble. "You walk into their office, they're so unfriendly, so unfriendly and cold . . ."

Everyone smiles lovingly at him. By now the sky outside is the color of his marble, but they are all reluctant about gathering up their books and magazines and records, about finding their car keys and ending the day, and by the time they are ready to leave Joan Baez is eating potato salad with her fingers out of a bowl from the refrigerator, and everyone stays to share it, just a little while longer where it is warm.

Part  4

FROM CIVIL RIGHTS
TO BLACK POWER

LITTLE MORE than a decade has passed since the movement began in Montgomery, Alabama. It seems far longer than that, as if an entire historical epoch had come and gone. And, indeed, with the murder of Dr. Martin Luther King in 1968 that is exactly what has happened. It is hard to recall how most people felt about racism and segregation before Montgomery. Negroes were often treated badly, it was agreed, but on the whole, outside the South at least, they were doing about as well as their limited capabilities permitted. Things in the South were sometimes deplorable, but nothing could be done about that because you can't change men's minds by passing laws. Anyway, Southerners did understand the Negro better than Northerners, and perhaps their social system was the best one possible under the circumstances. So went the customary refrain. The movement's emergence in 1956 was, therefore, a shock not only to Southerners but also to most other white Americans. Even more surprising was the rapid development of young Dr. King into one of the most important Americans of this century.

George Barrett's article reminds us that Dr. King's greatness was sensed from the outset by friend and foe alike. Liberals applauded him on several grounds. One reason was the guilty knowledge that a people who had been exploited and abused for so long ought to have launched a bloody revolution. Dr. King's first virtue, then, was that he saved us from our just desserts. In the long run, however, it became clear that his greatness derived not so much from his leadership of the civil rights movement as from the universality of his message. Dr. King meant to lead his people to freedom, but he also tried to save America from its own worst instincts—the violent ones that cause riots, lynchings, and murder at home and wars abroad. Although he was a Christian minister, the nonviolent ethic he devised owed as much to Thoreau and Gandhi as to the New Testament. The result was a creed of such flexibility that it appealed to Christian and non-Christian, the simple and the sophisticated alike. It had the effect, moreover, of making individuals larger than life and bringing them to moral heights they never expected to reach. Simple farmers and working people at first, and then a wide range of Northern as well as Southern activists found themselves performing heroic acts, standing up to danger and death, being beaten and going to jail. Their heroism had extraordinary consequences. The New Left was one, the Civil Rights Acts of 1964 another, a new crop of racist demagogues like Lester Maddox a third. Nothing was quite the same again.

And yet, in another sense everything stayed the same. Thousands, millions of people marched, picketed, protested, sat-in, swam-in, slept-in, and all the rest of it to pass bills and integrate facilities that hardly affected the lives of black Americans. The Establishment paid lip service to nonviolence while continuing to shoot looters in Newark and peasants in Vietnam. Working for freedom in Mississippi remained as dangerous as ever. The failure to secure a measurable improvement in black living standards, and the casualties suffered by the nonviolent armies, took their toll. If there was a particular moment when the nonviolent tide began to ebb, it was probably during the "freedom summer" of 1964 discussed in John Herbers' "Communiqué from the Mississippi Front." Herbers was interested in the impact of this attempted civil rights blitz on white Mississippians, but in time it became evident that the greatest impression had been made on black activists. Many now came to believe that as a tactic nonviolence was not paying off. Casualties were high in Mississippi, and progress minimal. Moreover, the inner costs of nonviolence were greater than anyone outside the movement could guess. Later it became known that the rage denied an outlet during public confrontations found expression in private combats between the activists. Obviously, they could not continue taking out their repressed fury on one another indefinitely, and they did not.

Black Power was, therefore, not simply a new strategy based on new experiences, but for young Negro militants a desperately needed psychological life ring. At last they were able to make their policies square with their feelings. This is an entirely understandable reaction to the stringent and painful self-discipline of the nonviolent movement. In the short run it has produced gratifying results for the militants. They obviously enjoy their swaggering new roles. Insulting liberals for fun and profit beats organizing in Mississippi any day of the week. And, as the Conference on New Politics demonstrated, some liberals can hardly be humiliated enough. Of course, Black Power has inflicted its own wounds. Paul Good's moving essay on John Lewis describes one such injury. Even more tragic than the individual losses has been the killing of Dr. Martin Luther King's vision of America redeemed. Both the chauvinism and the violence of Black Power make it seem unlikely that the American people will ever be disarmed and reconciled, as for a moment seemed almost possible.

But while the black militants have been successful in making some liberals crawl, and in forcing moderate civil rights leaders to take a somewhat harder line, they also have failed to raise the black standard of living. It is not true that the nonviolent movement was ineffectual, even though black militants insist that it was. It did what it set out to do. Racial segregation was overthrown in law and to a considerable extent in practice. All manner of opportunities that never existed before were opened up. The trouble was that poverty proved to be much more intractable than had been expected. It seems now that only massive sums of money will enable poor people, and especially poor Negroes, to take advantage of the movement's gains. Probably some form of guaranteed family income will have to be worked out. In order for this to be understood, however, the movement had first to knock down the walls of formal discrimination and ignorance. Only then could the scope of the problem and the magnitude of its remedy become apparent, and only then did the absurdity of Black Power become manifest. Black Power is not simply irrelevant to the task at hand, but subversive of it. What is needed are untold billions of dollars. Black Power's contribution is a stream of threats and abuse directed against that very "honkie" power structure from which the money will have to come.

In a real sense the black militants are setting themselves up for the slaughter. Now they are riding high. They can turn a serious effort like the Conference on New Politics into a nonpolitical happening. They can make their friends stand in for their enemies. In the long run, though, such posturing can lead but to disaster. Only the strong can commit violence, or threaten to, with impunity, and the black militants are only a tiny part of a weak minority. The ghetto uprisings which began in Watts, California, testify to this. The blacks rioted and the blacks died. After each outburst Negro casualties were ten or twenty times those of the white authorities. When they were over the ghettos were poorer and the police stronger than before. As city after city acquires armored vehicles and heavy weapons, the next round can only be more sanguinary and self-destructive for blacks. Thus far the reprisals have been comparatively slight. Armed white mobs have not attacked the ghettos lately. No leading Black Power advocate has been assassinated yet. But any or all of these things are certain to happen if the pressure is not eased. And if the black militants do not back off, they will surely discover, as so many radical groups from the IWW to the CPSUA before them have, that the power structure can only be pushed to a point. Once that point is reached (and the trials of Huey Newton and Eldridge Cleaver suggest that it is at hand), unlimited force is used to destroy the source of irritation. Thus, while it seems as if things could hardly get worse, they not only can but certainly will if Black Power and white blacklash are not abated.

"Jim Crow, He's Real Tired"

by George Barrett

MONTGOMERY, ALA.

NOT YET where the tar road ends and the mud ruts start, but far enough out where the whites never go, a Negro seamstress looked for a moment in silence at the folds of velvet that divided the choir loft in her church from the front-row pews. The velvet was worn, very worn, and the threads holding it to the brass rings around the choir rail were broken in many places. Sections of the drape yawed over, gave peep-hole views of the organ's pedal clavier and the choir's heating vents. Abruptly, she pushed aside her sewing kit, began pulling away at the drape. She talked to the drape as she pulled:

"Velvet, I'm sorry. But you're tired. And we've put up just about long enough with tired things. You gotta go." And down came the velvet. Then she turned the talk to Jim Crow, spoke without rancor, without defiance, without raising her voice: "I guess that's our answer. Jim Crow, he's more than 100 years old, and real tired, and like you just hear me tell this velvet, we figure we've about put up long enough with tired things."

That seamstress, a 57-year-old grandmother who left school before the eighth grade and still refers to her employer as "my white lady"; her Negro neighbor, a handyman who says "Yes SIR, Boss" and spends his evenings drafting and re-drafting an essay on the duties of

From the *New York Times Magazine*, March 3, 1957.

citizenship so sound that the white man's election board will no longer dare to hold back his ballot; their community leader, the 28-year-old Rev. Dr. Martin Luther King, Jr., whose fusion of Christianity, Hegelianism and Gandhism has spurred Montgomery's Negroes and set back Montgomery's whites in the opening battle here to end racial segregation; indeed, each of Montgomery's 50,000 Negroes shares an identical distinction.

Each is the South's "new Negro."

When the white man—the Northern white man—speaks, as he often does these days, of the "new Negro," he generally means the Dr. Kings, the Negroes who have left their back-hollow birthplaces, the "Jim Towns" and "Shanty Villages" in the Deep South, and gone North to collect their master's degrees and their doctorates from integrated universities. He means the Negroes who have found their first day-to-day reality of racial democracy in the armed services and in foreign duty, and are now coming back to mobilize the stay-at-home Negroes for the big march against the bastions of the Old South.

When the white Southerner speaks of the "new Negro" these days he means the same thing, except that if he's a reputable member of the community he will probably fiddle uneasily with a paper clip on his desk and say, "That communistic N. A. A. C. P. is sending them back down here to stir up our decent Nigras," and if he is not so educated or prosperous he will spit at the dirt in angry silence, or he will say, with unprintable interpolations, "That communistic N. C. double A. P. or whatever it's called is sending them back down here to stir up our niggers."

Example Number One here in Alabama, in fact in the entire Deep South, is Dr. King, according to most of the Southern whites who are fighting each new attempt to carry out the Supreme Court's mandates against segregation. They are convinced that the Dr. Kings—and particularly *the* Dr. King, who they are certain is regarded by most Negroes as a kind of latter-day Messiah—are basically causing All The Trouble.

But visit Negro night spots in Montgomery, attend midweek prayer meetings, go with them to their pep sessions, join them in their parlors: the "new Negro" is not only the Dr. Kings but the seamstress, the handyman; in fact, most of Montgomery's Negroes, who never went North. Negroes here who have traveled in the Deep South or have received letters from their friends and families in other

Southern states say that the forces that unified Montgomery's Negroes in the remarkable year-long bus boycott, the passive-resistance
campaign that broke down the first racial barriers in this "Cradle of
the Confederacy" a few weeks ago, are emerging also in other areas
across the Southern tier.

The "new Negro," in fact, is a phrase that brings quick looks
between Negroes here, then good-natured grins. A Negro mail carrier
put it this way: "New Negro? It's just us old Negroes, the same old
folks. It's not the 'new Negro'—it's the 'new times.' Only we know
it, that's all, and the white folks here haven't caught on to it yet."

The "new times," of course, means today, the culmination of long
years of better Negro education, of a fast-narrowing world with its
ready exchange of ideas and closer living patterns, of the Negroes'
emerging economic power, of spreading industrialization throughout
the Deep South, of the day-by-day absurdities involved in sectional
segregation in a nation tending naturally and swiftly toward integration on all levels, and finally of the Supreme Court's parade of bans
against Jim Crow, which for the Negroes here meant, as a quietly
jubilant Negro housewife said: "Before, we only thought we were
right—now we know we are right."

But the point they emphasize, a point which most of the Southern
whites fail to see and refuse to consider, is that there are many Mont-
gomerys in the Deep South; there are other Dr. Kings and other
communities also acutely aware of the "new times" and waiting now
for just the right moment to move as Montgomery moved. Dr. King,
Georgia-born and Boston-educated, is a cardinal example of the
aspiring Negro who reached the scholastic heights up North (he is a
doctor of divinity and a doctor of philosophy) and resolutely came
back to segregation in the Deep South to fight it. But he is convinced
that Montgomery's Negroes would have made their challenge without him.

In the living room of his small, white bungalow, as Beethoven's
Sixth played softly inside and searchlights played garishly outside to
protect him from night attackers, Dr. King recalled that Montgomery's Negroes "arose spontaneously" over the bus-segregation
issue, that for the whole Negro community a tired seamstress who
was asked to give up her seat to a white passenger suddenly became
a symbol.

"Actually, I was catapulted into the leadership," Dr. King said. It
was a matter of choosing him to direct a defiance that had already

erupted. During the early days of the bus boycott, before the Negroes had organized their car pools and when every one of them walked, and people like the president of Tuskegee left their cars at the city limits to walk also, the ministers and professors who began to take over the direction of the boycott were often accosted on the streets of Montgomery by Negroes who said they had been wondering how long it would take for them to catch on and act.

From his pulpit Dr. King has warned, softly, those who have three times now bombed or shot up his home: "Kill me, but know that if you do you have 50,000 more to kill!"

Two and a half years ago, Dr. King turned down two higher-salaried ministerial offers in the North to become the minister of Montgomery's neat, red-brick Dexter Avenue Baptist Church, at the broad approach to the State Capitol. As he puts it, "I wanted to turn my talents to our Negro cause down here, to do my part in this tense period of transition." He came here at the age of 26, brimming over with an intellectual eagerness that was in vivid contrast to the kind of Biblical bombast still popular in many Negro churches. He was not so much concerned with the happy crossings of the River Jordan, but preached sermons that drew lessons for his congregation from Toynbee, Shakespeare, Benedict, Hegel, Aristotle, Galileo, Socrates and Myrdal. Yet he is the first to deny that he is any more the "new Negro" than the "old style" folks who worked, often dangerously, toward the integration that is now beginning to evolve.

His congregation loves to tell the story of the minister who preceded Dr. King, a more old-fashioned man of God who some years ago decided suddenly to sit in a front seat of a Montgomery bus when front seats were still being reserved by law for white passengers. The white driver looked at him, told him to get up and sit in the back of the bus. The Negro minister said, "No," and did not move. A block later, the driver looked again, his face reddened, and he said, "Preacher, I thought I told you to get to the back of the bus!"

The minister glared back, answered, "And I told you I was going to sit right God-damned here."

The driver was flabbergasted and subsided into silence for the rest of the trip. The minister later told his congregation, "I looked up, and I said, 'God, You know I meant no blasphemy,' and I kind of suspect that God, He just looked down and He said to Himself,

'Now there's a real comer, yonder in Montgomery, I better keep an eye out on him.' "

Most of the whites here, who see nothing unusual about a member of the board of trustees of Tuskegee working as a chauffeur for his living, have never got past the porches of Negro homes, except on occasional paternalistic visits to see if Cora is coming along all right. If they had, they would have discovered that in the past as well as in the present minister of the Dexter Avenue Baptist Church, in the Jasons and the Rubys and the Anna Maes and the Sams who scrub their kitchen linoleum and change the oil in their cars, there has been for a long time a determined—if very quiet—resolve to get rid of Jim Crow.

"Funny thing," one Negro girl said recently after a prayer meeting, while other Negroes in the pews nodded in agreement, "our white families say to us it's such a terrible thing that a man like that Reverend King comes here and gets the colored people all stirred up, and we say, 'No, ma'am, the Reverend, he didn't stir us up, we've been stirred up a mighty long time,' but our white folks they just don't seem to hear us, because later at the dinner table they'll be talking to their friends and saying what a terrible thing it is for that Reverend King to come in here and stir up all us colored people and how they were just that morning talking to their maid, only they never say what it was we answered. I guess they just don't hear us."

The "stirring up" long pre-dates Dr. King's arrival in Montgomery. Out where the tar road ends and the mud ruts start, there is a Negro social club. The juke box pours forth garish tints and grinding tunes. But over the doorway leading to the dance floor, there is a prominent placard, brilliant under a spotlight. It reads: "Honor Roll of Registered Voters."

Night after night, when there are no dances, and in side-room booths on the nights when there are dances, Negroes bone up on their civics to try to get their names on the Honor Roll. In these "schools"—in night spots, in churches, in funeral sheds where the long pine boxes provide handy seats—the Negroes have for several years prepared for the day when they expect to be able, especially with the help now of F. B. I. agents on hand to walk up to the election board, be tested on the basis of merit instead of color, and get their ballots.

Much of Montgomery's white community, however, still thinking in terms of Uncle Rastus, or "that lazy shiftless, no-good nigger," would be incredulous at the news that the textile factory sweeper, the laundress, the truck driver are studying with such stern single-mindedness with their ministers, their professors and their high-school teachers. Here, as in most places in the Deep South, the whites insist that the Negroes want no change. Always, someone points to a prominent local Negro—"one of our own niggers"—who has made a good deal out of segregation and doesn't want to see it go.

There is a wealthy, long-resident Negro in Montgomery, a successful business man, who keeps his rough corduroys strapped with a diamond-studded belt. This is what he has to say: "The whites get angry about the Reverend King, they blame him for the troubles." He leaned forward in his chair. "They don't know what's going on. We need the Reverend King, that's true, and we've got things from his leadership nobody else could have given us. But there's something more important. The colored people know this is the right time, just like the Supreme Court knows this is the right time."

He got up and paced his shabby, cluttered office. "I own a Cadillac. When I was a little boy, I thought the most beautiful thing in the world was a big, long, black Cadillac. Now the Cadillac is low, wide, gleaming white, or silver, sometimes both. I had to look a long time before I bought mine. I had to study it, think about what I always liked in a Cadillac, think if I could give up my notions of the past. And I decided I liked the new look. A lot of people down here have got to do some hard looking now at the old living styles. And I guess they'll discover that the modern style is sure different, but kinda good-looking, too, when you get used to it."

The whites in Montgomery are still having trouble getting used to the new style, and again and again they blame the Dr. Kings, with their highfalutin' notions. They don't know how far they have spread. Another Negro with highfalutin' notions, a man who is helping to put his nephew through college, said:

"We've been waiting for this day a long time. We've been quiet about it, though, and I guess if the whites knew what we were feeling deep inside all the time they'd have called us 'uppity.' We used to joke about it, but we didn't feel like joking, when we'd say that for the kind of traveling our kids were gonna have to do in life all they needed was a rattletrap jalopy. Anyhow, that's all they got. Now our kids are beginning to get some of the latest models, like other kids, only we've been planning a little for this day and seeing to it that our kids knew how to drive these new models."

But the big question is: Why, of all the Deep South communities, has Montgomery become the first major testing ground? This is, after all, the "Cradle of the Confederacy," where Jefferson Davis took the oath as President of the Confederated States, where the Negro ratio of population—40 per cent—is well past the mark that is supposed to represent trouble for any community attempting racial integration.

Sociologists at Alabama State College are stumped on that one, as is everybody else here who has tried to find the rational or scientific explanation. Dr. King says he has tried to isolate the special factors but has found nothing that would not hold equally true for many other Deep South communities.

This writer discussed the astonishing initial shift in Montgomery's segregation patterns with Dr. King in the compact, tidy office of the Montgomery Improvement Association, the organization that is directing the Negroes in their struggle. Dr. King listened, nodded as, one by one, the sociological dimension, the economic dimension, the emotional dimension, the psychological dimension, the historical dimension were weighed and discarded.

"You have left one dimension out," he said, then added, softly, "the divine dimension."

For Dr. King, and there may be one or two Montgomery Negroes —but no more than one or two—who do not agree with him, the answer is God. "This won't satisfy the rational, materialistic inquiry," Dr. King said simply. "But God, we are convinced, has chosen Montgomery to lead the new way for Negroes. Remember, this is the 'Cradle of the Confederacy,' this is the symbol of all the things the Old South represents. It seems to us no accident— on the contrary, it seems to us most deliberate—that God should decide the place to start the New South is here in the cradle of the Old South."

This religious conviction is the most quietly dramatic aspect of the Negro story in Montgomery. Dr. King has been correctly described as the man who introduced intellectual dynamism to the Montgomery Negroes, who has transcribed Hegel's philosophy of strength through struggle, harmony out of pain, in terms of Negro living in the South, and thereby given the Negro a new awareness (and, therefore, a new strength). Many admit they don't always understand his words, but, as one of his own congregation put it, "We sure get the force of his meaning." ("He knows how to speak to the Ph.D.'s and the No D.'s," is a popular saying among the Negroes.)

And he has won world-wide recognition for the way he has translated Gandhi's philosophy of passive resistance into Alabaman terms, an adaptation that has administered a solid defeat to the segregationists. The Negro churches still show old movies of Gandhi to demonstrate again and again how victory—real victory—comes from non-violence.

But it is as a man of God, a man as profoundly religious as he is philosophically knowledgeable, that Dr. King has been chosen by Montgomery's Negroes to lead the way to the "new times." This is the Bible Belt and fundamentalism survives. It is the land of rousing hymns and camp-meeting tunes, the songs that cry of the Negro's suffering and his struggle.

Enter a Negro church any Sunday. The minister reads the prayer, slowly, and a single finger, then a foot, tap out the rhythm; swiftly, the congregation picks up the crescendo: "Hear our prayer, O Lord!" But it's no longer the old-style religion, no longer the way of escape from terrible realities. There is a sound now more than a cry; there is the ring of a deep conviction.

The words and the music are old—yet strangely new—as massed voices sing:

> *Thou hast made us willing,*
> *Thou hast made us free,*
> *By Thy grace divine,*
> *We are on the Lord's side.*

And this is the remarkable strength of the Negro in Montgomery: his conviction, so vivid in his face, that he must at last win because he is on God's side.

From the preaching of Dr. King, the Negroes have learned in the last year the hardest of Christ's truths—how to love, how not to judge, how not to hate—and found these precisely through their refusal to strike back when white men spat in their faces, slapped them across the mouth, hurled dynamite at their homes and churches.

Clearly—and this is probably the most stirring experience for the visitor to Montgomery—the Negroes' day-by-day acceptance and practice of Christ's principles, applied to the struggle against Jim Crow, have brought them a calm that seems unshakable, a humility that is formidable, a love that shatters hate and prejudice. The combination can only mean the ultimate—and not so distant—defeat of the segregationist cause.

One Negro woman said: "Did you ever dream of getting a million dollars some day, and buying all the things you've wanted? For us, right now, it's like suddenly getting a million-dollar check from the United States Government. We've waited a hundred years for it, only it's Friday afternoon and the bank won't open until Monday. It really doesn't matter if we don't get the cash until Monday. A weekend is not so long, now."

Communiqué from the Mississippi Front

by John Herbers

JACKSON, MISS.

A FEW NIGHTS AGO, 250 Negroes were holding a civil-rights rally in a building outside Indianola, a small town in the Mississippi Delta, when they heard a low-flying airplane overhead.

"It must be the K.A.F. [Klan Air Force]," someone said as several men started out the door to see. The plane dropped a flare, circled, and released a small explosive, which went off near the building without doing damage. Then it roared off into the darkness, leaving the meeting in a state of fear and confusion.

When several men were arrested in McComb, in southwestern Mississippi, on charges of bombing Negro homes, the authorities confiscated four high-powered rifles, several carbines and pistols, 15 dynamite bombs, a five-gallon can of explosive powder, several thousand rounds of ammunition, a stock of hand grenades and a number of clubs and blackjacks.

Recently, when the Atomic Energy Commission postponed an underground nuclear test in south Mississippi because of unfavorable weather, a joke made the rounds that the real reason for the delay was that the Ku Klux Klan had stolen the bomb and was threatening Washington with it.

Outside a "freedom house" in one small town white and Negro youths stand behind a barricade and try to record the numbers of

From the *New York Times Magazine*, November 8, 1964.

license plates as carloads of armed white men circle the building. Other civil-rights workers sit in jail in Belzoni, charged with "criminal syndicalism" for distributing handbills on the streets.

In Greenwood, so many cars on the streets are equipped with short-wave radios that it is difficult to tell at first sight whether they belong to segregationists or civil-rights workers; both use radio for instant communications. In Jackson, the state capital, the lights on the two top floors of a new office building, headquarters for the Federal Bureau of Investigation, burn all night long as agents pore over the latest intelligence.

These are the signs of the war in Mississippi, a struggle brought about by the efforts of both the Federal Government and civil-rights organizations to banish discrimination in the area where it has been most militantly defended. Although racial violence is not new to Mississippi, the conflict reached a new peak during the summer, when hundreds of civil-rights workers, mostly student volunteers, poured into Mississippi communities from throughout the nation to help the state's 900,000 Negroes advance politically, socially and economically. A number of the civil-rights workers stayed on into the fall, and more are being recruited for the months ahead. The struggle continues.

Casualties and Combatants

The cost of the war—in personal casualties and property damage—has been high. The Council of Federated Organizations (COFO), sponsor of the civil-rights drive in Mississippi, has compiled these statistics for the four-month period ending Oct. 21: three persons killed, 80 beaten, three wounded by gunfire in 35 shootings, more than 1,000 arrested, 35 Negro churches burned (two more were burned last weekend) and 31 homes and other buildings bombed. In addition, there have been several unsolved murders of Negroes that may have been connected with the racial conflict.

As in most wars, the number of actual combatants is only a small percentage of the total population, although virtually everyone—man, woman and child, white and Negro—is emotionally involved. The terror and violence are believed to be the work of small bands of whites, the night riders.

Some white leaders have suggested that they are delinquent teen-agers. But few teen-agers know how to detonate dynamite or burn churches without leaving a trace of evidence. The terrorists are not hard to find in most communities. They are the steely-eyed men— most in their 20's and 30's—who step out of a crowd and slug a civil-rights worker. They stand in bunches on a street corner and stare at Negroes lined up to register. They drive on the back roads in cars without license plates. Their education is limited; they generally are employed in laboring or service jobs. They have a certain amount of drive and intelligence; it takes some to escape detection by the F.B.I. Of those arrested in McComb and charged with unlawful use of explosives, several worked in the Illinois Central Railroad yards, one was a service-station attendant, another a store clerk, one a former Army demolition expert and one the son of a wealthy oilman.

The night riders' violence is directed against three categories of persons: whites and Negroes and their sympathizers engaged in the civil-rights effort; Negroes not engaged in civil-rights work but who just happen to be present; and whites who defend the segregated system but condemn the use of violence in attempting to preserve it. Only recently has the last group become a target.

Night Riders vs. Whites

It is one thing for Negroes and "alien whites" to be attacked, quite another for white officials who have supported segregation to be subjected to terror. Yet, the other night, Judge W. H. Watkins, an elected official who presides over several circuit courts in southwestern Mississippi, was startled to see a cross burning in front of his home. In Natchez, Mayor John Nosser had more cause for concern. He was seated in his living room with his wife and children one evening when a dynamite blast tore out a wall of the house.

Each was being "rewarded" according to his deeds. Judge Watkins, in a charge to a Walthall County grand jury in Tylertown, had made a plea for law and order. While he, too, opposed the new civil-rights law, he said, "We must live with it peacefully as law-abiding citizens," and he had harsh words for those who burn churches.

Mayor Nosser had gone a little further. As a moderate, he had surprised many by his re-election to office a few weeks earlier. He promised Negroes equal protection under the law and their right to vote if qualified. Also, he hired Negroes in his grocery business, against the wishes of white extremists. But he, too, favored segregation, and in no way had he directly challenged the system that Mississippians call "our way of life."

Another example concerns Mayor Charles Dorrough of Ruleville, a town of 2,000 in the heart of the Mississippi delta, a few miles from Senator James O. Eastland's cotton plantation. It has a large Negro population and a strong civil-rights movement, bolstered during the summer by student volunteers.

Mayor Dorrough clearly identifies himself with the white community, but he also is president of the Mississippi Municipal Association and he feels a responsibility for law enforcement. After the civil-rights law was enacted, he moved to set up a program to train Negroes to work in Ruleville industries that previously employed only whites. The Board of Aldermen hired a Negro policeman.

It was felt that neither of these acts would foster desegregation but would set a pattern of law enforcement and ease some of the pressures in the community. Nevertheless, a cross was burned on the Mayor's lawn, and literature attacking him and the aldermen as traitors was distributed in the white community.

Local business leaders, however, stood behind the Mayor. They posted a $500 reward for information leading to the arrest of those who burned the cross and passed out the literature in violation of state law.

The case of the Greenwood newspaper editor did not end so well. Thatcher Walt is a 35-year-old native of the Greenwood area. After working on newspapers elsewhere, he returned to become editor of The Greenwood Commonwealth. He was known as a responsible conservative who did not challenge the system.

Last spring, when the Ku Klux Klan became active in the area, Mr. Walt wrote a rather mild editorial criticizing cross-burning and similar activities. He and his family were immediately subjected to threats and harassment. Mr. Walt found it necessary to sit up one night with a shotgun across his lap.

The owners of The Commonwealth do not encourage taking stands on local issues and Mr. Walt never replied editorially. Instead, he went to leaders in the town and advised them to put down the terrorist threat before it became entrenched. He received little encouragement.

"I decided then I did not want to raise my children in this town," Mr. Walt said. During the summer, he found a job on another Mississippi daily where the climate was more inviting. He gave The Commonwealth two weeks' notice and was working out his time when he had another encounter with the Klan.

The Leflore Theatre, the best movie house in Greenwood, is owned by a chain. It was one of several in Mississippi to comply immediately with the new civil-rights law by opening its doors to Negroes. Gangs of whites congregated nightly in front of the theater, attacked Negroes who entered and warned whites to stay away. One night, Mr. Walt took his wife, two children and a neighbor's child to see a movie at the Leflore. They were confronted at the entrance by a picket line.

"Don't go in; there's niggers in there," one of the pickets warned. Mr. Walt replied that he was going in, and that if there was trouble he would notify the authorities.

After the movie, the family had barely returned home when the telephone threats began. There was an explosion on the front lawn. Mr. Walt asked for, but did not receive, police protection. Again, he had a long night with his shotgun.

The next day, a friend told Mr. Walt of overhearing at a service station a conversation about a plot to kill him. Mr. Walt packed up his family and left town immediately. He called the newspaper where he had taken a job and told the publisher he would not report to work as scheduled. "I felt like it wouldn't be safe for me anywhere in the state," he explained. Instead, he found a job in another state several hundred miles away.

A few days later, a reporter asked a Greenwood policeman about Mr. Walt. "He left town before we could get him," the officer replied.

Lost Liberals

For the majority of whites, the real war in Mississippi is going on in men's souls. One important factor is the fact that so many people are related. A resident of Jackson is likely to have a brother in Pascagoula, an uncle in Aberdeen and a third cousin in Clarksdale. And they all keep up with one another.

In almost every white family there are one or two persons who have thought their way out of the Mississippi orthodoxy. While they seldom express their opinions publicly, they frequently cannot restrain themselves in family gatherings. This leads to violent arguments, for it is a polarized society.

"I just don't talk about it any more when I go home," a young man in Jackson said. "But I find it hard not to when the subject is always under discussion."

The polarization of opinion is evident in every business office. The minority who do not agree with the "segs"—i.e., those who support the Mississippi way of segregation—simply remain quiet. The story is told of the girl who finally summoned the courage after several months to tell a fellow worker that she violently disagreed with the predominant opinion. "You do?" the companion said in surprise. "Why I do, too!"

These people—"liberals," they are called disparagingly—form little cells here and there and discuss "the subject" even more than do the segs. One difference is that the segs despair of both the Negroes and the liberals, while the liberals despair only of the segs.

The plight of the liberals, most of whom certainly would not bear that label in any other section of the country, is that they have no place to go. No one has found a way to activate them, even if they could be identified. They have nothing in common with the civil-rights workers coming into the state. Many of the latter are unkempt revolutionary types who seem alien to both Negroes and whites in the region. And even the liberals do not approve when they see a white college girl and a Negro man walking down a street hand-in-hand, stirring up the night riders.

Agonized "Segs"

Even among the segs, the night riders are a small minority. They see themselves as the last line of defense. They are said to feel that their former leaders, the men in high office, led them into battle and then deserted them.

They are the final splinters of the massive resistance that stood for a decade under the aegis of the white Citizens Councils. As the civil-rights movement focused on Mississippi, those who did not think the councils were militant enough broke away and formed Klan chapters and the Society for the Preservation of the White Race. There was further splitting between groups which favored violence and those which did not.

The night riders already find their organizations, like the Communist party they so detest, infiltrated by the F.B.I. They can carry on a guerrilla warfare for a time, but eventually they will be brought down, by Federal if not state authority.

Everyone in Mississippi is touched to some extent by the turmoil. But the nonviolent segs seem most in agony. They live in a world of rumor and fabrication. A few months ago, they were convinced that a number of Negro men, who would wear white Band-Aids on their throats, had been designated to rape white women. Negro restaurant employees, they were told, were contaminating the food. One current rumor is that the National Association for the Advancement of Colored People has instructed maids to harass their employers by hiding valuable items—so that the lady of the house would experience a moment of terror before discovering they were not stolen.

When three civil-rights workers were missing in Neshoba County, a good portion of the state's white population was certain they were in Cuba or, as one report had it, in a bar in Chicago, drinking beer and laughing at it all. When McComb was plagued by bombings, the authorities were convinced they were the work of integrationists, and had lengthy explanations to support their views. The whites attribute the most cynical motive to any step the Federal Government makes in the civil-rights field. The massive investigation of the Philadelphia murders was, according to many, not to bring justice but to win the election of President Johnson.

There is almost no middle ground. No one is more aware of this than Erle Johnston, the director of the State Sovereignty Commission. He is also a weekly newspaper publisher, and he can best be described as an unpolarized segregationist, or one who can look at the race problem objectively. There are not many of these left.

Mr. Johnston shies away from labels like "moderate," a word that has become packed with emotion in Mississippi simply because it implies the middle of the road. The agency he heads was created to preserve segregation, and Mr. Johnston is dedicated to that end. Because of the nature of his job he is an enemy of the civil-rights organizations. But also because he has tried to avoid violence and promote ethical methods, he has been attacked from the other side. "The Ku Klux Klan, the Americans for the Preservation of the White Race, the Citizens Councils, the John Birch Society—they're all against me," Mr. Johnston said. "Nobody is for me."

"The prime victims in this war are not the Negroes," one of the liberals said. "Violence is nothing new to them, and things are going their way for the future. It is what the white people are doing to themselves that disturbs me."

What Hope?

Yet there are paradoxes here. On the surface, there is a serenity. Most Mississippians live in pastoral scenes that suggest tranquility. In the early autumn, the sky is a deep blue and the green of the landscape has not been touched by frost. The haze of the summer has lifted, and the detail of field and forest is visible for miles. On the coast, there are white sand, shrimp boats and industry. Jackson, with a population of 150,000, has clean new buildings and virtually no slums. Greenville, on the Mississippi River, has more urbane, sophisticated people than most Northern cities its size. Everywhere, people are friendly and open. If there is hostility, it comes only after they get to know you.

William Faulkner, the man who could explain Mississippi best, found it necessary to use long, tortuous phrases saying what something was not, when logically it should have been, before he got around to saying what it was. This need, in itself, points up the risks of predicting what Mississippi will be in the future. But there have been more changes in the past six months than in the previous 10 years—and there will be more.

Probably the most significant change is the fact that Mississippi, like all other Southern states, has switched from massive resistance to gradualism in desegregation. The remarkable thing is that this switch has been accomplished as peacefully as it has after bitter-end resistance to any change in racial policy had become a cult, with politicians convincing a good portion of the populace that Mississippi would never have to yield.

In addition to widespread compliance with the public-accommodations section of the civil-rights laws, three public school systems have been desegregated and two Negroes are attending the University of Mississippi without the help of Federal marshals. These changes have given many Mississippians a chance to see that integration is not as terrifying as they had been told it was.

Much depends, of course, on how much pressure the Federal Government brings to bear in months to come. Negro leaders predict there will be enough of their race registered within three years to decide the next election for Governor. This may be an over-optimistic view, but few doubt that the day will come when Negroes will vote in significant numbers in the state. Some believe that a large Negro vote will have an immediate moderating effect in Mississippi, just as it has in other areas of the South.

While the segs are still determined to hold out, they are divided and confused. And a number of leaders are now talking about the need to improve Mississippi's image. They are moved, as usual, by economic losses. The coast, which had little to do with Mississippi's problems, suffered a severe cutback this year in tourist trade. Most coastal leaders are moderates, by Mississippi standards, and, with their pocketbooks hurting, they may bring considerable pressure for a change in Jackson. Other cities could follow.

An example of such pressure took place during the summer. The Jackson Chamber of Commerce, aware of the city's image, ignored the preachments of the Citizens Councils and urged compliance with the civil-rights law. In doing so, its members enlisted the help of Mayor Allen Thompson, who had been a council spokesman.

Some observers believe Mississippi is too emotionally wrought up and too entrenched in segregation to make a smooth transition to a new way of life. There is still a wide gulf between the few white moderates who have the power to make changes and the civil-rights groups. The young workers who come in from the outside, for instance, are teaching Negroes a brand of political and economic liberalism that repels most Mississippi whites. This increases the possibility of creating a white party and a black party—opposed, not only racially, but economically and politically.

There is a chance, however, as gradualism takes hold and as the Negro vote dispels some of the demagoguery, that the white liberals will be freed from their isolation. They would then be in a position to help establish a middle ground that both whites and Negroes could share. The question is whether there is time for this process to take place.

A Journey into the Mind of Watts

by Thomas Pynchon

LOS ANGELES

THE NIGHT of May 7, after a chase that began in Watts and ended some 50 blocks farther north, two Los Angeles policemen, Caucasians, succeeded in halting a car driven by Leonard Deadwyler, a Negro. With him were his pregnant wife and a friend. The younger cop (who'd once had a complaint brought against him for rousting some Negro kids around in a more than usually abusive way) went over and stuck his head and gun in the car window to talk to Deadwyler. A moment later there was a shot; the young Negro fell sideways in the seat, and died. The last thing he said, according to the other cop, was, "She's going to have a baby."

The coroner's inquest went on for the better part of two weeks, the cop claiming the car had lurched suddenly, causing his service revolver to go off by accident; Deadwyler's widow claiming it was cold-blooded murder and that the car had never moved. The verdict, to no one's surprise, cleared the cop of all criminal responsibility. It had been an accident. The D.A. announced immediately that he thought so, too, and that as far as he was concerned the case was closed.

But as far as Watts is concerned, it's still very much open. Preachers in the community are urging calm—or, as others are putting it: "Make any big trouble, baby, The Man just going to come back in

From the *New York Times Magazine*, June 12, 1966.

and shoot you, like last time." Snipers are sniping but so far not hitting much of anything. Occasionally fire bombs are being lobbed at cars with white faces inside, or into empty sports models that look as if they might be white property. There have been a few fires of mysterious origin. A Negro Teen Post—part of the L.A. poverty war's keep-them-out-of-the-streets effort—has had all its windows busted, the young lady in charge expressing the wish next morning that she could talk with the malefactors, involve them, see if they couldn't work out the problem together. In the back of everybody's head, of course, is the same question: Will there be a repeat of last August's riot?

An even more interesting question is: Why is everybody worrying about another riot—haven't things in Watts improved any since the last one? A lot of white folks are wondering. Unhappily, the answer is no. The neighborhood may be seething with social workers, data collectors, VISTA volunteers and other assorted members of the humanitarian establishment, all of whose intentions are the purest in the world. But somehow nothing much has changed. There are still the poor, the defeated, the criminal, the desperate, all hanging in there with what must seem a terrible vitality.

The killing of Leonard Deadwyler has once again brought it all into sharp focus; brought back long-standing pain, reminded everybody of how very often the cop does approach you with his revolver ready, so that nothing he does with it can then really be accidental; of how, especially at night, everything can suddenly reduce to a matter of reflexes: your life trembling in the crook of a cop's finger because it is dark, and Watts, and the history of this place and these times makes it impossible for the cop to come on any different, or for you to hate him any less. Both of you are caught in something neither of you wants, and yet night after night, with casualties or without, these traditional scenes continue to be played out all over the south-central part of this city.

Whatever else may be wrong in a political way—like the inadequacy of Great Depression techniques applied to a scene that has long outgrown them; like an old-fashioned grafter's glee among the city fathers over the vast amounts of poverty-war bread that Uncle is now making available to them—lying much closer to the heart of L.A.'s racial sickness is the co-existence of two very different cultures: one white and one black.

While the white culture is concerned with various forms of systematized folly—the economy of the area in fact depending on it—the black culture is stuck pretty much with basic realities like disease, like failure, violence and death, which the whites have mostly chosen—and can afford—to ignore. The two cultures do not understand each other, though white values are displayed without let-up on black people's TV screens, and though the panoramic scene of black impoverishment is hard to miss from atop the Harbor Freeway, which so many whites must drive at least twice every working day. Somehow it occurs to very few of them to leave at the Imperial Highway exit for a change, go east instead of west only a few blocks, and take a look at Watts. A quick look. The simplest kind of beginning. But Watts is country which lies, psychologically, uncounted miles further than most whites seem at present willing to travel.

On the surface anyway, the Deadwyler affair hasn't made it look any different, though underneath the mood in Watts is about what you might expect. Feelings range from a reflexive, angry, driving need to hit back somehow, to an anxious worry that the slaying is just one more bad grievance, one more bill that will fall due some warm evening this summer. Yet in the daytime's brilliance and heat, it is hard to believe there is any mystery to Watts. Everything seems so out in the open, all of it real, no plastic faces, no transistors, no hidden Muzak, or Disneyfied landscaping, or smiling little chicks to show you around. Not in Raceriotland. Only a few historic landmarks, like the police substation, one command post for the white forces last August, pigeons now thick and cooing up on its red-tiled roof. Or, on down the street, vacant lots, still looking charred around the edges, winking with emptied Tokay, port and sherry pints, some of the bottles peeking out of paper bags, others busted.

A kid could come along in his bare feet and step on this glass —not that you'd ever know. These kids are so tough you can pull slivers of it out of them and never get a whimper. It's part of their landscape, both the real and the emotional one: busted glass, busted crockery, nails, tin cans, all kinds of scrap and waste. Traditionally Watts. An Italian immigrant named Simon Rodia spent 30 years gathering some of it up and converting a little piece of the neighborhood along 107th Street into the famous Watts Towers, perhaps his own dream of how things should have been: a fantasy of fountains, boats, tall openwork spires, encrusted with a dazzling mosaic of Watts debris. Next to the Towers, along the old Pacific

Electric tracks, kids are busy every day busting more bottles on the steel rails. But Simon Rodia is dead, and now the junk just accumulates.

A few blocks away, other kids are out playing on the hot blacktop of the school playground. Brothers and sisters too young yet for school have it better—wherever they are they have yards, trees, hoses, hiding places. Not the crowded, shadeless tenement living of any Harlem: just the same one- or two-story urban sprawl as all over the rest of L.A., giving you some piece of grass at least to expand into when you don't especially feel like being inside.

In the business part of town there is a different idea of refuge. Pool halls and bars, warm and dark inside, are crowded, many domino, dice and whist games in progress. Outside, men stand around a beer cooler listening to a ball game on the radio; others lean or hunker against the sides of buildings—low, faded stucco boxes that remind you, oddly, of certain streets in Mexico. Women go by, to and from what shopping there is. It is easy to see how crowds, after all, can form quickly in these streets, around the least seed of a disturbance or accident. For the moment, it all only waits in the sun.

Overhead, big jets now and then come vacuum-cleanering in to land; the wind is westerly, and Watts lies under the approaches to L.A. International. The jets hang what seems only a couple of hundred feet up in the air; through the smog they show up more white than silver, highlighted by the sun, hardly solid; only the ghosts, or possibilities, of airplanes.

From here, much of the white culture that surrounds Watts—and, in a curious way, besieges it—looks like those jets: a little unreal, a little less than substantial. For Los Angeles, more than any other city, belongs to the mass media. What is known around the nation as the L.A. Scene exists chiefly as images on a screen or TV tube, as four-color magazine photos, as old radio jokes, as new songs that survive only a matter of weeks. It is basically a white Scene, and illusion is everywhere in it, from the giant aerospace firms that flourish or retrench at the whims of Robert McNamara, to the "action" everybody mills along the Strip on weekends looking for, unaware that they, and their search which will end, usually, unfulfilled, are the only action in town.

Watts lies impacted in the heart of this white fantasy. It is, by contrast, a pocket of bitter reality. The only illusion Watts ever allowed itself was to believe for a long time in the white version of what a Negro was supposed to be. But with the Muslim and civil-rights movements that went, too.

Since the August rioting, there has been little building here, little buying. Lots whose buildings were burned off them are still waiting vacant and littered with garbage, occupied only by a parked car or two, or kids fooling around after school, or winos sharing a pint in the early morning. The other day, on one of them, there were ground-breaking festivities, attended by a county supervisor, pretty high-school girls decked in ribbons, a white store owner and his wife, who in the true Watts spirit busted a bottle of champagne over a rock—all because the man had decided to stay and rebuild his $200,000 market, the first such major rebuilding since the riot.

Watts people themselves talk about another kind of aura, vaguely evil; complain that Negroes living in better neighborhoods like to come in under the freeway as to a red-light district, looking for some girl, some game, maybe some connection. Narcotics is said to be a rare bust in Watts these days, although the narco people cruise the area earnestly, on the lookout for dope fiends, dope rings, dope peddlers. But the poverty of Watts makes it more likely that if you have pot or a little something else to spare you will want to turn a friend on, not sell it. Tomorrow, or when he can, your friend will return the favor.

At the Deadwyler inquest, much was made of the dead man's high blood alcohol content, as if his being drunk made it somehow all right for the police to shoot him. But alcohol is a natural part of the Watts style; as natural as LSD is around Hollywood. The white kid digs hallucination simply because he is conditioned to believe so much in escape, escape as an integral part of life, because the white L.A. Scene makes accessible to him so many different forms of it. But a Watts kid, brought up in a pocket of reality, looks per-haps not so much for escape as just for some calm, some relaxa-tion. And beer or wine is good enough for that. Especially good at the end of a bad day.

Like after you have driven, say, down to Torrance or Long Beach or wherever it is they're hiring because they don't seem to be in Watts, not even in the miles of heavy industry that sprawl along Alameda Street, that gray and murderous arterial which lies at the eastern boundary of Watts looking like the edge of the world.

So you groove instead down the freeway, maybe wondering when some cop is going to stop you because the old piece of a car you're driving, which you bought for $20 or $30 you picked up somehow, makes a lot of noise or burns some oil. Catching you mobile widens The Man's horizons; gives him more things he can get you on. Like "excessive smoking" is a great favorite with him.

If you do get to where you were going without encountering a cop, you may spend your day looking at the white faces of personnel men, their uniform glaze of suspicion, their automatic smiles, and listening to polite putdowns. "I decided once to ask," a kid says, "one time they told me I didn't meet their requirements. So I said: 'Well, what are you looking for? I mean, how can I train, what things do I have to learn so I *can* meet your requirements?' Know what he said? 'We are not obligated to tell you what our requirements are.' "

He isn't. That right there is the hell and headache: he doesn't have to do anything he doesn't want to because he is The Man. Or he was. A lot of kids these days are more apt to be calling him the *little* man—meaning not so much any member of the power structure as just your average white L.A. taxpayer, registered voter, property owner; employed, stable, mortgaged and the rest.

The little man bugs these kids more than The Man ever bugged their parents. It is the little man who is standing on their feet and in their way; he's all over the place, and there is not much they can do to change him or the way he feels about them. A Watts kid knows more of what goes on inside white heads than possibly whites do themselves; knows how often the little man has looked at him and thought, "Bad credit risk"—or "Poor learner," or "Sexual threat," or "Welfare chiseler"—without knowing a thing about him personally.

The natural, normal thing to want to do is hit the little man. But what, after all, has he done? Mild, respectable, possibly smiling, he has called you no names, shown no weapons. Only told you perhaps that the job was filled, the house rented.

With a cop it may get more dangerous, but at least it's honest. You understand each other. Both of you silently admitting that all the cop really has going for him is his gun. "There was a time," they'll tell you, "you'd say, 'Take off the badge, baby, and let's settle it.' I mean he wouldn't, but you'd say it. But since August, man, the way I feel, hell with the badge—just take off that gun."

The cop does not take off that gun; the hassle stays verbal. But this means that, besides protecting and serving the little man, the cop also functions as his effigy.

If he does get emotional and says something like "boy" or "nigger," you then have the option of cooling it or else—again this is more frequent since last August—calling him the name he expects to be called, though it is understood you are not commenting in any literal way on what goes on between him and his mother. It is a ritual exchange, like the dirty dozens.

Usually—as in the Deadwyler incident—it's the younger cop of the pair who's more troublesome. Most Watts kids are hip to what's going on in this rookie's head—the things he feels he has to prove —as much as to the elements of the ritual. Before the cop can say, "Let's see your I.D.," you learn to take it out politely and say, "You want to see my I.D.?" Naturally it will bug the cop more the further ahead of him you can stay. It is flirting with disaster, but it's the cop who has the gun, so you do what you can.

You must anticipate always how the talk is going to go. It's something you pick up quite young, same as you learn the different species of cop: the Black and White (named for the color scheme of their automobiles), who are L.A. city police and in general the least flexible; the L.A. county sheriff's department, who style themselves more of an élite, try to maintain a certain distance from the public, and are less apt to harass you unless you seem worthy; the Compton city cops, who travel only one to a car and come on very tough, like leaning four of you at a time up against the wall and shaking you all down; the juvies, who ride in unmarked Plymouths and are cruising all over the place soon as the sun goes down, pulling up alongside you with pleasantries like, "Which one's buying the wine tonight?" or, "Who are you guys planning to rob this time?" They are kidding, of course, trying to be pals. But Watts kids, like most, do not like being put in with winos, or dangerous drivers or thieves, or in any bag considered criminal or evil. Whatever the cop's motives, it *looks* like mean and deliberate ignorance.

In the daytime, and especially with any kind of crowd, the cop's surface style has changed some since last August. "Time was," you'll hear, "man used to go right in, very mean, pick maybe one kid out of the crowd he figured was the troublemaker, try to bust him down in front of everybody. But now the people start yelling back, how they don't want no more of that, all of a sudden The Man gets very meek."

Still, however much a cop may seem to be following the order of the day read to him every morning about being courteous to everybody, his behavior with a crowd will really depend as it always has on how many of his own he can muster, and how fast. For his Mayor, Sam Yorty, is a great believer in the virtues of Overwhelming Force as a solution to racial difficulties. This approach has not gained much favor in Watts. In fact, the Mayor of Los Angeles appears to many Negroes to be the very incarnation of the little man: looking out for no one but himself, speaking always out of expediency, and never, never to be trusted.

The Economic and Youth Opportunities Agency (E.Y.O.A.) is a joint city-county "umbrella agency" (the state used to be represented, but has dropped out) for many projects scattered around the poorer parts of L.A., and seems to be Sam Yorty's native element, if not indeed the flower of his consciousness. Bizarre, confused, ever in flux, strangely ineffective, E.Y.O.A. hardly sees a day go by without somebody resigning, or being fired, or making an accusation, or answering one—all of it confirming the Watts Negroes' already sad estimate of the little man. The Negro attitude toward E.Y.O.A. is one of clear mistrust, though degrees of suspicion vary, from the housewife wanting only to be left in peace and quiet, who hopes that maybe The Man is lying less than usual this time, to the young, active disciple of Malcolm X who dismisses it all with a contemptuous shrug.

"But why?" asked one white lady volunteer. "There are so many agencies now that you *can* go to, that *can* help you, if you'll only file your complaint."

"They don't help you." This particular kid had been put down trying to get a job with one of the larger defense contractors.

"Maybe not before. But it's different now."

"Now," the kid sighed, *"now.* See, people been hearing that *'now'* for a long time, and I'm just tired of The Man telling you, 'Now it's OK, *now* we mean what we say.' "

In Watts, apparently, where no one can afford the luxury of illusion, there is little reason to believe that now will be any different, any better than last time.

It is perhaps a measure of the people's indifference that only 2 per cent of the poor in Los Angeles turned out to elect representatives to the E.Y.O.A. "poverty board." For a hopeless minority on the board (7 out of 23), nobody saw much point in voting.

Meantime, the outposts of the establishment drowse in the bright summery smog: secretaries chat the afternoons plaintively away about machines that will not accept the cards they have punched for them; white volunteers sit filing, doodling, talking on the phones, doing any kind of busy-work, wondering where the "clients" are; inspirational mottoes like SMILE decorate the beaverboard office walls along with flow charts to illustrate the proper disposition of "cases," and with clippings from the slick magazines about "What Is Emotional Maturity?"

Items like smiling and Emotional Maturity are in fact very big with the well-adjusted, middle-class professionals, Negro and white, who man the mimeographs and computers of the poverty war here. Sadly, they seem to be smiling themselves out of any meaningful communication with their poor. Besides a 19th-century faith that tried and true approaches—sound counseling, good intentions, perhaps even compassion—will set Watts straight, they are also burdened with the personal attitudes they bring to work with them. Their reflexes—especially about conformity, about failure, about violence—are predictable.

"We had a hell of a time with this one girl," a Youth Training and Employment Project counselor recalls. "You should have seen those hairdos of hers—piled all the way up to here. And the screwy outfits she'd come in with, you just wouldn't believe. We had to take her aside and explain to her that employers just don't go for that sort of thing. That she'd be up against a lot of very smooth-looking chicks, heels and stockings, conservative hair and clothes. We finally got her to come around."

The same goes for boys who like to wear Malcolm hats, or Afro haircuts. The idea the counselors push evidently is to look as much as possible like a white applicant. Which is to say, like a Negro job counselor or social worker. This has not been received with much enthusiasm among the kids it is designed to help out, and is one reason business is so slow around the various projects.

There is a similar difficulty among the warriors about failure. They are in a socio-economic bag, along with the vast majority of white Angelenos, who seem more terrified of failure than of death. It is difficult to see where any of them have experienced significant defeat, or loss. If they have, it seems to have been long rationalized away as something else.

You are likely to hear from them wisdom on the order of: "Life has a way of surprising us, simply as a function of time. Even if all you do is stand on the street corner and wait." Watts is full of street corners where people stand, as they have been, some of them, for 20 or 30 years, without Surprise One ever having come along. Yet the poverty warriors must believe in this form of semimiracle, because their world and their scene cannot accept the possibility that there may be, after all, no surprise. But it is something Watts has always known.

As for violence, in a pocket of reality such as Watts, violence is never far from you: because you are a man, because you have been put down, because for every action there is an equal and opposite reaction. Somehow, sometime. Yet to these innocent, optimistic child-bureaucrats, violence is an evil and an illness, possibly because it threatens property and status they cannot help cherishing.

They remember last August's riot as an outburst, a seizure. Yet what, from the realistic viewpoint of Watts, was so abnormal? "Man's got his foot on your neck," said one guy who was there, "sooner or later you going to stop *asking* him to take it off." The violence it took to get that foot to ease up even the little it did was no surprise. Many had predicted it. Once it got going, its basic objective—to beat the Black and White police—seemed a reasonable one, and was gained the minute The Man had to send troops in. Everybody seems to have known it. There is hardly a person in Watts now who finds it painful to talk about, or who regrets that it happened—unless he lost somebody.

But in the white culture outside, in that creepy world full of pre-cardiac Mustang drivers who scream insults at one another only when the windows are up; of large corporations where Niceguymanship is the standing order regardless of whose executive back one may be endeavoring to stab; of an enormous priest caste of shrinks who counsel moderation and compromise as the answer to all forms of hassle; among so much well-behaved unreality, it is next to impossible to understand how Watts may truly feel about violence. In terms of strict reality, violence may be a means to getting money, for example, no more dishonest than collecting exorbitant carrying charges from a customer on relief, as white merchants here still do. Far from a sickness, violence may be an attempt to communicate, or to be who you really are.

"Sure I did two stretches," a kid says, "both times for fighting, but

I didn't deserve either one. First time, the cat was bigger than I was; next time, it was two against one, and I was the one." But he was busted all the same, perhaps because Whitey, who knows how to get everything he wants, no longer has fisticuffs available as a technique, and sees no reason why everybody shouldn't go the Niceguy route. If you are thinking maybe there is a virility hangup in here, too, that putting a Negro into a correctional institution for fighting is also some kind of neutering operation, well, you might have something there, who knows?

It is, after all, in white L.A.'s interest to cool Watts any way it can—to put the area under a siege of persuasion; to coax the Negro poor into taking on certain white values. Give them a little property, and they will be less tolerant of arson; get them to go in hock for a car or color TV, and they'll be more likely to hold down a steady job. Some see it for what it is—this come-on, this false welcome, this attempt to transmogrify the reality of Watts into the unreality of Los Angeles. Some don't.

Watts is tough; has been able to resist the unreal. If there is any drift away from reality, it is by way of mythmaking. As this summer warms up, last August's riot is being remembered less as chaos and more as art. Some talk now of a balletic quality to it, a coordinated and graceful drawing of cops away from the center of the action, a scattering of The Man's power, either with real incidents or false alarms.

Others remember it in terms of music; through much of the rioting seemed to run, they say, a remarkable empathy, or whatever it is that jazz musicians feel on certain nights; everybody knowing what to do and when to do it without needing a word or a signal: "You could go up to anybody, the cats could be in the middle of burning down a store or something, but they'd tell you, explain very calm, just what they were doing, what they were going to do next. And that's what they'd do; man, nobody had to give orders."

Restructuring of the riot goes on in other ways. All Easter week this year, in the spirit of the season, there was a "Renaissance of the Arts," a kind of festival in memory of Simon Rodia, held at Markham Junior High, in the heart of Watts.

Along with theatrical and symphonic events, the festival also featured a roomful of sculptures fashioned entirely from found objects—found, symbolically enough, and in the Simon Rodia tradition, among the wreckage the rioting had left. Exploiting textures of charred wood, twisted metal, fused glass, many of the works were fine, honest rebirths.

In one corner was this old, busted, hollow TV set with a rabbit-ears antenna on top; inside, where its picture tube should have been, gazing out with scorched wiring threaded like electronic ivy among its crevices and sockets, was a human skull. The name of the piece was "The Late, Late, Late Show."

Odyssey of a Man – and a Movement

by Paul Good

JOHN LEWIS, former chairman of the Student Nonviolent Coordinating Committee in the days before black power, is 26, but he looks years older. He was among the first to sit-in, to be clubbed down on Freedom Rides, to be trampled at the Selma bridge. He has been in jail 40 times, in the White House six times, and these experiences have aged him. A few civil-rights leaders, including some who recently gathered in an urgent summit meeting as the tempo of race violence quickened in places like Tampa and Cincinnati, have experienced similar travail. But in the present welter of racial bitterness and threat, Lewis's experience uniquely illustrates important realities—not because he is singular, but because in his leadership role the part of Southern Black Everyman was played out to a melancholy conclusion.

As a boy Lewis chopped cotton on white man's land in Alabama and at 16 he was a Baptist minister, seemingly destined for a lifetime of preaching the gospel in a good black suit to "amen-ing" old ladies and drinking their lemonade from dime-store pitchers on sun-baked rural Sundays. Then the movement intervened and he found himself preaching civil rights to Catholic nuns in Wisconsin and downing martinis with Westchester liberals. For five years the movement became his life, he helping to shape it, it molding him. And suddenly one night, a year ago, it was all over.

On the night of June 24, 1966, both Lewis and the movement

From the *New York Times Magazine,* June 25, 1967.

he epitomized reached the symbolic and literal end of the road in Canton, Miss. No formal announcement was made that something was over in American life. To the public at large, Canton was just another stopping place on the Meredith March, that meandering trek through Mississippi begun after James Meredith tried to demonstrate that a controversial Negro could walk safely through the state and, for his temerity, was shot near the town of Hernando, Miss. (Meredith, his temerity undiminished, announced a few days later that he would resume his walk next weekend.) A few weeks before the march began, Lewis had been defeated by Stokely Carmichael for re-election as S.N.C.C. chairman. But beyond the fact of lost leadership, there would be deeper loss in Canton.

The march that arrived there had been plagued by disunity almost from the start with S.N.C.C. and CORE generally on the militant side, the N.A.A.C.P. blaring at them in bourgeois tones from the other side, and Dr. Martin Luther King's Southern Christian Leadership Conference somewhere in the middle. The press had harped on the differences until they seemed a stigma instead of a reflection of the natural economic and philosophic divisions among 25 million people in different stages of social development. During the march, the fusion of two words, black and power, had further divided blacks and antagonized whites the country over.

The marchers reached Canton on June 23. That evening Mississippi lawmen routed them when they tried to set up tents at the McNeil Elementary School, still segregated, like most Mississippi schools, 12 years after the U.S. Supreme Court decision. The Federal Government had reacted to this with legalisms, chiding march leaders for having broken state law by trespassing on school grounds. Law, after all, was law, even in a state where law, very often and despite the work of Congress and the Court, was not law.

The logic might be fuzzy, but in the hardening racial context of 1966 the Washington message seemed clear: America was a country tired of confronting its conscience. A majority of white people were sore from probes into racial nerves. The political emphasis was on image, not reality. Something that flared briefly in the national soul, a confession of racial guilt and a penitential urge toward reform, was now feeble.

A mantle of common cause still was draped over the march but it was slipping fast on that night of the 24th when men, women and children who had been clubbed and tear-gassed the previous evening returned to the school again in protest. But the leadership —split over black power, nonviolence and its judgment of the prevailing American mood—had decided against new confrontations in an acrimonious council. The knowledge of disunity was in the dark air as people stood and waited for their leaders on ground made soggy by state troopers who had opened water pipes in a final act of petty harassment.

The people wanted to do something, but no one knew what. The chunky form of Lewis rose on a shaky box. "Fellow freedom fighters," he said. "The whole man must say no nonviolently, his entire Christian spirit must say no to this evil and vicious system. . . ."

Even as he spoke, listeners sloshed away. The speaker's credentials were in order, but his time was out of joint. He spoke the old words of militant love, but the spiritual heart of the movement that for years had sent crusaders up and down American roads, trusting in love, was broken and Lewis had become that most expendable commodity, a former leader. It was not so much that he was losing his audience; the audience was already lost.

"That night in Canton I felt like the uninvited guest," Lewis says in a choppy Alabama accent. "It's hard to accept when something is over even though you know things have to change. In the beginning, with the sit-ins and Freedom Rides, things were much simpler. Or we thought they were. People just had to offer their bodies for their beliefs and it seemed like that would be enough, but it wasn't. By the time of Canton nobody knew what would be enough to make America right, and the atmosphere was very complicated, very negative."

About a month later the front page of The New York Times carried the headline: LEWIS QUITS S.N.C.C.; SHUNS BLACK POWER.

The headline's partial truths fitted the rationale of a white society that had tolerated racial injustice for a century, yet denounced "black power" in a day. At the same time, some in the society were paying sentimental homage to the good old days when Negroes faced fire hoses and police dogs with beatific smiles. Moderates lamented. If only Carmichael hadn't raised his raucous voice or Dr. King had stuck to nonviolence in the South instead of messing with Chicago housing or Vietnam. The rationale comforted Americans who had never been black, since it subtly shifted blame from oppressor to oppressed. Lewis, it followed, was a victim of his own kind.

Today he works for the Field Foundation, which supports civil-rights and child-welfare programs. He lives in a one-room apartment in Manhattan's crowded Chelsea district, an area of urban renewal and civic decay where civil rights are guaranteed but human destinies are often circumscribed. The apartment walls bear mementos from his life in the movement—a photograph with Senator Robert Kennedy, a Kenyan antelope-skin drum from an African tour and, next to it, a snapshot of two water fountains in an Alabama courthouse that shows a big electric cooler labeled White and a dinky bubbler marked Colored. The picture leads Lewis to talk about his origins as he sits on a daybed, his face habitually serious, his manner somewhat formal, befitting a properly brought up Southern boy.

Lewis was raised in Pike County, Ala., in a family with six brothers and three sisters. The landscape is red clay and green pine, the population 60 per cent white and the rest black. Pike and its county seat of Troy exist on a hard-scrabble economy of cotton, lumbering, peanuts, cattle and credit.

"When I grew up, white kids went to high school, Negroes to training school," he says. "You weren't supposed to aspire. We couldn't take books from the public library. And I remember that when the county paved rural roads they went 15 miles out of their way to avoid black-topping our Negro farm roads."

He also remembers watching Tarzan movies from the segregated balcony, he and his friends identifying with the tribesmen and cheering them on against Tarzan. These memories of clay roads dusty in summer and gluey with fall rain, of books denied and movie heroes with bones through their noses are only about a dozen years old. Yet many white Americans are impatient when Negroes don't forget all this promptly or when their recent past makes them wary of present white promises and advice.

Somehow, Lewis became converted to (some would say hooked on) nonviolent love early in life. He is not sure why.

"My mother is a good Christian but nonviolence was never a family topic," he says. "Sometimes my father wanted me to do chores instead of go to school, and I'd hide out to get the school bus. He'd catch hold of me later and he wasn't nonviolent."

Lewis was already a teenage preacher when the civil-rights gospel began spreading over the South. In 1957, he tried to apply to all-white Troy State College. His mother, fearful, wouldn't sign the papers. The classic ingredients of black American drama that so often ended in tragedy were beginning to mix: a boy moved to rebel against injustice, parents fearing the unknown content of change more than the reality of oppression.

In a broader American tradition, the cornball tradition of the poor boy who leaves the farm to struggle for an education in the big city, Lewis obtained a work scholarship at the all-Negro American Baptist Seminary in Nashville. Working as a janitor and pursuing a bland ministerial education, he encountered a transcendent personality in another student, James Lawson. A pacifist who had served time as a conscientious objector, Lawson is the generally unheralded spiritual father of the movement's belief in nonviolence and was a major influence on Martin Luther King.

"Lawson didn't talk much about demonstrations," Lewis recalls. "But he philosophized about keeping in harmony with the Christian faith until Christ's example wasn't something remote anymore. Your flesh could suffer like Christ's out of love. This was a strong current in the Nashville Student Movement that evolved into S.N.C.C. in 1960. You have to understand this to understand what S.N.C.C. was in the beginning."

By 1960, the Montgomery bus boycott was four years in the past. But aroused black emotions still were searching for direction and Nashville was the center of the ferment, particularly among young people filled with both urgency and frustration as they watched their slow-moving elders.

"When I'd come home and preach civil rights," says Lewis, "my mother would say: 'Preach the Bible, preach the Scripture.' She'd talk about my 'call,' and I'd say, 'Mama, if I'm called by God, why can't I do what He tells me to preach?' "

Lewis was arrested half a dozen times during the 1960 sit-ins, but that was only a prelude to the 1961 Freedom Rides. For many veterans of the movement, those days were a combination of Dickens's French Revolution ("... the best of times . . . the worst of times . . .") and America's own frontier days. The risks were so grave, the rewards to the spirit so satisfying that it was difficult for many participants, and impossible for some, ever to adjust to the prosaic tasks of black political and economic organization. Lewis himself may be a victim of that fearful glory.

It seems a very long national time ago when CORE sponsored 13 volunteers who left Washington, D. C., on two regularly scheduled buses heading into the territory of Jim Crow. It was May 4, 1961, only six years ago. One bus was burned in Anniston, Ala., and riders were beaten at other stops. The atmosphere was murderous.

"CORE called off the rides as too dangerous," Lewis recalls. "Robert Kennedy was Attorney General and he wanted a cooling-off period. The Nashville Christian Leadership Council—an affiliate of Dr. King's Southern Christian Leadership Council—said it was suicidal. A group of mainly young people decided we had to go on. On Wednesday morning, May 18—no, May 17—three young ladies and seven guys left Nashville for Birmingham. Eight Negroes and a white young lady and a white boy. Jim Zwerg was his name. All those names come back of people you never see again."

They were arrested in Birmingham, went on a hunger strike and two days later, in the predawn hours, were driven by the police to the Alabama-Tennessee line and dumped out near the town of Ardmore. "It was still dark. We didn't know if whites were waiting to welcome us, so we hunted up the railroad tracks because colored families always live by them. There was an old Negro couple in a shack, scared to death, but they took us in.

"At first light, the old man went out to get some food. He went to half a dozen stores, buying a little bread, a little milk and baloney in each one so as not to arouse suspicions. We called Nashville to send a car, talking in a kind of code. You know, 'Pick up the packages in Ardmore.'

"A boy—Leo Lillard; he lives in Brooklyn now and I just spoke to him the other day for the first time again—drove down and we started back to Birmingham to get another bus. A bulletin came in on the car radio with the exact highway we were on and saying we were going to Birmingham. We were plenty frightened. But we took side roads and managed to get into the city."

On the morning of May 20 the bus reached the apparently empty Montgomery terminal. Scores of whites, hidden in doorways, rushed out and in the absence of protective Federal presence or local police (the terminal was half a block from police headquarters) they went to work. Lewis was knocked unconscious for 45 minutes. As he came to, an Alabama official served him with a court order barring integrated travel.

The battered riders regrouped, although black and white elders again counseled against continuing. With some Northern reinforcements, including a cool New Yorker named Stokely Carmichael, they took the bus to Jackson. There were more beatings, arrests and sentences to the state penitentiary.

"I came out very disturbed that America had left it up to a few students to do what had to be done," says Lewis. "But I was still convinced that nonviolence was the right way. The whole idea of beating people into submission should have died out with the early Christians and Romans. You're not submitting when you're a victim of violence. You're exerting a much greater force."

Each year of the movement has had a special flavor. After 1961, characterized by improvised daring, 1962 was largely a time of regrouping to plan attacks on the monolith of Southern segregation. In Mississippi, a campus-sized Civil War erupted when James Meredith enrolled at Ole Miss with the legal backing of the N.A.A.-C.P. and an army of U.S. marshals. The nation at large was outraged by the violent Mississippi defiance and white public opinion outside the South allied emotionally with the movement. In 1963, a year of horrors as well as hope, the magnetism of epic change in the making drew Lewis from Fisk University, where he was studying philosophy, into permanent action.

The S.N.C.C. chairmanship fell vacant and he was elected unanimously. He became titular head of an organization already in flux, its original Southern element stirred by Northern recruits. Bohemianism was rubbing shoulders with old-time religion; nonviolence was alternately a creed and a tactic. Black Southern youth who saw salvation in the right to vote heard disillusioning Northern tales of ghettos that generations of black ballots could not vote away. Lewis was the embodiment of a deep paradox. Here was a young man of rural courtliness and moral high-mindedness, a square even, leading a group that generally disdained bourgeois manners and morals as just another American hangup.

His cherished concept of nonviolence passed through one crucible after another. Soon after his election, Mississippi N.A.A.C.P. leader Medgar Evers was murdered. Demonstrations in Birmingham made police dogs and fire hoses synonymous with Southern repression, the orgy of white violence culminating in the Birmingham church bombing that killed four Negro girls. Lewis—only three years off an Alabama farm—was called to the White House with other civil-rights leaders for emergency meetings with President Kennedy.

Despite violence and sluggish Federal reaction, the movement in

1963 drew hope from press and television coverage which dramatically presented a modern morality play to the nation. Good was clearly black people, marching lamblike and singing hymns; evil was the white face that spat and sneered. In August, the March on Washington struck an exultant chord. Lewis, for all the innate contradictions between himself and S.N.C.C., was God's angry young man in the original speech he prepared for the march:

"We will march through the South, through the heart of Dixie, the way Sherman did. We shall pursue our own 'scorched earth' policy and burn Jim Crow to the ground—nonviolently."

The tone so upset white liberal sponsors like Walter Reuther and Negroes like Roy Wilkins that the program at the Lincoln Memorial was held up until Lewis changed it to:

"If we do not get meaningful legislation out of this Congress, the time will come when we will not confine our march to Washington. We will march through the streets of Jackson . . . Danville . . . Cambridge . . . Birmingham. But we will march with the spirit of love and with the spirit of dignity that we have shown here today."

By 1964, President Kennedy was dead and the Johnson Administration, convinced that Federal inaction would bring internal disorder and international obloquy, pressed for a civil-rights bill to open up public accommodations. Negroes following Dr. King in St. Augustine sought to spur passage by inviting racist excesses as they sang "God Will Take Care of You" into the teeth of white mobs. The bill passed but many Negroes thought such nonviolence a singular way to lobby for legislation in a democracy.

That spring Lewis was unanimously re-elected S.N.C.C. chairman. S.N.C.C. and CORE decided to attack the stoutest segregationist bastion, Mississippi, and planned the Freedom Summer of 1964 to send volunteers into the state.

They cast a net of conscience over American youth and gathered in a mixed bag—young people wise and witless, God-inspired and beat, reformers and social renegades. The catch recalled the self-descriptive words written by an abolitionist 100 years before: "We are what we are. Babes, sucklings, obscure men, silly women, publicans, sinners and we shall manage this matter just as might be expected of such persons as we are. It is unbecoming in abler men who stood by and would do nothing to complain of us because we could do no better."

The press was beginning to prove itself an undependable chronicler in depths beyond the episodic. With few exceptions, it observed with fascinated repulsion the surface aspects of volunteers' beards or black boy–white girl pairing instead of digging deep into the social and economic cul-de-sac into which America's history had forced black men throughout the country. Adult newsmen—attitudes slightly corpulent and bedeviled by their mature anxieties over careers, sex and money —were suspicious of and, in turn, scorned by volunteers going their lean, instinctual way, indulging their sexual vigor, making progress and mistakes with the same reckless abandon, with nothing much at stake. Except possibly their lives.

After three rights workers were murdered in Neshoba County, F.B.I. Director J. Edgar Hoover arrived in Jackson to decry what he called an "overemphasis" on civil rights, declaring his bureau "most certainly" would not offer protection to volunteers. Such sentiments had a traumatic effect on Negroes in general and S.N.C.C. members in particular since they were under the gun. S.N.C.C. skepticism about American justice became institutionalized. Many white "friends" deplored the attitude, but they had not been there.

Lewis skipped around the country fund-raising, and, he concedes, often losing touch with troops in the field. Meanwhile, the independent Mississippi Freedom Democratic party ran into the facts of political life at the 1964 Democratic convention in Atlantic City. The regular Mississippi Democratic party historically had disregarded nondiscriminatory laws when choosing delegations and had disloyally backed Republican and Dixiecrat nominees.

But when the M.F.D.P. sought to unseat it, columnists and commentators warned that the movement was naively seeking a moral solution to a political problem. President Johnson confirmed their judgment by ordaining a "compromise" that tossed two at-large seats to the rebels while seating the regulars. Negroes were left to ponder: If morality and politics were mutually exclusive, then why go on with hymn-singing forbearance? Atlantic City was a milestone on the movement's road to final disillusion in Canton.

By 1965, though Lewis was still doggedly following his star of brotherhood through nonviolence, many in S.N.C.C. weren't following him. The John Lewis who on March 7 led a band of black people across the Selma bridge toward Montgomery bore little relevance to his own organizations. Trudging toward a motley posse of helmeted men, Lewis wore a light coat, dark suit, shirt and tie, and had a bedroll neatly slung over his shoulders. He looked like a minister leading his Sunday School class on a jolly outing. But anyone watching who knew Lewis might have bled for him, since he made no secret of the fear he felt that faith could not quiet.

The first truncheon cracked his head in the same spot as the blow that felled him on the Freedom Ride, and he slumped to his knees with a concussion. America saw it all on television and was predictably, though momentarily, appalled. But many Negroes in S.N.-C.C. thought that John Lewis was a Christ-loving damn fool to have crossed that bridge.

"I felt after Selma that it was my last demonstration," Lewis said later. "We're only flesh. I could understand people not wanting to be beaten anymore. The body gets tired. You put out so much energy and you saw such little gain. Black capacity to believe white would really open his heart, open his life to nonviolent appeal was running out."

Faster than he knew. Lewis was re-elected chairman of S.N.C.C. in 1965, but this time there were many opponents, Carmichael among them. A massive deterioration of white credibility in Negro eyes was taking place and Lewis could no more prevent it than nascent black nationalism could take credit for it. White conscience seemed to need black sacrifice to stimulate it, and often lapsed when black militancy insisted on human prerogatives beyond the letter of the law. White conscience, many Negroes were concluding, was a sometime thing.

The Voting Rights Act of 1965 passed. Whites predicted a black wave. But figures showed that in five Deep South states, only 60 of 418 counties had a potential Negro voting majority. Nothing less could break racist control and experience would demonstrate that in only a dozen of those counties could barriers of tradition and economic intimidation be surmounted.

S.N.C.C. limped through a desultory year in 1965, frustrated and edgy with black-white internal tensions. It needed revitalization but John Lewis could not provide it. The body *was* tired.

"I came to believe that maybe the scars of racism couldn't be erased in my lifetime," he says. "But some people inside S.N.C.C. were moving into a fantasy world where mountains had to be moved right away. They were filled with self-righteousness and closed themselves off from anyone who disagreed. The ideal of nonviolence came under question. But as far as I was concerned, with a goal of the the world community at peace with itself, methods had to be consistent with the goal. Maybe I was at fault because I couldn't adapt. But I couldn't.'"

"Some old S.N.C.C. veterans still respected him," says John Wise, now S.N.C.C.'s executive director. "But a lot of new ones didn't have that feeling. The old day of love was gone."

S.N.C.C. began last year by denouncing the draft and the Vietnam war, and Lewis concurred. Despite the fact that Negroes were over-represented in Vietnam and underrepresented on draft boards, the position assured S.N.C.C.'s continued unpopularity on the American scene. Lewis himself was the first Negro in Alabama history to be granted C.O. status. The Justice Department successfully intervened in his case after an obdurate local board chairman told Lewis: "But *we're* all Baptists and *we're* not C.O.'s."

S.N.C.C. still was receiving White House invitations in 1966 and Lewis planned to participate in the June conference President Johnson had scheduled under the title, "To Fulfill These Rights." He went to a preliminary meeting in March under the impression that the conference and pending civil-rights legislation would be discussed.

"But all the President wanted to talk about was Democratic losses in the coming Congressional elections," says Lewis. "He kept saying, 'I need your help, you have to help me.' It was embarrassing. Consensus. He must have used that word a dozen times. But there wasn't any consensus anymore. Why should all Negroes think alike? And who could be patient seeing the war getting bigger and the poverty program tightening up?"

What had begun simply with a bus ride was foundering on domestic and foreign complexities. On April 21, 1966, in Nashville, Lewis was defeated for re-election by Carmichael in an atmosphere charged with racial polarity. Lewis had favored a black-directed movement, with whites taking their place inside it. Carmichael sought the essence of insularity that had characterized the political battles of other minority groups. When the Irish in New York, for example, had originally formed their political organizations, Italians and Jews were not invited in. Whether the analogy was valid could be debated, but the notion that Negroes, in the best American tradition, had to do for themselves, by themselves, was not as radical as it was made to appear.

Carmichael's cry of "Black Power" caught the nation in a mood of rearoused racism. White Chicagoans were furiously opposing open housing, and new civil-rights legislation that would affect North and South was bogged down in Congress. The press pounced on Carmichael's careless rhetoric and establishment Negroes like Roy Wilkins equated Black Power with Nazism.

The movement, like a gem scored for cutting, had long been ready to come apart and Black Power supplied the final tap. Bitterness among all parties accompanied the split, and John Lewis decided his role was no longer effective. He resigned from S.N.C.C.

"Part of it I can see now was ego," he says. "Losing the election hurt. Part of it was Canton, reviving all the white violence and making black people so disillusioned. But mostly it was the bitterness all around that turned me. Some people wanted retaliatory violence. But even as a practical measure, how many people are you going to attract to a program based on violence? It might deliver some quick solutions, but in the long run it debases you. I felt I owed an allegiance to a higher principle than S.N.C.C. It was as simple as that."

The consequences weren't simple. He was charged with running out. His highest S.N.C.C. salary had been $40 a week and he was broke. The limited life of a church pastor no longer would satisfy. During years when other young men were perfecting educations or starting careers, he was sitting-in, going limp, getting jailed. As it did for many movement veterans, it all made peculiar reading on a job résumé.

The Field Foundation offer meant leaving the South and Lewis took a long train ride up to New York, the kind where the landscape of a young man's country and his years slip by. "It was lonesome, leaving the movement," he says. "I kept thinking, 'Where am I going, and why, why?' But I also felt liberated. I thought it was ordained because there was nothing left for men to do in the movement. And truthfully, it was good to be going toward a real job and to know that for the first time I'd be earning enough to send something home to my family."

Today, Lewis is learning to live with ambivalence. When Tampa Negroes riot after police shoot a black suspect, he feels he should be on the scene. But he is puzzled over what he or anybody else can do as the racial climate seems inexorably to worsen. Lewis is proud of S.N.C.C.'s accomplishments when he was chairman but painfully aware of its failures and its present debilitated condition.

The organization he left is now a small, embattled group of about

50 young pariahs struggling to stay alive. The only offices still functioning are in New York, Washington, Atlanta and San Francisco,
and while there is brave talk of programming, the programs are not
much in evidence. Carmichael—swashbuckler of Black Power—has
been replaced by Rap Brown, an experienced Southern field organizer but an unknown quantity as leader. Persons close to S.N.-
C.C. believe that Carmichael had become too hot for even S.N.C.C.
to handle if it wanted to maintain liaison with other black and white
civil-rights groups. Lewis does not know Brown well. Those who
do say he is philosophically a Black Power militant but determined
to be less visible and vocal than Carmichael. But the question of his
qualities may be academic. Without a power base, alienated from
most white liberals and a target of opportunity for forces out to
squelch any sign of black self-assertion, S.N.C.C. in its present form
has a limited life expectancy.

Looking back on the year since that night in Canton, Lewis sees
a steady growth of reaction in the North and South—the election
victories of Lester Maddox in Georgia and Lurleen Wallace in
Alabama, the defeat in New York of a police review board, the viru-
lent press campaign against Dr. King's Vietnam position.

"The Vietnam debate lets a lot of plain racism come out as patriotism," he says. "The Government is contradictory, telling oppressed black men not to be violent in the streets while it carries
out the terrible slaughter in Vietnam and finances it with money it
should be spending to get things right at home.

"Black conditions in the rural South are desperate. In Mississippi,
Negro faith in the democratic process is being strained. The Johnson Administration has been out to break the Freedom party ever
since Atlantic City, deliberately using programs like Head Start to
lure people away from their first hope for political independence and
back under the white thumb. And at the same time, Vice President
Humphrey takes the arm of Lester Maddox to show there is Democratic consensus."

Not long ago, Lewis returned home for a visit. After all his wan-
derings, the illusion of permanence moved him—the house of concrete blocks with its wide breezy porch looking out on his father's
fields and a pecan grove.

A few things in Pike County had changed for the better and it
was satisfying to know he had played a part. His parents were voting for the first time, albeit for white-picked candidates, and his

brothers were taking books from the library. But they still attended segregated schools and no jobs were available except the old ones, like bagboy in the local A&P. Most of the men in his family still at home would eventually go North, following the established pattern. One 24-year-old brother married early, has four children and lives in a rented shack.

"He works cutting pulpwood." Lewis says. "That's all there is. No factories and nobody to build them. The only wealth is land and the good land stays in white hands. He's going to be working hard for nothing the rest of his life."

Lewis felt stymied by these realities. He looked into white Southern faces and saw no spiritual change, only grudging retreat from the old authoritarianism under pressure of law whose enforcement depends on the white national mood.

While he cannot conceive of Negroes slipping back as they did after Reconstruction, he is fearful that the opportunity for the creation of the "beloved community" of black and white together is being lost to bitterness. Black hopes would be again betrayed. On his way back to New York, he rode the integrated bus from Troy to Montgomery and at the terminal he walked to the spot where he had been beaten on that Saturday morning in 1961. He says he stood there, letting his memory flow back and forth over all that had happened since then. He had taken his various beatings dry-eyed. But in that moment, John Lewis almost cried.

When Black Power Runs the New Left

by Walter Goodman

If things begin to get out of hand—if for example your child begins to take advantage of your permissiveness—it's harder to find your way back onto the right track. The child makes you mad, all right, but the madder you get the guiltier you feel for fear you'll step into the very pattern you were determined to avoid. Of course, I'm making all this sound too black and white.
> —"Baby and Child Care" by Dr. Benjamin Spock.

FOR THOSE PAST the age of 30 who wish to understand wherein the New Left differs from the old Left and from its own ideal of itself, the National Conference for New Politics (N.C.N.P.) "Convention on 1968 and Beyond" which met in Chicago over a frenetic Labor Day weekend presents a mine of enlightenment. Some 3,000 people from 200-odd groups working for peace in Vietnam (Women Strike for Peace), justice for the black man (Mississippi Freedom Democratic Party), electoral victories (Berkeley-Oakland Community for New Politics) and a better life for the poor (Summit County [Ohio] Adequate Welfare Committee) gathered in the Palmer House to decide on the course of the movement.

Votes were allocated among the delegates depending on how many activists their organizations had back home—200 votes for the Bergen County Democratic Council, 31 votes for the Camden Citizens for Peace in Vietnam. On that basis, of the 33,500 votes distributed in the convention, about 5,000 represented black organizations. There were also "observers" from sympathetic organizations such as the National Lawyers Guild and freelance "representatives" —people who belonged to no organization but received one vote apiece for putting in an appearance.

The convention call—"Don't Mourn for America—ORGANIZE!" had been issued by the N.C.N.P., a group of prominent and obscure advocates of a new structure which would transfer power from the various Establishments to the poor and voiceless. Its co-chairmen were Julian Bond, the solitary black member of the Georgia House of Representatives, and Simon Casady, a dissident Democrat from California. On the 25-man steering committee were David Frost, who ran for the U.S. Senate on a peace ticket in New Jersey; Arthur Waskow of the Institute for Policy Studies in Washington, D. C.; Benjamin Spock, M.D.; as well as representatives of the Student Nonviolent Coordinating Committee, the Southern Christian Leadership Conference and several local New Politics organizations.

Any democratic group committed "to some form of organizing work in the community" and willing "to conceivably endorse an independent candidate at some time" was eligible to participate in the convention. Some of those in attendance harbored hopes of a third party Presidential ticket in 1968 led by Martin Luther King, Jr., and Dr. Spock.

The convention had some features predictable at such gatherings. IMPEACH JOHNSON CENTENNIAL buttons ran a close second to BLACK POWER buttons. A couple of hippies called on those who would listen to free themselves from personal hang-ups before they undertook to free the world. Two photographers were slugged and rude words were scratched on the elevator doors. There were pleasing juxtapositions, too. On Sunday, this put-down of the middle class was flanked by a bridge tournament and a Jewish wedding reception.

The most striking and attractive aspect of the meeting was its youth. Even if we include several score ladies from Women Strike for Peace, gentlemen from SANE, remnant trade unionists, and Communist party personages looking indecently old, most delegates were under 30. There was even a high school caucus.

For voting purposes the delegations were grouped in the ballroom by states, but most of the young people were affiliated with exceedingly local enterprises. Activists rather than ideologues, their vista was the neighborhood rather than the nation, and they had little in common with most of the names signed to the convention call. But though the young were the heart of the assembly (as they are the heart of the movement) the remarkable events that churned around them originated elsewhere in the body.

Symptomatic of the occasion was the opening night rally on Thursday, Aug. 31. While the New Politicians inside the Chicago Coliseum were being soothed by Martin Luther King, entertained by Dick Gregory and informed by William Pepper, executive director of N.C.N.P., that they were taking part in "the most significant gathering of Americans since the Declaration of Independence," outside a bongo group was chanting "Kill Whitey . . . Kill Whitey . . . Kill Whitey . . . Kill Whitey. . . ."

As events turned out, Whitey seemed to share the bongo group's sentiments.

The N.C.N.P. steering committee, composed of persons on the cooler end of the New Left's vivid political spectrum, lost control of their convention even before its official opening on Thursday evening.

As delegates were gathering on Tuesday to start preconvention consideration of resolutions, credentials and such, about 100 youths from Chicago's black ghettos confronted the organization with its first crisis. The youths complained that they had not been consulted in the planning for the affair and demanded separate, if not entirely equal, facilities for their own deliberations.

According to irate N.C.N.P. leaders, a large number of the intruding blacks were "Chicago crazies," "thugs," "ghetto psychotics," "suicidal types." But they also included spokesmen from CORE and Chicago ACT who were sufficiently sophisticated to charge the radical sponsors of the convention with the mortifying liberal crime of "political paternalism." The sponsors, pledged to an "open convention," could hardly renounce for their own convenience the principle of black power which they endorse. They provided the protesting youths with accommodations in a hotel meeting room, hoping that more moderate black delegates would soon take over. (In radical politics, the term "Negro" is reserved for members of the N.A.A.C.P. and the Urban League.)

But when the more moderate blacks arrived they were drawn into the entrenched group—some, it was rumored, by threats of violence, some simply by the pressure to show that they could be as tough as the toughest Black Nationalist in dealing with a white power structure. Thus was conceived the Black Caucus that was to rule the convention from tumultuous beginning to fatigued end.

Shortly before proceedings began a staff member was asked whether there was any danger that the meeting would fall under the control of some particular group, say the Communists (whose presence in the Palmer House gave The Chicago Tribune something to expose for several days running). He replied, "We've structured this meeting so that it's uncontrollable; the question is whether it's manageable."

In the resolutions committee, delegates were encouraged to pitch in with their notions about L.S.D. and free sexual play as well as about Vietnam. They abused the privilege enthusiastically. On the floor, which contained few black faces at the first plenary session on Friday, the delegates got themselves into a tangle of points of order and points of personal privilege and motions and amendments to motions that Sam Rayburn himself would have been hard put to sort out. "Will the body cool it, please?" the even-tempered young chairman, Gary Weissman, appealed as chaos periodically descended.

One after the other, the speakers delivered their condemnation of American society from top to middle, bringing to mind the remark that Caesar is supposed to have made on first hearing Brutus speak in public: "I know not what this young man intends, but whatever he intends he intends vehemently."

But order, of a kind, was soon to be restored, with a vengeance. The impending discipline was proclaimed by Floyd McKissick of CORE: "Black people can't be a plank in someone else's platform. They must be the platform itself."

In the early hours of Saturday the convention received the black platform, a 13-point document which, among other things, called for 50 per cent black representation on all committees; condemnation of the "imperialist Zionist war" (which "does not imply anti-Semitism"); efforts in white communities to "humanize the savage and beastlike character that runs rampant through America, as exemplified by George Lincoln Rockwells and Lyndon Baines Johnsons"; and support for all resolutions passed by the recent black power conference in Newark, which, so far as a generous sampling of opinion could determine, nobody in the Palmer House that Saturday had read. The Black Caucus demanded that its program be accepted unamended by 1 P.M.

"This whole thing has been a nightmare to me," said Dr. Carlton Goodlett, a Negro member of the California Democratic Council and the N.C.N.P. steering committee, who argued for moderation within the Black Caucus on the grounds that "no revolution has ever succeeded without the middle class and professionals." Despite substantial differences of opinion among black delegates, Dr. Goodlett wistfully reported, "My advice wasn't too well taken."

Among whites, opposition centered on the character of the ultimatum and the reference to "Zionist imperialism." A New Jersey organizer told the meeting that if a bunch of whites had presented him with 13 points on a take-them-or-leave-them basis, he would have replied, "Shove it!" He saw no reason to respond differently to a bunch of blacks. "We're being asked to flagellate our liberal consciences," declared a young man from Oakland, Calif., who plans to try for local office in his middle-class community.

Robert Scheer, an editor of Ramparts who ran well in a 1966 Democratic Congressional primary in California, suggested modifying the resolution on Israel to call on Israel to withdraw to her pre-June borders in return for a commitment from the Arabs to respect those borders, but the body's mood was such that he withdrew the proposal. "What right has the white man got amending the black man's resolution?" yelled a member of the Black Caucus. A young man stomped away from the Indiana section after a hot argument with the cry, *"Goyim* do not understand Zionism!"

As for the proponents, they took their lead from Mrs. Septima Clarke, an elderly lady associated with the Southern Christian Leadership Conference, who put it to whites that this was a test of their "social barometer."

Most whites on hand agreed. "I'm not going to quibble over words," said a girl from New York's Lower East Side, "while Negroes are dying in the streets of Newark and Detroit." The secretary of a handful of trade unionists called a "labor caucus" said the 13 points were "a cry for help from people who are bleeding." A lady from Arlington, Va., who tried to get in a few words for "little Israel" was roundly booed.

The Black Caucus scorned requests to clarify any provision of their manifesto. "Who speaks for the Black Caucus?" called the chairman, seeking answers to delegates' questions, but no one replied. It was quite mysterious.

The convention's planners were shaken by the ultimatum. One major figure in the N.C.N.P. told me he doubted that most of the delegates understood the consequences of their vote on the 13 points: "We don't have any urban blacks and if we pass the black resolution we ruin ourselves among white liberals." But the delegates couldn't have cared less about the embarrassment of the N.C.N.P., an organization that barely exists apart from the ambitions of its founders.

A principal founder, Arthur Waskow, a portly figure with the most impressive beard of the occasion, bustled about trying to put through a compromise on the ultimatum. It would have acknowledged the 13 points as a statement of the Black Caucus rather than the position of the entire body, but he could not even get it introduced on the floor. If such a resolution had been introduced and passed, the Black Caucus was prepared to make a dramatic exit—as its most militant element was urging in any case.

Even whites who disagreed with one or two or more of the 13 points were eager to vote for them as a gesture of trust and sympathy for a suffering people who, it was argued, were leading America's forces of liberation. Other whites had other reasons. Some wanted to prevent a public split at any cost. A few, like the representatives of California's minuscule Peace and Freedom party, had politics on their minds—"If we don't vote for this resolution, we're dead in the black areas of Los Angeles."

But it was passion, not strategy, that carried the day. As one N.C.N.P. planner described it, "An extraordinary development took place. The walls of the Palmer House began to drip with guilt."

So the 13 points were accepted by a 3-1 majority. The ladies from Women Strike for Peace, somewhat taken aback by the reference to Israel, abstained. At least two Jewish members of the N.C.N.P. board were poised upon the brink of resignation but did not jump. A delegate from Manhattan's Riverside Democrats expressed the minority's bitterness after the vote: "They came in and said, 'Accept this or we'll fix you!' Well, they'll fix us anyway." But the large majority treated themselves to a standing ovation.

Having come together in a convention pledged to "reflect your goals, your programs and your plans . . . through the process of participatory democracy," the new Jacobins acclaimed their compliance with an ultimatum.

Sunday's session further enhanced the dominant mood of the meeting—the desire to show that the whites at this convention were of a different breed from liberal Democrats, who play up to blacks only in order to manipulate them.

Having been invited to appear, James Forman of S.N.C.C. filled the stage with his entourage, which starred bodyguards in what appeared to be African garb. They stood at the rostrum while their leader spoke, grimly scrutinizing the white radicals below. Many of the prominent New Politicians—Waskow, Scheer, Paul Booth, Martin Peretz—left the room during Forman's performance, but the remaining whites fairly tingled with pleasure under the whiplash of his demagogy. H. Rap Brown declined to appear before an integrated audience, thereby depriving himself of an ovation from the honkies.

A flurry of dissent met Forman's method of cajoling the body into passing impromptu resolutions, such as one calling for a boycott of all General Motors 1968 models, without going through the parliamentary niceties. He simply told people to stand up if they agreed with him and declared the resolution carried. "That's dictatorship," a Chicago lady objected. "All right, I'm a dictator," called back Forman. This, finally, prompted cries of protest, whereupon Forman clowned, "Jesus Christ, man, can't we have *any* fun?" The audience chuckled itself back into a condition to cheer when he told them, "We're going to liberate you whether you like it or not!"

His promise was redeemed a few hours later when the Black Caucus returned to the ballroom with its second major demand. Now they wanted 50 per cent of the voting power on the convention floor. That is, instead of settling for the 5,000-odd votes which black groups had been accorded on the basis of the numbers of activists they allegedly represented, the Black Caucus wanted 28,498 votes—as many as all the white delegations put together. Since the Black Caucus was acting as a bloc, this meant control of the convention.

"I hope they have the guts to turn it down," said an N.C.N.P. planner evidently not attuned to the spirit in the hall.

The justification for acceding to the Black Caucus owed less to the philosophy of Dr. Spock than to that of the more permissive Dr. Gesell. Again it was a case of trust. "These guys want to be trusted," explained co-chairman Simon Casady to a delegate who felt that the black humor was wearing thin. "We have to show them we trust them." (Casady's co-chairman, Julian Bond, had the good luck or good sense to leave Chicago before the first plenary session was called to order.)

No member of the Black Caucus participated in the 50 per cent debate; they were under instructions not even to applaud as their white advocates called for trust, trust, trust. A big white war veteran hollered at the audience that 50 per cent of the front line troops in Vietnam were blacks and niggling now over democratic processes would lead to the victory of fascism. The Black Caucus, joined for a time by James Forman and bodyguards, occupied a reserved-seat section up front, under a standard marked BLACK, like players in the Reconstruction scenes of "The Birth of a Nation." When one black man, or perhaps he was a Negro, attempted to speak, two others ran over to him, whispered a few words in his ear and he sat down.

Waskow, disputing the argument that the blacks would cooperate once they had charge of things, declared fervently: "If you castrate a man, you don't sleep with him afterwards." Though perhaps the highpoint of a weekend excruciatingly short on eloquence, his indignation proved ineffective.

The demand for 50 per cent of the vote swept through by a 2-1 margin, with the W.S.P. ladies casting more than 800 of their 1,000 votes for the proposition.

"We have just shown the nation that black people can fight," announced Carlos Russell, a Brooklyn antipoverty worker who identified himself as chairman of the Black Caucus. Then he formally took over the meeting on behalf of a group which represented, at best, a sixth of the convention's constituency and had no noticeable program beyond the humiliation of their white comrades.

A woman from Wisconsin stood up and sadly burned her delegation card, good now for 15 worthless votes. "This is the old politics, not the new politics," she said and went home.

Lending a nostalgic note to the coup was the sudden open appearance of the Communists. "My God," exclaimed a staff member as one after another got the microphone to urge 50 per cent of the vote for the Black Caucus, "they've surfaced!" The Communists and a number of egregious fellow travelers were conspicuously present in the Palmer House, but until Sunday they had conducted their inimitable machinations in private.

During the 50 per cent debate, however, C.P. members and their young allies from the W. E. B. DuBois Clubs came forward as the chief spokesmen for the black demands. The first one to surface, a portly lad from the party's youth division, received an ovation when he argued for the 50 per cent proposal on the grounds that blacks constitute a separate nation in America and hence are entitled to the same number of votes as the white nation.

The reasons for the show of fraternity were not hard to fathom. The Communists mainly sought from the convention a commitment to a third party race in 1968 which could give them their first opportunity since the 1948 Progressive party debacle to break out of political isolation.

The proposed King-Spock ticket had been scotched early when it became clear that the black militants would not accept Dr. King, whom they consider a milquetoast. Nonetheless, the Communists hoped that the Black Caucus, in which they had representatives, would evidence its gratitude for support on the 50 per cent issue by voting in favor of the principle of a third ticket.

In fact, the third-ticket question had already come before the delegates on Saturday afternoon, while the Black Caucus was out caucusing. (When Manhattan Councilman Theodore Weiss, a previous guest speaker, raised the possibility of working through the Democratic party to defeat Lyndon Johnson, he was booed by everyone for committing the sin of "lesser evilism." References to Robert Kennedy, incidentally, evoked louder hoots than references to Barry Goldwater.)

The chief supporters of a third ticket were predominantly middle-aged delegates, a number of whom had fond memories of Henry Wallace and all that. Most young local activists vehemently opposed an independent ticket, fearing that a national race would divert money and energy from their grassroots work. Some of them were prepared to leave the convention if the N.C.N.P. committed itself to a third ticket. The proper concern of the New Left, argued a spokesman for Ohioans for a Reasonable Settlement in Vietnam, "is not to capture the old structure but parallel it with a parastructure in neighborhood, factory, Congressional district and—perhaps —even in Congress."

Finally, a compromise was reached in the form of a resolution that put the N.C.N.P. on record as opposing a national third party or ticket, but favoring independent Presidential slates in 1968 in states (namely California) where local groups felt the basis for a campaign existed.

This was the situation on Sunday, which the Communists tried to undo. They were blocked by a surprising development.

The 50 per cent victory had strengthened the moderates within the Black Caucus; the white brothers, after all, had demonstrated incontestably their willingness not only to cooperate with blacks but to serve under them. The most militant blacks, who had been seeking an excuse to break away ("We don't want no more of this jive!") had by now drifted off to their own convention in a South Side church from which whites were barred, and representatives of the Southern Christian Leadership Conference took over.

To the dismay of the Communists, the moderate black leaders came to an agreement with N.C.N.P. planners to support the old compromise. At the same time, it was amended by a provision, written by Arthur Waskow, which set up two new groups: one to consider a third ticket, the other to work with local organizers. Both groups will be half white, half black.

Such rags of unity could not conceal the fact that few blacks will find much worth discussing with white radicals.

The issue of Vietnam, which brought most delegates to Chicago, is not of consuming interest in black ghettos. The single whole-hearted display of radical togetherness came on Sunday, in response to the appearance of a black private, a W. E. B. DuBois Club member from Philadelphia who announced that he was refusing to go to Vietnam (and has since been arrested for his refusal). For a few minutes, as whites and blacks chorused "Hell no, we won't go!" the convention was one. The blacks could cheer the soldier for his color, the Communists for his affiliation, the peace fighters for his act, but such a combination of qualities is not likely to come along every day.

As for the white radicals, whether they are disposed to national politicking or neighborhood rallying, black power is a commodity they cannot hope to sell. "We are a movement of people with radically different needs," argued Rennie Davis, an alumnus of Students for a Democratic Society who now works with the poor on Chicago's North Side. "A supercoalition makes no sense."

The events of the weekend constituted an argument for a kind of apartheid, with the old goals of civil rights and integration being written off as stale promises of phony liberals.

On Monday the convention ran briskly through its resolutions—immediate withdrawal from Vietnam, an end to the draft, restoration of Adam Powell's seat in Congress. A resolution that would have touched off a debate over nonviolence was shelved.

The delegates, who had repeatedly cheered the principle of each man "doing his thing," showed how politely they could do the things arranged for them by others.

As each resolution was ready to be voted on, a lad in the front row of the Black Caucus raised the large pink card that represented 28,498 votes. Occasionally his attention wandered and he had to be reminded to lift his arm so that democratic procedure might prevail. In this way, on Monday evening, ended the "free and swinging" convention that Simon Casady had promised a few days earlier.

Considering all they had endured at this convention, which obscured the better part of the movement and exposed the worst, people left Chicago in good spirits.

Two W.S.P. women from the suburbs of New York told me how heartened they were by the impressive display of opposition to the Vietnam war. The blacks, having conducted a ceremony in which their friends were made to stand for their enemies, returned to the real world feeling that they had won something and, psychologically speaking, perhaps they had. The Communists could look forward to participating in meetings of the third-party committee and so retain some flickering illusion of political life.

Waskow, who had represented the fading voice of decency at the convention, rhapsodized over the conciliatory outcome. Now that the worst is over, he predicted, black and white radicals will work together in a man-to-man way. Waskow found no humor in the pair of earnest girls who approached him with the suggestion that 51 per cent of the convention's votes be given to women to make up for their centuries of inequality.

William Pepper said that the convention's action "gives us an entrée into the ghetto." He was less sanguine about his entrée into the middle class, where the money is, unless "the false taint of anti-Semitism is overcome." And good Dr. Spock, whose participation in the affair consisted of being applauded on public occasions, allowed that everything is "more reasonable, pleasanter" now—although he was concerned over the dirty words scratched on the elevator doors. He is ready as ever to stand for Vice President or perhaps Senator from New York, but his candidacy would create problems because Dr. Spock still uses the word "Negro."

Among the younger delegates joy was not unconfined. They liked the workshops, bull sessions of local organizers with common interests which met during the convention's off hours. But many voiced a sense of having been enmeshed willy-nilly in a project that was not of their making. "The whole point of S.D.S. was to go our own way, not to be controlled," a Georgetown University graduate said almost tearfully. "And here we let these other people control us."

But if a disquieting sense lingers among the young of having been pawns in an exercise that would have been ludicrous had it not stunk so of totalitarianism, the Labor Day experience may turn out to be useful for people who still have a lot of politics ahead of them.

Part 5

WHERE ARE WE NOW?

THE SINGLE ITEM in this section is abridged from a three-hour discussion. Usually something so mutilated would not be worth reprinting, but the panel was composed of three brilliant men, each of whom envisions a different future for American society. Arthur Schlesinger, Jr., Pulitzer prize-winning historian and Special Adviser to President Kennedy, is an unusually gifted Establishment liberal. Norman Mailer is not only a great novelist but a social critic of long standing now in the unique position of seeing the "existential radicalism" he demanded all through the sterile fifties come to pass. As his special contribution to the current unrest he has just produced a remarkable book, *The Armies of the Night,* which stands by itself as an original reinforcement to our battered sensibilities. Herbert Marcuse is a philosopher of much subtlety and obscurity who has nonetheless become the New Left's chief intellectual resource. His most influential book is *One-Dimensional Man,* a difficult work so cumbersomely written that it defies comprehension. An important virtue of the discussion that follows is that it forced Marcuse to speak plainly, as Mailer and Schlesinger always do. The resulting exchange (moderated by Nat Hentoff) was extraordinarily illuminating, if not prophetic.

Democracy Has/Hasn't a Future...a Present

The Theater for Ideas is a group of some 60 prominent New York intellectuals who meet, usually privately, for evenings of experimental drama, music, films or political debate. Recently, the group held a panel discussion open to the public at the Friends Meeting House on Gramercy Park. The topic: the nature and future of democracy. Herewith, an abridged transcript of nearly three hours of debate and of questions from the floor.

HENTOFF—This first question has to do with what is presumably the reaffirmation of the Democratic processes, the fact that because of Eugene McCarthy and Senator Kennedy various young people have become convinced—some say for the last time, if it doesn't work—that the political processes are viable, that you can change things that way. Do you three on the panel agree with this assessment: that there is a reason to be reasonably optimistic about the processes of democracy in terms of what's been happening politically? Does it make you hopeful about the future of democracy?

Norman, do you want to start?

MAILER—All right. If this question had been asked six months ago, the consensus, if I may use that gentleman from Texas's favorite word, would have been altogether more pessimistic. In

From the *New York Times Magazine*, May 26, 1968.

fact, it's hard almost to conceive of a forum of this sort in New York City with this panel six months ago.

It's obvious that there's been an extraordinary shift in the tempo of events. When McCarthy began to run no one believed that he had a chance. We were all drenched with a sense of defeat. People went through the ritual of democratic gestures, democratic moves, democratic stands. They attempted to express dissent in one form or another. It never amounted to anything.

Suddenly we've had this incredible phenomenon. McCarthy, while not winning a majority in New Hampshire, nonetheless, comes close enough to take the delegates. Kennedy comes out. Johnson, if he does nothing else, reveals to us that he's a man of incredible political imagination.

Even if his resignation from the Presidency was done for Machiavellian reasons, at least he's a Machiavellian, which you couldn't say before. And I work on the firm theory that a democracy depends upon having extraordinary people at the helm—even if they're villains, because an extraordinary villain can sometimes create an extraordinary hero. Just as a doctor is no better than his patient, so a hero is no better than his opposition.

I think the answer to the question, then, has to be in the affirmative. Now, the next point to consider is what is actually going on in American life. I would suggest that Technologyland tends to create a psychic condition which is the equivalent of plastic. And just as plastic objects work well and show no sign of age until the moment when they cease to work—and then they give no warning; they just split—so certain things in American society are breaking—with no warning at all.

HENTOFF—I wonder if Professor Marcuse is that optimistic.

MARCUSE—He is not. He disagrees with Norman Mailer. He is where he was six months ago. He is optimistic if the question means that the American democratic process will go on. The American democratic process, which I do not consider a democratic process [*applause*]; at least it is not what the great theoreticians of the West understood by democracy.

We see shifts. We see even important shifts. But they are all shifts within the same mess. We say, in favor of the democratic process, that the people's will makes itself felt. It makes itself felt up to the point where the will of the people would threaten the established institutional and cultural framework of the society. So changes we have indeed. But they are changes within the established framework.

So I would say democracy certainly has a future. But in my view it certainly does not have a present.

SCHLESINGER—I would like to distinguish between what one might call the practical and the pure democratic process.

The practical democratic process deals with the possibilities existing within the kind of industrial society which prevails in the developed countries of the West. I would say that the practical democratic process as it has established itself in political procedures implies, for example, the First Amendment of the Constitution. It implies freedom and discussion, and it implies in particular the inability to change things in a decisive way unless you have a majority of the people with you.

In general, it seems to me the values associated with civil liberties and with the effort to persuade majorities to shift from one position to another are more useful to a society than the values associated with short-run decisions in the interests of what one group or another believes to be absolutely right. I believe that the views of those who were deeply opposed to the Vietnam policy but were willing to rely on the democratic process to achieve a change in that policy have had a certain vindication. Because what has happened, as Norman Mailer pointed out, is that in January of this year this country appeared to be locked in, so far as the Presidential contest in November was concerned, to a choice between the two most disliked and mistrusted politicians of the 20th century. In the weeks since, the political situation has changed. President Johnson accepted the case of his critics and we now have—rather than a choice between the worst among the Presidential possibilities—a choice from among the best. [*Loud hissing.*]

Now let me distinguish between the practical model of democracy and the pure model. The pure model, I suppose, is a democratic system which would instantly reach infallible results. This pure model of democracy has never existed anywhere on earth.

You have to make a choice. We have, for example, a system which always has a lot of dolts and idiots who have to be brought along. Either you exist in this system and you do your best through every kind of pressure and persuasion to make the maximum gains within that system, or you abandon that system. Herbert Marcuse has written with great eloquence about an alternative system. This would be a system which would abrogate, for example, the Bill of Rights, which would deny freedom of expression to those who took views which Herbert would consider antipublic views.

MARCUSE—Here, a correction. I certainly haven't said there should not be freedom of expression for those opinions with which I do not agree or which I consider as damaging to the public cause. I have suggested there should be discriminating tolerance— that is to say, movements which are obviously and objectively aggressive and destructive, not in my personal view but objectively, should not be tolerated. I think that is a very different thing.

HENTOFF—The term you used was "objectively" determined?

MARCUSE—Yes.

HENTOFF—How does one accomplish this?

MARCUSE—Let me give you the example which I myself gave long before Hitler came to power. It was clearly beyond the shadow of a doubt that if the movement came to power there would be a world war, there would be the extermination of the Jews. That was not a personal opinion. That was objectively demonstrable. If the Weimar Republic had not tolerated the Hitler movement until it was too strong to be suppressed, we would have been spared the Second World War and the extermination of six million Jews. I think that is one case where you can say the definition of this movement as not deserving democratic tolerance is more than a personal value judgment.

Similarly, you can very well decide today in [Vietnam] who is the aggressor and who is not the aggressor. Again, not in terms of personal preference, but objectively.

SCHLESINGER—I would not, perhaps, disagree with Herbert Marcuse on his substantive judgments on the war in Vietnam. Where we do disagree is in the way a democratic society should confront a problem of this sort. It is my belief that a democratic society should confront a problem of this sort as we have confronted it, with all the defects and messiness of this confrontation, and that is through some form of public argument and political pressure, and not through some system of exclusion and control.

Herbert [has written] that in a proper democratic society there should be: "the withdrawal of toleration of speech and assembly from groups and movements which promote aggressive policies, armament, chauvinism, discrimination on the grounds of race and religion or which oppose the extension of public services, social security, medical care, etc." These people would be denied protection under, for example, the First Amendment. Moreover, the "restoration of freedom of thought may necessitate new and rigid restrictions on teachings and practices in the educational institutions." All this seems to me a high price to pay.

Let's take, for example, Herbert's proposal that racist arguments and teachings should be automatically suppressed. Now, this contains for anyone, since I assume we're all antiracist, a certain flavor of acceptability. But there are two problems with it. First, if you accept this, you have to have a mechanism which is going to effect the suppression, and this implies the concentration in our society of an extraordinary degree of power; and you have no assurance that the power is going to be used disinterestedly, for the suppression of racist teachings rather than for the benefit of the men operating the mechanism. In the second place, the actual judgments: Even if you are persuaded of the disinterestedness of any central authority, what, for example, would happen to Stokely Carmichael or Rap Brown under this proposition?

HENTOFF—I would like to ask Norman, as a conservative, a rather singular conservative, what his reaction is to the quotation from the essay on sin.

MAILER—From Dr. Marcuse? Oh, I think it's too much! [*Laughter*.] Let me make my side of the argument.

Democracy consists of the resolution that comes out of a play of forces. The moment you legislate what is part of the game and what is not part of the game, you are entering into the most dangerous territory of all. Now, of course, every society does precisely that. It legislates. It cuts off part of a terrain. It says, for example, you cannot kill, you cannot steal, and so forth. So that there is not a free play, if you will, of every human desire. To that extent, a society is not democratic.

If we're going to talk about the nature of democracy and whether democracy has a future, we've got to consider the problem in some depth rather than should we legislate against this or legislate against that, because I can give one immediate answer to Marcuse, which is that not every racist is void of ideas, of human content. Sometimes a profound idea is buried in a particularly ugly notion.

The moment one starts wiping whole ideologies off the board and giving them no chance to enter into a civilized dialogue, one may be losing untold intellectual fertilities of the future. We just don't know. It's an incredible arrogance to assume that one knows what should belong in the game and what shouldn't. So in that sense, I'm completely against what Marcuse says.

On the other hand, I think that Marcuse is absolutely right to this extent: that the sort of things that have been going on in the last six months have been going on in democracies so-called. What's fascinating about the game is not that we have been having true democratic expression these last six months. What is fascinating is that the old tricks that used to be used to pen us up and keep us away from any kind of democratic expression at all are not working any more. In other words, I grant you that the forms that are used now are not democratic. But what's interesting is that the old forms that were able to contain us ever since the Second World War are just not working. There is something loose, and this something can go on to break down those old forms and create new ones.

This brings us back to the whole notion of what I talk about when I talk about democracy. You might say the great democrat of them all was de Sade because de Sade said that everybody should have absolute rights over everybody else. Now, what does that mean? That means when a man is walking down the street, he goes up to a girl and says, "I want to have you." And, according to de Sade— this is where de Sade is a little bit impure as a democrat—she is supposed to say, "All right, you can have me," and de Sade's theory was that the woman might make it sufficiently distasteful so that the man would never approach her again. We Americans prefer a more direct riposte; we prefer the girl to say, "Get lost, mother——." Now, the point I'm making is that if you go down the street and you do that to a girl in life, what happens? If she's attractive enough, the odds are she has a boyfriend—and he's a real stud. And you're in trouble. In other words, democracy consists of a play of forces and some of these forces are not altogether divorced from violence.

If we're going to start to think about democracy, we have to start to think about it as a process which consists of much more than people getting together and voting on where they want to go with the next step. Democracy consists of an open play of human forces with the end unknown. Its essential affirmation is that a good rather than an evil society will eventually emerge. For the first time in years I feel there is a hope for this to emerge in America.

MARCUSE—Well, that was very illuminating. This notion of democracy I accept completely—that it is an open play of forces. My criticism was precisely that it isn't open.

The word that occurred again and again in Norman Mailer's presentation was "game"—"playing the game"—and precisely here is, in my view, the unbridgeable gap between what I and my friends stand for and what he stands for. We don't want to play the game any more. We consider it a rigged and a brutal game. I would be ashamed to call it a game.

MAILER—That's all marvelous, but Marcuse misread me 180 degrees. I said that, to the extent that society is a game, it is not democratic. To that extent, democratic forces are cut off. You just misread what I said.

MARCUSE—I misheard.

MAILER—Misheard. We're finally going to get arbitrary: O.K.

SCHLESINGER—May I say something?

The problems which we confront today are not peculiar to the United States. One need only read the newspapers to know that every form of frustration—for example, of student protest, of bitterness about the devaluation of human values—appears in societies all over the world at a certain stage of industrial development, quite regardless of whether they're capitalist, Communist, Socialist or whatever.

The problem is not something specifically related to the United States, to the military-industrial complex or whatever else one likes to attribute all original sin to, but is a worldwide phenomenon which exists in all highly organized societies.

QUESTION—What would happen if Columbia . . . [*Hisses.*] I'm sorry to bring up Columbia. It seems to me that here you have clearly a question of people who resorted to force instead of sitting down and talking. You have people who did not have any power, could not control force, setting up a situation where they did finally have some power to confront a people who normally in a society do have power. That's why this whole discussion of the forces is unrealistic. There isn't an equality of forces.

HENTOFF—Would you, Norman, focus on what's been happening at Columbia—in terms of your idea of the play of forces?

MAILER—All right. I support that strike at Columbia completely. I support it because it was existential, because these kids went out and did something that they had never done before, and they did not know how it was going to turn out.

If they end up making an institution of this strike, and disrupting that particular campus year after year, I'll probably end up being against it.

But what's interesting about this is it was a new way of forcing the administration to recognize that they had no sense at all of how powerfully the students felt about a great many issues. These students had gotten to the point where they recognized that any number of polite protests were going to mean nothing with the Columbia administration. They'd obviously been doing this for years. So they broke a whole series of rules, and profoundly shocked the administration, and in return got beaten up by the police. So they then learned something else about themselves.

What is necessary for democracy is that you must learn more about yourself. Sometimes, in a democracy, one will need peaceful modes, because there's nothing more boring, more debilitating of the real resources of a whole cadre of students than to be on perpetual strikes. Listen to those meaningless speeches for hour after hour, week after week, year after year. That's no way to spend a college education when you could be reading a great many things. But to do it once—to do it that brilliantly, with that much force, that much conviction—was marvelous.

It's just that, next time, they're going to have to do something else. I think some of them decided that they'd had enough. I think others decided that they were going to go back with more. The fact of the matter is that if this technological society which rules us and brainwashes us is as bad as we all say it is then there's no way to get around it. There's going to be violence before that society is cracked to the point where we can begin to breathe a little more.

That [Columbia] strike was a good one because it had an air of the unexpected. It was bold; it was passionate, and the causes were good. Another strike in another school might just be a disaster—a dull disaster, like the one in Harvard, where 700 kids penned one man in a room, a man from Dow Chemical. I mean, that's not the way to show the administration that you're fed up with them.

MARCUSE—The thing I was interested in hearing is that apparently Norman Mailer believes, at least in this case, that the democratic process wouldn't work unless from time to time broken by extrademocratic and nondemocratic action.

I believe that you can transform the democratic process we have today only by this injection of extrademocratic, extraparliamentary actions for the simple reason—now I use the word "game"—that the game is rigged. The play of force is not the play of equal forces. I can hardly imagine a concentration of power which is more overwhelming than the concentration of power we have right now in this country.

HENTOFF—Dr. Schlesinger, the terms now that have been introduced are "extrademocratic," "extraparliamentary." What's your reaction to Columbia in that context?

SCHLESINGER—There is nothing that the students at Columbia did which was not wholly consistent with the American version of democracy.

MARCUSE—Then why the police?

SCHLESINGER—This has nothing to do with the police. There is nothing—and I will repeat it—"there is nothing in what the Columbia students did which is in the slightest degree extrademocratic." We do not in the United States identify the democratic process with the parliamentary process. Ours is a rich and complex conception of democracy in which the right to strike—by labor, by students or whatever—is a basic part.

The democratic process in any sense in which a historian has to deal with it includes a wide variety of means of pressure. I don't think any serious student of the American democratic process would say that the sit-down strikes [of the nineteen-thirties] were not a contribution to the democratic process.

One of its great qualities is the diverse means by which the democratic process absorbs public protest and converts it to a change of policy. I am unwilling to settle for a definition of the democratic process so restrictive that it would exclude what the Columbia students did, or what the sit-down strikers did, or what the abolitionists did. To have so impoverished and legalistic a definition of the democratic process is against what the American democratic tradition is about.

MARCUSE—May I ask one question (because I am afraid that we may agree here)? Do you consider the forcible occupation of buildings and the invasion of private property a part of the democratic process?

SCHLESINGER—Yes.

MARCUSE—Then I agree with you on the definition of democracy.

QUESTION—I am struck with the agreement between Norman

Mailer and Arthur Schlesinger. I think that Norman Mailer is amoral. I think that Arthur Schlesinger is immoral.

I can give a few examples. Norman Mailer said, about the Columbia thing, he liked it. He constantly referred to its novelty, its newness, its daring. At no point did he talk about the Columbia thing in terms of its issues. If it was a right-wing thing, if it was reaction, if it was against students' rights, if it was just as novel, I think he would have enjoyed it, too. I think that is amoral.

I think that Arthur Schlesinger has been extremely immoral and dishonest. For instance, the way you talk about Herbert Marcuse's discussion of democracy. It's the kind of activity that's to be permitted or not to be permitted that must be discussed, not who has the right.

MAILER—I think that charge has a great deal to it. What characterizes totalitarianisms is that they are no fun. One of the reasons it's very, very hard to get pro-Russian for more than a few weeks is that we keep coming face to face with the fact that the Soviet Union must probably be the most boring country in the history of nations.

But the young lady, like many mechanical leftists—I'm using an old-fashioned phrase—is extraordinarily inaccurate in her indictment, because I was concerned with these issues. I said several times over that I thought they were excellent issues. If some right-wing kids were going up and saying they didn't want any Negroes allowed in Morningside Park do you really think that I would applaud equally? If you believe that then a certain portion of the left has become psychotic.

I'm perfectly willing to go down in a leaky rowboat with Arthur Schlesinger—so long as we're both for Kennedy, that is—but let one thing be understood, which is that Schlesinger and I are not at all in any kind of profound agreement.

He is talking about the institutions that we have, and he's saying that he thinks there's much more vitality in those institutions than most of you believe. I feel there's much less than he feels.

If we are amoral we are each amoral in our own separate ways.

QUESTION [*by Robert Lowell, a Pulitzer prize-winning poet*]— I'm going to ask a short, concise question of Arthur Schlesinger, but I'm going to cheat and make a statement.

The only definition of democracy that makes any sense to me is that you have the power to vote people out of office. That's a very profound rule. But the democratic process is something much deeper, and I want to ask Arthur this: Do you think the police were acting within the democratic process at Columbia, or should they have been put on trial?

SCHLESINGER—I fear I must seem to cop out of this question. I've been out of town. [*Hisses.*] O.K. The question is a perfectly legitimate and searching question which, when I have had a chance to get caught up on The New York Times and Jimmy Wechsler and Nat Hentoff and the facts, I'm prepared to answer [*hisses*] but I'm god-damned if I'm going to answer to please an audience on the basis of no knowledge of what the facts are.

HENTOFF—I'm going to move on to another question. Herbert Marcuse has written that American society is "an explosion of insanity." Norman Mailer writes that he had to come to decide "that the center of America might be insane." Now, is democracy possible in a society of madmen? How serious are you, both of you, in these diagnoses, and how do you apply them to what we're talking about?

MAILER—Insanity consists of building major structures upon foundations which do not exist. I think American society has become progressively insane because it has become progressively a technological society. A technological society assumes that if it has a logical solution to a problem then that is the entire solution. If it decides that the problem, for instance, is to keep food in such a way that it may be eaten six months later, then it proceeds to freeze it, and then it points out to you that six months later when you unfreeze that food you can still eat it. What it does not decide scientifically —although it pretends that this has been a scientific operation—is what portion of that food has been destroyed, what unknown ailments may possibly be inflicted upon the generations of the future.

This is a tiny example of it. But if you start going through every single manifestation of American society you find that it's just an endless series. There's architecture, there's food, there's the incredible fact that in a supposedly rational society we've come to a point where it's almost literally impossible to breathe the air in the city. That's a sign of a society that's mad.

The question is: How do you take a society away from madmen? Well, you take a society away from madmen by getting weapons and charging the castle where the madmen have barricaded themselves and are terrifying the countryside.

The point of the impasse in which we find ourselves is that no one knows where the castle is, no one knows quite who the madmen are, because every time we think we've found a madman, he disclaims himself on television.

For instance, we have this enormous hope that maybe Richard Nixon is the madman. But he gets on television: He's as reasonable as you or I. He cannot be the madman.

Can it be our own dear Governor Rockefeller, who has never said anything interesting that any of us can remember? It certainly can't be Jack Armstrong, our Mayor. He's not the madman. Or is it General Motors then? Yes, conceivably. Now we're getting a little closer. Where in General Motors?

The point is that what we are getting into is not a revolution which is going to take over the seats of power. We're going to have a revolution which is going to be a reconnaissance to find out where the power is located. That's what the sense is of all these operations. That's why I approve of the Columbia strike, because everybody at Columbia now knows a lot more about where the power is located.

So, as I say, the way in which you discover the madmen is that you have a slow continuing revolution which consists of artful moves that expose the madmen, or expose some of the places where they've buried their power, their techniques, their secrets, their fears—because they're terribly afraid.

That's the one thing we've won in these six months, Marcuse, that you give no credit to. The people who have the power are terribly afraid. Which one of us thought that Lyndon Johnson would cave in? The fact of the matter is that the man was suffering from that barrage we were giving him. The barrage we were giving him is much more powerful than he, than any of us, believed. That's the incredible fact.

HENTOFF—Professor Marcuse, do you think it's that difficult to find out where the men involved are?

MARCUSE—No. I don't think we need a revolution to find out where the power lies in the country today. The problem is not: "Who are the madmen?" It is the society that is insane.

I would consider a society sane—or, rather, not insane—which uses the available resources—technical, material, intellectual—not for increasing waste and destruction and unnecessary consumption, but for the abolition of poverty, alienation and misery all over the world. And inasmuch as this society disposes over resources greater than ever before and at the same time distorts and abuses and wastes these resources more than ever before, I call this society insane—not the people in it.

QUESTION [*by Elizabeth Hardwick, writer; advisory editor, New York Review of Books; Mrs. Lowell*]—As a resident of Manhattan I can't have too much of Norman Mailer and Arthur Schlesinger, but I'm fascinated by our visitor from the West. I don't want to ask a stupid question, so I'm trying to think of one that would be cogent so that he could talk about it.

Well, does it bother you, Professor Marcuse, when you talk about the inequalities in our society, that perhaps the real left as we all think of it isn't a very large thing in American society? Perhaps it has as much power as the people want it to have, maybe a little more?

MARCUSE—Well, I think that is about the most important question you could ask in this context because it involves what is really, in my view, the problem of democracy today. Namely, whether we can still say, with good conscience, that the majority is right. I think we cannot say it any more.

Within the established society we no longer have a majority constituted on the basis of the completely free development of opinion and consciousness. We do not have a majority constituted on the basis of free and equal access to the facts and all the facts. We do not have a majority constituted on the basis of equal education for all.

However, we do have a majority which is standardized and manipulated and even constituted by standardized and administered information, communication and education. In other words, this majority is not free, but it belongs to the very essence of democracy that the people who are sovereign are a free people. That was the notion of Rousseau and John Stuart Mill. That was also the way the great fighters for democracy understood it from the beginning—not the people as people, but the really free people, the people who are allowed to think for themselves, to feel for themselves and to form their own opinion, not subject to the terrific pressure of lobbies, political parties, the whole power structure as it exists today.

SCHLESINGER—The implication of Herbert's proposition is that there was some golden age of democracy in which the majority was pure, unfettered and wise, and that this golden age has——

MARCUSE—If you want me to make it perfectly clear once and

for all, I do admit such a democracy has never existed and does not exist in any society today. But I do believe that we could have it.

SCHLESINGER—All right. Herbert has made it clear that the indictment he has made of American democracy in the nineteen-sixties is something he would level equally at American democracy at any stage in its history, at the time of Jefferson or whatever.

MARCUSE—No, because we didn't have mass media at that time. The technological society has means of control that never existed before.

SCHLESINGER—There are two mild points I would like to make if no one minds. One of them is this: Herbert Marcuse has said that the democracy of an immaculate majority has not existed, does not exist, but he hopes it may sometime exist. Is that correct?

MARCUSE—I not only hope it may sometime exist. I say today that all the resources are available so that it can be translated into reality.

SCHLESINGER—In order to bring about the democracy of the immaculate majority, I take it that the policy which you would advocate in the transition is the suppression of those views which you think are incompatible.

MARCUSE—No.

SCHLESINGER—Well, do I misread you?

MARCUSE—I'm afraid so.

SCHLESINGER—I don't want to read that quotation again, but I gather you feel that those who are "opposed to the extension of the social services" and so on . . .

MARCUSE—Yes, but what has this to do with the question whether the majority today is a free majority or not?

SCHLESINGER—My second point is this, and perhaps it's a different or a deeper problem: If there is any society which, far from being arrogant and tyrannical, is confused, has a bad conscience, is vulnerable to argument and, in fact, is condemned by its critics because of its pathetic desire to come to terms with its critics, it is this one. Even Herbert is embarrassed by the fact he's being celebrated by Time and The New York Times Magazine. Critics resent the fact that they are hailed by the society.

MAILER—The danger of this technological society is that it appropriates everything that's new. It does not appropriate Marcuse's thought. But it takes one piece of Marcuse's flesh and it introduces it into the machine. It appropriates him to the point where people who couldn't begin to understand one of his sentences can use his name at a cocktail party.

MARCUSE—Your name, too.

MAILER—Yes. Now this is a debasement of nature. It's debasement of the Gothic intricacies of Mr. Marcuse's style.

MARCUSE—You write much better.

MAILER—Thank you.

MARCUSE—But I write deeper.

MAILER—Yes, you write deeper. . . . The point I might like to get to is this: Someone asked whether the left wing we have now is a reflection of what the democratic majority wants—I'm talking about the orthodox left wing. But the orthodox left wing really doesn't matter because that's not the left that I think anyone is really talking about now. That's not the left wing that produced this particular, odd, nascent revolution in American life. This nascent revolution in American life popped out to everyone's amazement. It came out of the youth. It came out of a very basic reaction. Untold millions of this youth began to say, "They are snowing us. They are burying us." And they said, "We cannot put up with it any more. We're going to overthrow it." Now there are two perspectives in all this. One is a revolution from the top and, in fact, it's a revolution that's impossible, given the present state of American life. It's a revolution which would come to pass only if worldwide Communism won everywhere and then some of you might inherit the mantle here and be as unhappy as all those guys with names like Norodny or Novotnick or whatever his name is.

The real revolution that's going on in American life is a revolution that no one in this room can predict. No one can say which way it will turn. It's a revolution, I submit, that comes out of the very marrow of the human condition—which is what is exciting about it. And the reason it cannot be put down is that no one comprehends it. That's its strength.

The horror of the technological society is that the moment it comprehends something it acquires it. The moment it understood how to freeze food it acquired that act of freezing food without knowing the rest of what was going on. The moment it knows how to sell an idea it sells an idea, whether it cares about the rest of the idea or the consequences of the idea or not.

One of the ways in which the society would be overthrown is for this revolution to be directed against the mass media. For instance, how about occupying some of the television stations? [*Applause.*] How about occupying some of the newspapers? [*At this point a young man approached Mailer and offered what appeared to be a marijuana cigarette.*] Are you joining me? Thank you, I don't smoke. You've unmasked me. I'll tell you why I didn't take a puff on that stick. I see no reason to arm the police while I'm feeling a state of euphoria. The action of the gentleman coming up to me was marvelous and interesting. He revealed the conservative side of my nature. Thank you.

HENTOFF—We've been talking about new institutions, new structures, as the only way to get fundamental change. What would that mean to you, Mr. Marcuse, in terms of the university, in terms of Columbia?

MARCUSE—I was afraid of that because I now finally reveal myself as a fink.

I have never suggested or advocated or supported destroying the established universities and building new anti-institutions instead. I have always said that no matter how radical the demands of the students and no matter how justified, they should be pressed within the existing universities and attained within the existing universities.

I believe—and this is where the finkdom comes in—that American universities, at least quite a few of them, today are still enclaves of relatively critical thought and relatively free thought. So we do not have to think of replacing them by new institutions. But this is one of the very rare cases in which I think you can achieve what you want to achieve within the existing institutions.

Suggested Reading

The period since 1945 has been rich in social analyses and social documents. The following brief list is made up of books that have been important or influential, but it would take many pages to indicate the wealth of such material available. Although the citations here refer to first editions, each of these books has also been reprinted in one or more paperback editions.

James Baldwin, *The Fire Next Time,* New York, Dial, 1963.

Betty Friedan, *The Feminine Mystique,* New York, Norton, 1963.

John Kenneth Galbraith, *The Affluent Society,* Boston, Houghton Mifflin, 1958.

Paul Goodman, *Growing Up Absurd,* New York, Random House, 1960.

Norman Mailer, everything, but especially *Advertisements for Myself,* New York, Putnam, 1959; and *The Presidential Papers,* New York, Putnam, 1963.

C. Wright Mills, *The Power Elite,* New York, Oxford University Press, 1956.

David Riesman, et al., *The Lonely Crowd,* New Haven, Yale University Press, 1950.

William H. Whyte, Jr., *The Organization Man,* New York, Simon and Schuster, 1956.

Malcolm Little, *The Autobiography of Malcolm X,* New York, Grove, 1965.

There are as yet no formal histories of American society since 1945, but the following books deal with the historical roots of matters of urgent contemporary interest.

Richard Hofstadter, *Anti-Intellectualism in American Life,* New York, Knopf, 1963.

David M. Potter, *People of Plenty,* Chicago, University of Chicago Press, 1954.

Arthur I. Waskow, *From Race Riot to Sit-In,* Garden City, Doubleday, 1966.

Index